DEMOCRACY AND MUSIC EDUCATION

COUNTERPOINTS: MUSIC AND EDUCATION

Estelle R. Jorgensen, Editor

Democracy and Music Education

*Liberalism, Ethics, and the
Politics of Practice*

Paul G. Woodford

INDIANA UNIVERSITY PRESS

Bloomington and Indianapolis

This book is a publication of

Indiana University Press
601 North Morton Street
Bloomington, IN 47404-3797 USA

http://iupress.indiana.edu

Telephone orders   800-842-6796
Fax orders   812-855-7931
Orders by e-mail   iuporder@indiana.edu

The paper used in this publication meets the minimum
requirements of American National Standard for Information
Sciences—Permanence of Paper for Printed Library
Materials, ANSI Z39.48-1984.

Manufactured in the United States of America

Library of Congress Cataloging-in-Publication Data

Woodford, Paul, date
   Democracy and music education : liberalism, ethics, and the
politics of practice/Paul G. Woodford.
      p.   cm.—(Counterpoints : music and education)
   Includes bibliographical references and index.
   ISBN 0-253-34516-2 (cloth : alk. paper)—ISBN 0-253-21739-3
(pbk. : alk. paper)
   1. School music—Instruction and study—Social aspects.
2. Education—Philosophy.   I. Title.   II. Counterpoints
(Bloomington, Ind.)

   MT1.W89 2005
   780.'71'073—dc22   2004010949

1   2   3   4   5   10   09   08   07   06   05

I Hear America Singing

I hear America singing, the varied carols I hear,
Those of mechanics, each one singing his as it should be
    blithe and strong,
The carpenter singing his as he measures his plank or beam,
The mason singing his as he makes ready for work, or leaves
    off work,
The boatman singing what belongs to him in his boat, the
    deckhand singing on the steamboat deck,
The shoemaker singing as he sits on his bench, the hatter
    singing as he stands,
The woodcutter's song, the ploughboy's on his way in the
    morning, or at noon intermission, or at sundown,
The delicious singing of the mother, or of the young wife at
    work, or of the girl sewing or washing,
Each singing what belongs to him or her and to none else,
The day what belongs to the day—at night the party of
    young fellows, robust, friendly,
Singing with open mouths their strong melodious songs.

    —Walt Whitman

Let us admit the case of the conservative: if we once start thinking no one can guarantee where we shall come out, except that many objects, ends and institutions are doomed. Every thinker puts some portion of an apparently stable world in peril and no one can wholly predict what will emerge in its place.

    —John Dewey

CONTENTS

PREFACE

Educators in the western democracies have long believed that education should ultimately lead to the development of personal autonomy in students so that they can realize their individual potentials. As John Dewey expressed it in *Reconstruction in Philosophy* (1950),

> Government, business, art, religion, all social institutions have a meaning, a purpose. That purpose is to set free and to develop the capacities of human individuals without respect to race, sex, class, or economic status. And this is all one with saying that the test of their value is the extent to which they educate every individual into the full stature of his possibility.[1]

Dewey's remarks were particularly aimed at the school, as it was through its agency that future social progress could most readily be obtained. Of late there has been a renewal of interest in Dewey's philosophy, as philosophers such as Richard Rorty and Richard Shusterman have gone beyond analytic philosophy in search of models providing greater insight into larger social, cultural, and political problems.[2] Indeed, Rorty identifies Dewey as one of the three most influential philosophers of the twentieth century.[3] North American educational philosophers had never completely abandoned Dewey, but between 1950 and the mid-1980s Dewey's pragmatism was outside of the philosophical mainstream.

Given the recent resurgence of interest in Dewey, it seems appropriate to revisit the more salient aspects of his educational and political philosophy as means of introducing the democratic theme of this book. Dewey had a lot to say about the arts, but while his book *Art as Experience* (1934) has long been a staple of graduate philosophy of music education courses, the democratic theme in that particular book is less explicit than in, for example, *Democracy and Education* (1916) and *Reconstruction in Philosophy*. Music educators may be less familiar with the latter two books and with Dewey's many other publications addressing wider political and educational concerns.

My own doctoral dissertation at Northwestern University (1994) was a musical and educational exploration of Dewey's concept of reflective or critical thinking (the term "reflective thinking" that Dewey used has since been largely supplanted by "critical thinking"). I defined musical reflective thinking as a form of musical and social inquiry whereby individuals and groups constructed a musical worldview and corresponding sense of musical identity. But while acknowledging that musical reflective thinking necessarily took place within social and cultural contexts in which competing beliefs and values needed to be sorted out and understood, I failed to fully appreciate and develop the moral and political aspects of Deweyan educational philosophy. Musical reflective thinking was narrowly conceived as a form of general intellectual skill or musical problem-solving ability, albeit one that was an extension of personality.[4] I somehow lost sight of Dewey's larger social and educational purpose and vision, which was that education ought to prepare students to participate in democratic society and thereby contribute to the common good. Reflective thinking, as Dewey understood it, was as much a moral and political kind of thinking as a type of intellectual skill or form of social inquiry. It was an intellectual means of engaging with the world as a moral agent of change.

The chapters in this book were written after the completion of my dissertation and reflect a growing awareness of, and concern for political, moral, and ethical issues in music education philosophy and practice. My own developing philosophy, though, is not simply a working out of Dewey's ideas as they apply to music education. Philosophers including Hans Georg Gadamer, John Rawls, Richard Bernstein, Lawrence Cahoone, Charles Taylor, John Ralston Saul, Martha Nussbaum, and Jean Bethke Elshtain have also been influential, as have music education philosophers of differing political stripes whose arguments have helped shape my own thinking during the past decade or more. To a significant extent, the chapters in this book represent my own attempts at making sense of the philosophical, political, and sociological debates that have racked the music education profession, at least at the university level, during the past two decades. The arguments presented by various music education and other scholars in the professional literature provided a necessary stimulus to my own creative efforts.

Nevertheless, my own thinking remains indebted to Dewey, as was driven home not too long ago when I read Robert Westbrook's *John Dewey and American Democracy* (1991). That wonderful book gave me a much better appreciation of both the scope and genius of Dewey's thinking, particularly as concerns his radical liberal vision of democracy. I was also struck by the realization that my own philosophical project thus far mirrors in some small way Dewey's own quest for understanding. At some level, whether conscious or unconscious, Dewey's project has served as a model and moral framework for my own thinking. Like Dewey's, my own writings are intended to be neither definitive nor authoritative. They should be interpreted as generative and provisional, as potentially helpful but tentative, intended only for application in our own time and place.[5] There can be no final or definitive concept of democracy and thus no final or definitive understanding of what a democratic purpose for music education might imply for professional practice.

This, however, should not be interpreted to mean that democracy is an "empty" concept. Rather, it is an ideal, or set of ideals, into which each generation must breathe new life. The democratic project depends on public conversations in which people assert and share their stories and ideas while working together to reach consensus on important matters of mutual concern such as health care and education. Thus, if music and other teachers are to provide the necessary educational leadership in democratic society, and if they are also to be held accountable by government for the attainment of realistic educational goals, then they had better learn how to communicate with the public in ways it can understand.[6] Music education philosopher Estelle Jorgensen expresses the problem this way:

> If music education is to remain a vital element of public education, today's challenge is to shape public understanding to such a degree that educational policymakers are impelled to provide conditions under which music education can proceed with integrity. This demands a persuasive political philosophy of music education, one in which political reasons for music education's place in the schools are clearly articulated.[7]

The aim of this book is to invite music educators to begin reclaiming a democratic purpose for music education by contributing to wider intellectual and political conversations about the nature and significance of music in our lives and those of our children. This kind of political philosophy and action, I believe, is essential to securing a place for music education in public schools. Unless music teachers contribute to public conversations about the nature and purpose of education in general and music education in particular, thereby asserting and establishing their political legitimacy, they will continue to be marginalized and excluded from educational decision making at the governmental level. Music teachers need to reconceive themselves as opinion leaders and champions of the public good and not as just another special interest group.[8] Possibly this was what Max Kaplan meant when calling during the 1960s for the development of a larger social vision for music education, one in which music educators played an important role in contemporary education and democratic society.[9]

Today's music educators, though, remain ambivalent about the coupling of democracy with music education. While the democratic purpose of public schooling is usually acknowledged by them, autocratic educational models and methods continue to prevail in music teacher education programs and in public school music programs. One probable explanation for this discontinuity between political purpose and actual music education practice is that the concept of democracy in music and music education remains little under-stood. All too often it is wrongly equated with anarchy or with a relativistic laissez-faire attitude toward other people and their respective musical and pedagogical beliefs, values, and practices. Both views are potentially danger-ous because they distort the nature and purpose, and thus also the value, of music education in democratic society by rendering individuals passive and incapable of individual or collective action. Music educators like to think that they are above politics, but politics just refers to the ways people engage in collective decision making.[10] Avoidance of politics in education serves no one well, except perhaps those who would dominate and control. Much of this book is accordingly dedicated to examining how and why music ed-ucators and other teachers and academics have avoided, or been excluded from, political debates within the public sphere and how this has contributed to the weakening and stultification of the profession. This is preliminary to suggesting ways in which they can begin reclaiming their place and role in democratic society as political beings and moral agents in public deliberations about musical, educational, and other values.

Music educators, though, can hardly be expected to pursue democratic ends or values unless they have some sense of what democracy might mean for them, for their pupils, and for society as a whole. As Dewey expressed it, intelligent control of means implies knowledge of ends, and vice versa. Each informs and guides the other. Knowledge of ends, or perception of possible consequences, can provide direction and guidance to educational thought and action, that is, provided those ends are the subject of conscious or purposeful intent. Those ends, in turn, are rooted in the world and qualified through the various means that teachers employ.[11]

Given the above observation about Dewey's philosophy providing a moral framework for my own work, it is appropriate that we begin in chapter 1 with an overview of some of the more salient aspects of his educational and political thinking before considering previous, and largely failed, attempts at applying democratic ideals to music education practice. While inspired by Dewey and motivated by a democratic interest, early-twentieth-century American music educators generally failed to realize their democratic inten-tions and ideals in the schools and wider educational community. It is worth examining some of the reasons why and how those early-twentieth-century music educators failed to live up to their democratic intentions and ideals, as that information should be taken into account when attempting to apply democratic ideas to current practice.

Chapter 2 presents my own interpretation and understanding of what a liberal education means and entails for professional practice. It is my mani-festo. Although often associated with study of the classics, a liberal education more properly implies thoughtful criticism and mediation of all experience coupled with a moral obligation to others. Criticism, while essential to understanding and to personal and civic responsibility, is motivated by compassion and love of humanity. Underlying Dewey's educational and political philosophy, for example, is a feeling of love and compassion for his fellow citizens, a feeling that is perhaps revealed most explicitly in his 1934 book, *A Common Faith*.[12] Like the poet Walt Whitman before him, Dewey believed that the pursuit of democracy was an expression of love and a moral obligation to one's fellow men and women.

Martha Nussbaum has returned to this theme in her recent books, *Poetic Justice* (1995) and *Upheavals of Thought: The Intelligence of Emotions* (2001). It was only after having read the latter book that I was able to fully appreciate Whitman's democratic vision and commitment to democratic principles and ideals as revealed especially in his poem "I Hear America Singing" in which, to the consternation of elitist culture critics, individuals from different walks of life, occupations, and social classes sing their own songs in their own ways.[13] What first drew me to Whitman's poetry, though, aside from the obvious democratic themes, was his use of musical metaphors for illustrating those political ideas, just as I was struck by Benjamin Barber's use of musical metaphors in his book *Jihad vs. McWorld: How Globalism and Tribalism Are Reshaping the World* (1996). Surely, if music can serve as a metaphor for politics and cultural problems, there must be some shared element of meaning? Music is not socially abstract or transcendental but *of* the world. If, as is now commonly believed, music is a badge of identity and form of cultural representation, then it is strongly implicated in politics and the culture wars.

Literary critic Gregory Jay writes that the culture wars in the American academy can be understood as a struggle for representation.

> This struggle is multifaceted, plural, complex; it includes struggles over the theory of representation as well as over the actual cultural and political distribution of representation. The questions can be put this way: Who represents what to whom, for what reasons, through what institutions, to what effect, to whose benefit, and at what costs? What are the ethics of representation? What kinds of knowledge and power do authorized forms of representations produce? What kinds of people do such representations produce? Who owns or controls the means of representation? And what new ways of representation might better achieve the goals of justice and democracy in the overlapping worlds of education and politics?[14]

The concern here is less with *what* groups or meanings are represented through literature, music, and art than *how* they are represented, whether they are misrepresented or simply excluded altogether from public deliberations.

Nussbaum argues that "good" literature, because it promotes self-examination, identification, and empathy, can challenge individuals and groups to confront their own preconceptions, limitations, and moral failings. For this reason it should be included in the study of law (and by extension education). "Good" literature has an important moral role in public deliberations. But while acknowledging that music has narrative properties and emotional content, Nussbaum doubts that music is sufficiently determinate to be of much use in public deliberations. It is just too vague and abstract to be of much practical value.[15]

Plato certainly didn't think so, however, any more than do radical feminists and many postmodernist thinkers. I have written elsewhere, and at length, about some of the claims of radical feminists and postmodernists regarding musical representation and identity. My own view, as expressed in chapter 3 especially, is that music education in both school and university should be dedicated to the exploration, critical examination, and mediation of these and other sometimes conflicting philosophical, musical, and pedagogical claims. Ironically, implicit in all such claims is an appeal to reason. Radical critics of reason are fond of dualistically depicting it as "cool" and "disembodied," as divorced from emotion. But we need to get beyond such destructive polarizations if progress is to be achieved in addressing educational and social problems. That is what Nussbaum is proposing when arguing for the cognitive role of emotions like empathy, compassion, and mercy in public judgment and deliberation.[16] Emotions, albeit carefully circumscribed, are essential to good ethical judgment. Here Jay appears to be saying something very similar:

> While each [cultural or other group] seeks the skill and power to represent its own interests, each must also render its representations accountable to others. Each should consider how the production of its own self-representation affects others, sometimes to the point of distorting or destroying the others' power to represent their own different interests. This self-examination about how we represent things cannot be limited to questioning the effects of oppressive words or practices. It should also consider effects of too quickly jumping to accusations of racism, sexism, homophobia, harassment, or some other judgment that puts all the responsibility on the shoulders of someone else, turning difficult political and personal issues into simplistic moral dramas of good and evil.[17]

My own view of public deliberation as a form of democratic social practice dedicated to fostering a climate of reconciliation and mutual respect is intended as an antidote to these problems and to the politics of blame. First published in the *Philosophy of Music Education Review* (Spring 1999), that essay, which appears as chapter 3 in this book, remains largely unchanged. Public reason is a tool of understanding that individuals and groups employ to make sense of their complex and constantly shifting musical worlds. A key term in democracy, it implies recognizing similarities and differences but also striving to achieve mutual understanding and respect. Understanding, used this way, implies knowledge of both self and others. But it means more than just that. As Alfred North Whitehead expressed it, "By understanding, I mean more than a mere logical analysis, though that is included. I mean 'understanding' in the sense in which it is used in the French proverb, 'To understand all, is to forgive all.'"[18] Rather than simply blaming others for their transgressions, we should seek reconciliation and friendship. Democracy is, or ought to be, the attempted expression of our fondest hopes for the improvement of the human condition. Public reason, as an expression of social intelligence, is ultimately concerned with the pursuit of social amelioration and thereby the building of a sense of democratic community. This entails reaching out to, connecting, and empathizing with others. That ought to be as much an aim of music education as any other area of the curriculum.

Music might or might not have literal content along the lines of what Nussbaum proposes with respect to "good" literature—it might or might not of itself build character and virtue—but its emotional content can easily overwhelm thought, thereby leaving individuals more susceptible to manipulation and control by the powerful or by those who would distort or pervert. That is why music remains the political tool of choice of tyrants but also of media moguls and others wishing not just to represent but to autocratically impose their values on others. It is also a primary reason why music ought to be subjected to serious scrutiny in the home, school, and public arena. For the world, as Barber writes, is racked by struggle between the opposing forces of "the market's universal church" and "the retribalizing politics of particularist identities." Neither of these choices is a friend to democracy and civil liberties. "They both make war on the sovereign nation-state and thus undermine the nation-state's democratic institutions. Each eschews civil society and belittles democratic citizenship, neither seeks alternative democratic institutions. Their common thread is indifference to civil liberty."[19]

If music is implicated in this struggle between globalism and tribalism, then both its potential content and uses (including the ways that it is taught and sold) ought to be the subject of continuous critical examination and public deliberation and not just left to the experts, Wall Street financiers, government, the entertainment industry, or self-styled musical or educational gurus to use or abuse according to their own whims. Considerable attention is thus given in this book to the dangers of autocratic, absolutist, and extremist thinking but also of laissez-faire attitudes of musicians, music students, and teachers with respect to what and how music is taught. As is explained, music education has all too often contributed to the musical disfranchisement of children and the public by serving to indoctrinate them to the canon of genius or, more recently, to consumer culture. Music educators also have a long history of colonizing the music of other classes and peoples, modifying their music and performance styles to suit their own bourgeois musical tastes and sensibilities. Music education is thus far from innocuous and, owing to its capacity for misuse, something that should profoundly matter to society.

Far from being "just" entertainment or skill building, music and music education (interpreted in the widest possible sense) are important in ways that most people probably fail to understand. Music, owing to its ubiquity, is simply taken for granted. As I explain in chapters 4, 5, and 6, one of the tasks awaiting music educators is to challenge students, parents, and others to attend to the subtle and not so subtle ways they are shaped and controlled in their musical thinking and tastes—or the ways they are not really thinking at all, unconsciously accepting or imposing their musical values on others. The aim of music education, however, is not to upset or overthrow the musical and educational establishments. Rather, it is to seek a dynamic social equilibrium or creative tension between the traditional and the seemingly new or strange. This means preparing children to function as moral agents in public deliberations about the appropriate content and use of music in the public sphere. Elshtain relates in *Democracy on Trial* (1993) how upon visiting a beautiful French Romanesque church she was struck by the realization that the historical statuary had been vandalized by eighteenth-century revolutionaries.

> These defaced relics had fallen prey to eighteenth-century political zeal. It was a breathtakingly simple response, and it reminded me, once again, of why I am not a revolutionary convinced that I have the right to destroy that which others, past and present, hold dear.

That is entirely to my own way of thinking. Elshtain adds:

> In America today we hear pitiless assaults on the past: all was oppression and domination and racist or sexist horror. But what happens to our obligations to the dead? Are we modern democrats not thus obliged? Wholesale assaults on the past enjoin and legitimate a vulgar willfulness of the present moment. That is not what the drama of democracy is all about. Rather, it is about permanent contestation between conservation and change, between tradition and transformation.[20]

This remonstration is equally applicable to music and music education practice in democratic society. Given the events of 11 September 2001 and the continuing culture wars in western society, there can be arguably no more important educational task than helping children simultaneously explore and shape their world in pursuit of mutual understanding, reconciliation, respect, and forgiveness—in short, in pursuit of their common humanity. Music education, as a form of ethical encounter involving the application of reason and conscience, can contribute to that project.

Doubtless some critics of this book are going to label me as naïve for attempting to reclaim a democratic purpose for music education. Critics of democracy often complain that it has not served women and minorities particularly well. Democracy, however, need not always devolve into a tyranny of the majority. Nor does the fact that democratic societies often fail to live up to their ideals constitute a sufficient justification for trashing the Enlightenment. That would be tantamount to abandoning the commitment to egalitarianism and the liberal ideals that made the civil rights, New Left, and women's liberation movements possible in the first place. Simply abandoning those ideals would only benefit a conservative social agenda or those wishing to monopolize power.[21] Like many philosophers cited in this book, I believe that the solution is not to abandon but to build on the gains of the Enlightenment.

My concern here is not with criticism, which is after all a liberal ideal. Rather, it is about what has been termed "the anxiety of appearing naïve." Today, it is not fashionable to promote any principles save "those that maintain the inevitability of aporia, contradiction, and nihilism."[22] Many academics, out of fear of being summarily dismissed as naïve for attempting to address complex issues, are reluctant to challenge the currently prevailing orthodoxy. This accounts for much of the trendy jargon, cliché, and slavish imitation to be found nowadays in the academy (a point that is raised in chapter 3) and the lack of intelligent conversation about political issues that really matter.

For my own part, and while acknowledging that the coupling of democracy with education is difficult and no longer fashionable, I choose to face professional and social problems head on and courageously while seeking improvement. Rather than surrendering to the "inevitability of aporia, contradiction, and nihilism," I prefer to live in hope that this book will initiate a long overdue and inclusive conversation about the public good and how music educators can best serve that end. The philosophical literature on democracy as an intellectual and political concept is vast and ancient. Yet in music education, and with the exception of a handful of relevant publications by writers such as James L. Mursell during first half of the twentieth century, the literature is practically nonexistent. Other music educators with their own voices, ideas, and understandings of what is democracy and what it might imply for music education need to be forthcoming if music education is to be revitalized and made more socially relevant in today's western democratic societies.

DEMOCRACY AND MUSIC EDUCATION

Intelligence in the World

John Dewey's Moral Project

> Democracy: Political, social, or economic equality: the absence or disavowal of hereditary or arbitrary class distinctions or privileges... A state of society characterized by tolerance toward minorities, freedom of expression, and respect for the essential dignity and worth of the human individual with equal opportunity for each to develop freely to his fullest capacity in a cooperative community.
>
> —*Webster's Third New International Dictionary*

The School and Society

As Dewey observed at the outset of *The School and Society* (1900), "Nothing counts as much as the school."[1] The school placed the accomplishments and dreams of previous generations at the disposal of future generations so that society could re-create itself while realizing its collective potential. It provided the means for society to simultaneously preserve, transform, and transcend tradition. This aim, however, could only be achieved if students were free to develop their individuality and native intelligence. Individualism and socialism were one, and it was by allowing and encouraging students to develop and pursue their own interests, enthusiasms, and convictions that they could become fully functioning members of democratic society able to contribute intelligently to its continued development.

Dewey, however, was not advocating the kind of freedom of thought and action usually associated with libertarianism, the right to think and do as one pleases so long as it does not infringe upon the rights of others. Education should foster *freedom of mind* such that students are empowered to exert some degree of intelligent or conscious control over experience. Without this facility, and without the freedom of intelligence necessary to foresee and weigh possible consequences of action, freedom of action was sure to manifest itself in confusion and disorder.[2] Freedom of mind had important social and moral dimensions and ramifications, for unless students considered the morality of their actions, freedom of action could just as easily lead to selfishness and terror. Democracy was not just a political platform or form of government but an ethical ideal and communal way of life. At its highest level, democracy was "a form of moral and spiritual association."[3] Thought and action did not occur in a moral or social vacuum.[4] Ultimately, freedom of mind was a means of pursuing and maximizing the public good. It was a form of social and cultural critique. Like the utilitarians, Dewey believed that society's institutions should be subjected to continual scrutiny and critique. But whereas the utilitarians defined good in terms of the pain, pleasure, or happiness of existing individuals, Dewey conceived of it as the releasing of human capacity for communal action.[5]

The keynote of Deweyan democracy was the necessary participation of every mature citizen in the formation of common social values regulating the lives of people.[6] Critical of institutional systems (including both capitalist and Marxist ones) that stifled individual and collective participation and initiative, Dewey proposed that those governed by regulatory agencies should have a say in their design, implementation, and management. Because knowledge arose from experience, no one was justified in managing others without their consent. And coercion only discouraged individual responsibility and creativity.

Possessing an abiding faith in human nature and the power of "pooled and cooperative experience," Dewey believed that, should sufficient numbers of people achieve freedom of mind, society could "generate progressively the knowledge and wisdom needed to guide collective action."[7] Students and the masses were conceived not as passive receptacles of received or expert knowledge but as potential sources of new knowledge and expertise. Without their participation, each according to his or her abilities, society would be deprived of potentially valuable ideas and resources. Individuals might not be especially wise or talented, but they were positioned to reflect on, and to act intelligently to improve, the quality of their own lives and of those around them.

Democracy, as Dewey noted, was a relatively recent addition to the political scheme, the social world having been governed for the greater part of human history by autocratic and authoritarian regimes. Even in those countries in which democratic governments existed, the populace, through long ingrained habit, too often only continued to place its collective faith in a hierarchical leadership imposed from above. In those cases, democracy remained tenuous. Autocratic and authoritarian social schemes were inimical to participatory democracy because they discouraged independent thinking and were based on an assumption of superiority, whether of family, race, gender, color, creed, ability, wealth, or social status. Dewey's, however, was not a theory of equality of natural endowment. People were naturally varied, or unequal, in their respective talents. They were not created equal. This was all the more reason why a democratic principle of equality was needed as a guide to the rule of law. For unless all individuals were treated as equals before the law and by the institutions governing society, the strong and the gifted would use their power to oppress the weak and the less gifted, thereby suppressing the latter's potential contribution to society. Equality was thus an important legal and political doctrine and not a psychological one. As Dewey explained, "All individuals are entitled to equality of treatment by law and in its administration. Each one is affected equally in quality if not in quantity by the institutions under which he lives and has an equal right to express his judgment, although the weight of his judgment may not be equal in amount when it enters into the pooled result to that of others."[8]

Individuals were free to develop their capacities to their fullest extent and to contribute to the institutions governing them, but the quality and extent of their contributions could only be assessed in the hurly-burly of lived social experience. It was not for the privileged, or an elite, to decide what was of social value. No one had a monopoly on truth or value, and autocratic and elite regimes and entrenched, taken-for-granted traditions only discouraged individuals from engaging in the kinds of reflection and moral decision making that were the foundation for personal responsibility and creativity.[9]

Dewey envisioned a community of cooperative inquirers with each individual empowered to contribute according to his or her own abilities in a spirit of service to others.[10] In a true democracy, a reciprocal relationship existed between the individual and society. Just as democracy depended on the active participation of every mature person in forming common social values, the full flowering of individuality required the right kind of social environment.[11] Individuality was not something that existed in a moral or social vacuum, nor was it something that could be handed ready-made to another. Rather, it had to be fostered and continually reconstructed through lived and shared social experience. The means to accomplish that end was reflective thinking, otherwise referred to by Dewey as "socialized intelligence."[12]

Reflective thinking was virtually synonymous with the scientific method. Dewey's critics were quick to seize upon his fondness for the scientific method as evidence of scientism. Dewey, though, "understood the dangers of using the authority of science to consecrate 'special interest' as something appropriate for all."[13] Reflective thinking was conceived by him not as an abstract, objective, or formulaic set of intellectual tools but as a socially situated, flexible, and fallible way of thinking that varied according to the nature of the problem and needs of the individual. The scientific method only made sense when it was framed within a context of human values. There was no such thing as "value-free" inquiry.[14] Human values gave rise to and shaped inquiry. They also determined what counted as knowledge, thereby setting the standards against which the fruits of inquiry were to be judged. Reflective thinking was an experimental way of thinking, a form of means-ends analysis the ends of which were ultimately social. Like Hans Georg Gadamer's hermeneutic circle, reflective or critical inquiry was a means of bridging, assuaging, or clarifying personal, historical, social, or cultural differences.[15]

Implicit in Dewey's socialized intelligence were the Aristotelian virtues of neighborliness, tolerance, and mutuality, as without them there could be no possibility of cooperative inquiry free from intimidation and ridicule. "Intolerance, abuse, calling of names because of difference of opinion about religion or politics or business, as well as because of differences of race, color, wealth, or degree of culture," Dewey wrote, "are treason to the democratic way of life."[16] Nor were legal guarantees sufficient to ensure freedom of expression if the relationship between the various parties was not based on a feeling of mutual respect coupled with a commitment to achieving mutual understanding and solidarity.

These conditions applied equally to all segments of society, including the school and scientific and business communities. As James Kloppenberg explains, Dewey's scientific community was conceived as "a democratically organized, truth-seeking group of independent thinkers who tested their results against pragmatic standards, but those standards always reflected moral rather than narrowly technical considerations."[17] Freedom of mind was both an end and a means with authority rooted not in a scheme of absolutes or tradition but in experience.

Dewey's emphasis on the development of a community of cooperative inquiry has been criticized on at least two related points that, as will become evident in subsequent chapters, are important to the theme of the present book. The first criticism is that his emphasis on community and solidarity might discourage diversity, while the second is that it might encourage or validate elitist tendencies in scientific and intellectual communities. With respect to diversity, Kloppenberg writes that, to Dewey, "a democracy without difference was a contradiction in terms, . . . he believed passionately that all individuals, in their uniqueness, make different contributions to democratic life. The richer the mix, the richer the culture that results from the interaction."[18] Individuals and groups with different agendas could still work together to clarify or resolve disputes while working toward common goals, that is, so long as they shared an interest in egalitarianism.

The charge of elitism originally arose during the 1920s, when behavioral and empirical social scientists invoked his pragmatism in support of social engineering proposals. Dewey's characteristic response was that it was folly to rely on elites. While acknowledging that elite communities possessing expert knowledge could demonstrate how cooperative inquiry might work in pursuit of narrow ends, Dewey reiterated that the purpose of such inquiry was to expand democracy, not to cause its retreat or contraction.[19] Further, and contrary to the prevailing opinion among American philosophers at the time, he viewed philosophy and science as properly allied in pursuit of solutions to human problems.[20] Philosophy, as a form of cultural practice and criticism, could provide much needed moral guidance to science. Practical science, for its part, could free philosophy from "vain metaphysics and idle epistemology," rooting it in experience and the world.[21]

Given Dewey's faith in the native intelligence of the common man and woman, and his democratic principle of participation by individuals in the institutions governing them, the challenge for philosophers, scientists, and other intellectuals, including teachers, was to become more inclusive with respect to the ethical, moral, political, and other forms of decision making affecting society. Dewey's antidote to many of the problems afflicting society was that socialized intelligence should become more widespread and habitual; that children, and eventually society as a whole, should learn to overcome the limitations of "past experience, received dogmas, the stirring of self-interest, the arousing of passion, sheer mental laziness, a false social environment steeped in biased traditions or animated by false expectations, and so on."[22] This was an ethical call for the cultivation of a democratic character and ethos that would "sustain and spread the rational or common good."[23]

The School and the Democratic Ethos

Realizing that socialized intelligence had to be nurtured and encouraged, Dewey turned his attention to the school in order to explain how it might be inculcated. Observing that schools often only reproduced social inequities, he reconceived education as a form of embryonic democracy in which teachers were authoritative but not authoritarian and in which the aim was to produce mature thinkers capable of participating as full-fledged members of democratic society. Children required guidance if they were to acquire the skills, knowledge, and attitudes necessary to participate as members of a democratic community of cooperative inquirers. Although often identified as a supporter of child-centered education, in reality Dewey believed that such practices were "really stupid" because they led to a relativizing of authority that quickly degenerated into authoritarianism.[24]

Education entailed some form and degree of social control by the school but also personal responsibility on the part of children. Teachers were moral and intellectual leaders who were to "direct by indirection," which meant that they were to establish the right conditions for inspiring, inculcating, and guiding the development of socialized intelligence.[25] They were to teach students not so much "what" as "how" to think.[26] They were not to impose on children any particular social or political agenda, other than the aforementioned democratic framework. Education, like philosophy, was a form of social and cultural criticism derived from a comprehensive social interest, not from an interest in a particular class struggle. As Dewey wrote in the *Social Frontier* in 1936,

> Yet what is the point of the class concept as a determining factor in educational procedure unless it is to have such a controlling influence on the latter that education becomes a special form of indoctrination? And in that case what becomes of the plea for freedom in teaching? Is it a plea merely for freedom to inculcate a certain view of society, logically entailing lack of freedom from other views?[27]

It was important to acknowledge that social injustices and inequities existed, but solutions to those problems were to be sought in the interests of all society, not just those of a particular class or group.[28]

In the end, it was up to individual children to develop their moral and ethical character through their own efforts. The role of the school and teacher was to create and maintain a social and intellectual environment conducive to that end. Just what that educational environment should look like Dewey was reluctant to say. Although deeply concerned about matters of curriculum theory, particularly the nature of reflective and critical inquiry and the kinds of problems that engender it, Dewey was wary of overprescribing to teachers. No doubt this had to do with his distaste for technical rationality, but he also expected teachers to think for themselves.[29]

Dewey's democratic ideal of participation demanded that teachers also play a role in the organization and structure of the school and its curriculum. As he stated in 1937, "Every teacher should have some regular and organic way in which he can, directly or through representatives democratically chosen, participate in the formation of the controlling aims, methods, and materials of the school of which he is a part."[30] One of the arguments against teachers becoming more involved in the governance of the school was that they were not sufficiently prepared or competent for such a role. But, as Dewey replied, if such were the case, then it would hardly be possible for them to understand and implement the curriculum, let alone follow directions. The fact was that teachers were in continuous contact with their students, whereas administrators and curriculum developers were usually removed from direct experience with children. If nothing else, the exclusion of teachers from participation in the formation of guiding aims was a waste of a valuable human resource. Viewed properly, experienced teachers were potential sources of knowledge about needed changes to education. Including them in the planning and implementation of the curriculum and other aspects of the school would encourage educational initiative while also contributing to a sense of community.

Eventually, as teachers learned to exert a degree of increased control over their school and classroom environments, teaching would improve. Of course, the opposite was also probably true. The absence of democratic methods in school administration would engender a spirit of passivity and rebelliousness among teachers leading to the abdication of personal responsibility and the dissolution of a sense of community.[31]

Another important reason for incorporating democratic methods into school administration and governance was that children required access to appropriate models of democratic and cooperative behavior. The work of administrators, teachers, and students would have to be organized to promote and facilitate the growth of a cooperative social environment. This meant encouraging association and the free exchange of ideas among all concerned. Dewey actually applied these and other democratic principles to an experimental Laboratory School he founded in 1896 at the University of Chicago. There "cooperative social organization applied to the teaching body of the school as well as to the pupils. . . . Association and exchange among teachers was our substitute for what is called supervision, critic teaching, and technical training."[32] Teachers helped shape the curriculum while also meeting regularly to collaborate and discuss their work.

Finally, as far as this very brief overview of Dewey's educational philosophy is concerned, he encouraged interaction between the school and wider community as means of helping children to understand things in relation to their social environment. Society and its problems gave education purpose and direction. If the school was to act as an agent for social change, then it must necessarily engage with and, to some extent, reflect social reality. Dewey's solution to the problems of social engagement and relevance was to incorporate real-life kinds of occupational activities and problems into the school curriculum. The school, he stated in *The School and Society* (1900), should be "active with types of occupations that reflect the life of the larger society and permeated throughout with the spirit of art, history, and science."[33] By this means, students were to be gradually inducted into the larger social community.

Dewey, of course, was not advocating technical or vocational training for its own sake. While acknowledging its relevance, he believed that such training, divorced from a liberal education, bred passivity while serving to perpetuate social divisions and inequities. The converse was also true, that an overemphasis on intellectualism was detrimental to society because it worked to conserve aristocratic and elitist regimes and tendencies.[34] Dewey's project was the overcoming of the many dualisms that plagued society, between school and society, theory and practice, science and common sense, and thought and action.[35] Education should train both the mind and body in the service of society. Intelligence was thus eminently practical because it implied a unity of mind and body in pursuit of social ends.

Dewey also observed "that there ought to be an interaction between all the parts of the school system."[36] Complaining that too much of what was taught in the elementary and secondary schools was trivial or outdated, he looked to the universities to provide the necessary guidance. The universities possessed greater resources and were dedicated to research in the pursuit of knowledge and truth. The school system pursued the same end. This end, however, could only "be reached as the most advanced part of the educational system [was] in complete interaction with the most rudimentary."[37] Dewey might just as easily have replaced the word "system" with "community." The school and university were both communities unto themselves while simultaneously members of the wider educational and social communities. Both school and university depended on, and were expected to foster, a spirit of inquiry in the service of society. Even more, Dewey envisioned the school and university as existing in symbiosis. The university placed its resources at the disposal of the school in the development of new theories, subject matter, and methods, while the latter acted as a laboratory in which those innovations were tested and critiqued in the crucible of experience. In the best of all possible worlds, Dewey believed, there should be a unity of educational experience in which there were no barriers separating school, university, and society and in which all contributed to the continued evolution of new social truths. There should be no "lower" and "higher" in education, "but simply education."[38]

Dewey and Music Education

Throughout much of the twentieth century, American music educators aspired to democratic ideals. Influenced by Dewey and the early Progressive Education Movement, they became convinced that all children could benefit from musical instruction, not just the gifted, and that the social function of music education in the schools was primarily avocational rather than vocational. Whereas previously the purpose of music education had been to train future musicians and music teachers, it now became the development of all children's musical abilities such that they were able to "make cultural use of leisure time."[39]

This acknowledgment of music education's social function eventually gave rise during the first half of the twentieth century to the music appreciation and community music movements. Both of those important movements were motivated by democratic ideals and intentions. However, the music appreciation movement, with its emphasis on the development of good musical taste in all children, was decidedly un-Deweyan and, by his standards, even undemocratic in nature. Music education was a means of socializing or indoctrinating students to the works of the great masters. "The goal was to develop musical taste along the lines of Western art music, ... to propagate and socialize the musical tastes of the socially elite class among all classes."[40]

Dewey frowned on social and educational schemes that were based on prior assumptions of superiority or that derived their authority from tradition. He was also critical of elitist artistic agendas because they stifled independent thought while leading to the reification of art and its consequent separation from ordinary experience. Concerned about the growing irrelevance of art in the lives of ordinary people, Dewey wrote in *Art as Experience* (1934) that "even a crude experience, if authentically an experience, is more fit to give a clue to the intrinsic nature of esthetic experience than is an object already set apart from any other mode of experience."[41] It was more important that people create their own musical and artistic experience and not just worship or imitate the masters. Art arose out of and was connected to ordinary experience, and "no amount of ecstatic eulogy of finished works [could] of itself assist the understanding of the generation of such works."[42]

Dewey doubtless approved of the music appreciation movement's attempt to make art, including so-called serious music, an integral part of communal life, although he probably would have disapproved of attempts by many of those same teachers to exclude popular music and jazz from the curriculum.[43] Rejecting both the western metaphysics underlying the western musical canon and crass commercialism, he conceived of music, too, as a form of social and cultural criticism that arose out of, and idealized, "qualities found in common experience," including that of the ordinary man and woman.[44] Music, like all other forms of human experience, was a complex social dance that depended for its continued existence and social health on the generation and inclusion of multiple perspectives that had to be tested through application to experience. Diversity was the keyword.[45] It was not for some social, intellectual, or musical elite to say what was or was not of musical value to society. Ordinary people, too, had potentially important musical and artistic contributions to make.

From Dewey's liberal democratic standpoint, communal musical values and standards were continually forged anew through the crucible of shared social and musical experience.[46] They were not fixed and immutable but constantly shifting in response to society's changing needs. There were no musical absolutes, but neither were all musical perspectives and accomplishments necessarily equal. Music and art were not merely subjective. Dewey, of late, has been associated with the postmodernists, thanks to Richard Rorty and other contemporary philosophers' interest in Deweyan pragmatism.[47] Unlike postmodernists such as Jacques Derrida and Michel Foucault, though, Dewey retained a healthy faith in the possibility of human progress. Everything depended on the exercise of intelligent judgment, which, while not infallible, was better than relying on "ignorance, whim, prejudice, imitation, or authority."[48]

The proper aim of music education was to help children understand music and its role in civilization, which was to "break through conventionalized and routine consciousness."[49] Music and the other arts were the primary means by which individuals and society as a whole enhanced the quality of experience, making it more purposeful, intense, and enjoyable. Art education demanded of children that they exercise good judgment in sorting out the meaningful from the merely mediocre or trivial and imagination in the generation of new and extended possibilities.[50] Insomuch as thinking, including musical and artistic varieties, was framed within a context of human values needing to be sorted out and understood, music education was essentially social and moral in nature. It was concerned with the development of moral character. Implied was a maturational process whereby students gradually learned how to explore, negotiate, and contribute to the complex and constantly changing social and musical world around them. The arts were organs of vision that gave depth, meaning, and moral direction to experience. As such they were not luxuries "but emphatic expressions of that which makes any education worth while."[51]

The community music movement was more in keeping with Dewey's philosophy, although in the end it, too, failed to live up to his democratic ideals. The purpose of the community music movement was to effect a symbiotic relationship between the school and community.[52] The school gave direction to community musical groups while receiving public support for its endeavors. The school provided much needed musical guidance to community groups with respect to methodology and standards while the community music movement "brought to school music its spirit of free expression, of joy, of fellowship, of universality, and of service."[53] No longer cloistered and shut off from the larger community, the school took its cue from society while, at least theoretically, becoming a positive force for needed social change.[54] The goals of both school and community music were seen as interdependent.

But while acknowledging that music education should have a social purpose and agenda, early-twentieth-century music educators, including those associated with the community music movement, failed to develop the insights needed to show how music in education could transform school and society. In part, this was because music educators continued to subscribe to the older aesthetic and utilitarian rationales.[55] The problem with aesthetic rationales is that they tend to treat music and music education as divorced from worldly affairs and thus not practical. Music exists and is worth studying for its own sake. Utilitarian rationales, on the other hand, justify music in the curriculum because it prepares students for musical careers or provides needed entertainment for school or community events. Music, of course, has utilitarian value, but what is generally missing from such approaches is an appreciation of far-off goals. Music education serves present and not future needs. Neither aesthetic nor utilitarian rationales, though, adequately prepare students to question and challenge authority and thereby to transform musical society.

Of the two rationales, probably the utilitarian is more problematic, as it assumes that music education ought only to replicate society. This problem continues to plague western music education down to the present. Too many music teachers still believe that music education is or ought to be primarily vocational or that it exists to serve entertainment purposes. Contemporary music education has no intellectual and social purpose along the lines of what Dewey proposed. Then, too, music educators have not been forthcoming with new ideas and philosophical explanations with respect to music education's social value. They continue to lack direction or vision. This is perhaps to be expected since, as Max Kaplan wrote in the 1960s, music educators have always "tended to live now and think later."[56]

James Mursell was a notable exception to this rule. In his book *Music Education: Principles and Programs* (1956), Mursell explained how music was a social art that lent itself well to participatory democracy. Participatory democracy, though, required a particular kind of leader if it was to succeed in accomplishing its aims.[57] Contrasting participatory democracy with autocratic and laissez-faire educational regimes, Mursell conceived of music teachers as democratic leaders whose function was to help children to deliberate, choose, and act cooperatively. Vision was an important aspect of democratic leadership, including teaching, because groups required guidance if they were to learn to act cooperatively. As Mursell expressed it,

> The music specialist who goes into an elementary school classroom with a set lesson and proceeds to push it through on a preconceived line is missing a chance. The band or choir director who treats his group simply

as an instrument is missing a chance. We must not relapse into a feeble laissez-faire or abdicate our leadership. Far from it! We must try to exercise the kind of leadership that evokes the thinking, the planning, the choosing, the deciding, the cooperating of others—the sort of leadership that does not treat others as passive followers, but that builds up in them a sense of active, responsible cooperation in a common enterprise.[58]

Democratically minded music teachers did not impose their will on others, nor did they leave them to their own devices. Rather, they sought to promote informed public deliberation and musical participation.[59] They possessed a social conscience and vision. Their job was not to entertain or pander to the masses, giving society what it wanted, or to replicate preexisting musical standards or conditions. Rather, it was to foster and guide personal and collective musical growth through shared social experience.[60]

Much like Dewey, Mursell conceived of education as a form of social and cultural inquiry and criticism whereby children gradually explored and made sense of their worlds and the range of choices available to them. An important aim of music education was to broaden the social and cultural horizons of children such that they gained increased awareness of the full range of human musical experience.[61] Music educators were leaders charged with pointing children in potentially productive new directions and with guiding them in the making of effective musical choices and decisions. True learning and growth arose out of active involvement in decision making and was organized according to the children's individual and collective developmental needs, not a preset and rigid curriculum.[62] Further, music specialists, as distinct from general classroom teachers who often assisted with music instruction, were charged with providing the necessary leadership to organize and coordinate other teachers, instructors, administrators, and parents involved in the music program. The music program, as Mursell ideally conceived it, was a cooperative venture involving all manner of people who needed to be cultivated and then coordinated in their pursuit of common social, musical, and educational goals. Music specialists, or teachers, were agents of social change in the sense that they worked to achieve personal and social integration.[63]

The Need for Educational Reform

Mursell's contributions notwithstanding, music educators during the early twentieth century acknowledged that social reform was needed, and they were successful in meeting society's immediate utilitarian and aesthetic needs with respect to socializing immigrants, developing community outreach programs, and promoting good citizenship. What they lacked was the realization that social reform demanded that education itself be reformed.[64]

They ultimately failed to change their ways and to provide the kinds of democratic and visionary leadership needed to challenge children and community
groups to develop to their full potential and thereby to transform musical
society. Rather than developing new musical and pedagogical ideas, methods, and repertoire that promoted personal and collective growth within a
democratic framework, music teachers all too often reverted to "tried and
true" approaches and materials. While paying lip service to democratic aims,
they continued to defer to the authority of tradition and the professional
status quo. Even today music teacher "training" still emphasizes traditional
pedagogical knowledge over social or other forms of inquiry, while academics have yet to adequately conceptualize music education's role or function in democratic society.[65] They have yet to consider what a commitment
to democratic principles and values might mean or entail for professional
practice.

Allen Britton may have hit upon one root of the problem—the lack of
meaningful reform in music education methodology, repertoire, and teacher
education—when he observed in 1966 that music education in the United
States (and presumably also in Canada and other western democracies) has
traditionally been somewhat removed from the real musical world. It has
existed in a sort of musical limbo suspended between folk and popular music
on the one hand and classical music on the other. Whereas popular music was viewed with distrust, for its lack of gentility, classical music was
little understood. Music educators found themselves in the peculiar situation of having to find or invent a kind of quasi-classical music that was
intelligible to the masses and to those in authority yet "could be taken as
'classical.'"[66]

What they elected for, and what the public wanted, was polite music that
was uncontroversial and guaranteed not to offend or ruffle anyone's feathers.
Parents wanted this music in their schools because they believed that it led to
social advancement, while music educators gained increased prestige through
association with the upper classes.[67]

Music education was both conservative and class-based. No one, it seems,
was especially worried that this approach might deaden music education
practice while serving to pacify and indoctrinate children. Contributing to
the lack of development of democratic vision and pedagogical models among
American music teachers were the decline of interest in sociology beginning
in the 1930s and the retreat of teacher training institutions into technical rationality and logical positivism. During the 1950s and 1960s, psychology pre-
vailed over philosophy, and when interest in philosophy began to reawaken,
it was aesthetics that once again came to the fore. Music education was a
means of training children to appreciate the beautiful and thereby transcend

the real world. Music educators dissociated themselves from the music of the street and countryside in the pursuit of the beautiful. It was only with the rise of the New Left in the 1960s, whose ideas eventually percolated down to the music education establishment with the rise of leftist and feminist scholarship in the late 1980s and early 1990s, that music educators began to develop a more comprehensive social interest and to seriously question the morality of their musical and educational actions.

During the past decade or so, critical theorists and radical feminists have contributed significantly to our understanding of some of the failings of professional music education philosophy and practice. Many of their teachings and criticisms of tradition and the status quo are now considered common sense by academics—for example, that power privileges, that knowledge and identity are socially constructed, and that the Enlightenment with its notions of individualism, reason, justice, and democracy has not always been favorable to women and minorities. These and other criticisms are usually directed at liberals, who typically try to ignore them while avoiding controversy. In consequence, liberal music educators and their detractors have yet to have many of the kinds of sustained and generous professional debates or conversations wherein these and other conflicting issues, ideas, and understandings of professional practice are worked out, let alone actually applied to practice. This lack of conversation between liberals and their critics is unfortunate, not just because the profession risks becoming increasingly stagnant and fragmented but also because there is a failure in communication and mutual understanding and thus also in common purpose. Critics malign "savage liberalism," but until now no one in the field of music education has attempted a spirited defense of a liberal music education. Nor do critics seem interested in challenging conventional notions of liberalism or asking whether so-called liberals in music education are actually living up to their ideals.[68] The concepts of liberalism and the liberal are simply taken for granted and all too often misrepresented by critics who mistake their "difficulties and misuses" for essences.[69] Some of the more radical of these critics would rather that the Enlightenment be thrown out and replaced with something of their own choosing. These self-appointed guardians of righteousness would reshape society to their own liking.[70]

The defense of liberalism in chapter 2 is offered as an antidote to this failure of communication and mutual understanding among music educators and as a check to those who would throw the baby out with the bathwater by trashing the very same Enlightenment ideals that have made their own criticisms possible. We need to get beyond such destructive polarizations if progress is to be made in addressing pressing professional and social problems and thereby ensuring the future of music education in the schools. One pragmatic response to the current impasse between liberals and their critics is to renew and strengthen our commitment to egalitarianism and participatory democracy by defining liberalism differently, "in ways that better accommodate the claims of individual, social, and cultural diversity."[71] This, as I try to show in subsequent chapters, effectively means that liberals should live up to their ideals by intellectually engaging with their critics and the public in search of a more inclusive, just, and humane musical society.

Intelligence in the Musical World

Defining Liberalism Differently

A Liberal versus Performance-Based Music Education?

2 Liberals of the Anglo-American philosophical tradition believe that the political legitimacy of democratically elected governments and civic leaders rests on an informed citizenry that is able to participate in public deliberation and, thereby, the shaping of communal values. A liberal education is supposed to contribute to that end, that is, to prepare future citizens "to function in a democratic culture beyond the specific frame of any profession or specialized knowledge."[1] Music education philosopher David Elliott, though, doubts that a liberal education is appropriate for all children or even "sufficient for future academics."[2] The future happiness of children, he says, depends on their ability to pursue the life values of self-growth, self-knowledge, and musical understanding and enjoyment through performance—"in short, a certain musical way of life."[3] In several important respects, Elliott's philosophy can be understood as reactionary to the "liberal" education advanced by educational leaders such as William Bennett, Allan Bloom, and E. D. Hirsch Jr.[4] Thus conceived, Elliott complains, a liberal education involves the self-indulgent study of very general and "inert" formal knowledge of the classics divorced from practical and vocational matters.

Peter Kivy, too, equates a liberal education with study of the classics or the great artistic and intellectual achievements of western civilization. He thinks the function of a liberal education is to initiate or socialize students into their tribal identity. If music is a form of ritual, music education is a rite of passage. "Rites of passage . . . are part of the function of art. In teaching us about ourselves, our symbols, the metaphors by which we live, art seems to humanize us in a quite literal sense of the word. It makes us human beings by helping us pass into our tribal identity."[5] This, Kivy thinks, is essential to personal happiness. But while a liberal arts education conceived thusly suggests both breadth and depth of certain kinds of knowledge (i.e., study of the western artistic and musical canons of genius), it is very narrow and conservative by today's standards. It also smacks of intellectual idol worship in that students are to be inducted into a preexisting and merely asserted social and cultural system.[6] In Kivy's Platonic view, students are expected only to accept and emulate the artistic representations found in the classics, not criticize, reject, or improve upon them.[7] Kivy and Elliott, however, are both being overly reductive with respect to the nature and value of a liberal education. Moreover, Elliott wrongly assumes that a liberal education is distinct from, or in some ways antithetical to, a vocational one.

Liberalism has been defined in many ways, but above all it is a philosophy for a democratic way of life in which primacy is given to the civil and political rights and responsibilities of individuals (although liberals also concede that there may be exceptions when group rights take precedence over those of individuals). There is a "fusion of freedom and responsibility," meaning that the rights of individual citizens are only protected to the extent they exercise their obligation to intelligently participate in public life.[8] The most important of those rights have to do with various personal freedoms, including freedom of speech, choice, association, occupation, conscience, etc. Among the important responsibilities of the liberal is a willingness to engage in shared public life by monitoring political authority, defending the rights and freedoms of both self and others, and exercising self-restraint in political demands. In short, liberals have a strong sense of solidarity and commonality that is motivated by "a shared commitment to liberal principles of freedom and equality."[9] Thus understood, the goal of liberal education is to "cultivate people who are willing and able to be self-governing in both their personal and political lives."[10]

Liberals also want to justify themselves to their "earlier selves."[11] That is why (in literature, for instance) the study of so-called great books is often emphasized in a liberal education. But, as Amy Gutmann admonishes,

> Liberal education, an education adequate to serve the life of a free and equal citizen in any modern democracy, requires far more than the reading of great books, although great books are an indispensable aid. We also need to read and think about books, and therefore to teach them, in a spirit of free and open inquiry, the spirit of both democratic citizenship and individual freedom. The cultivation of that spirit is aided by immersion in profound and influential books, like Plato's *Republic,* which expose us to eloquently original, systematically well-reasoned, intimidating, and unfamiliar visions of the good life and good society. But liberal education fails if intimidation leads to blind acceptance of those visions or if unfamiliarity leads us to blind rejection.[12]

Great books and music have the potential to provoke change and growth, but it would be a grave mistake to assume that a liberal education is only or even primarily concerned with the tried and true or the pinnacles of literary, musical, or other achievement. That is actually contrary to the political goals of liberalism. Rather, as Dewey expressed it, liberalism implies "thoughtful valuation," or criticism and mediation, of all experience, including the so-called classics but also the seemingly mundane.[13] Only through criticism and mediation of all experience can determinations of value be made. Music educators and other teachers ought to be constantly on the lookout for new works, too, including ones from other social groups and cultures, the study of which can also inform while provoking self-examination, reflection, and mutual growth—which can motivate conversation.

Although connoting negativism to some, the word "criticism" more properly implies breadth and depth of experience coupled with a commitment to careful research, analysis, and judgment about things that matter. It is an expression of intelligence, caring, and social responsibility in which the goals are growth and awareness of possible consequences of beliefs and actions. As Dewey wrote,

> Because intelligence is critical method applied to goods of belief, appreciation, and conduct, so as to construct freer and more secure goods, turning assent and assertion into free communication of shareable meanings, turning feeling into ordered and liberal sense, turning reaction into response, it is the reasonable object of our deepest faith and loyalty, the stay and support of all reasonable hopes.[14]

Criticism seeks the improvement of society. Surely, Dewey argued, this is "a better method than its alternatives, authority, imitation, caprice and ignorance, prejudice and passion."[15] Given that a liberal democracy depends on individual citizens engaging in public deliberations about shared values, one would hope that music education would contribute to the end, that it would prepare children for democratic citizenship. Unfortunately, "criticism" has become something of a dirty word in contemporary music education circles, thanks perhaps to the growth of relativism, postmodernism, multiculturalism, and political correctness in musical academia. Music, philosophers and professional leaders exhort, is both subjective, or in the ear of the beholder, and a badge of tribal identity. Either way it is beyond criticism and reproach. At worst, music is characterized as a battleground or Darwinian struggle in which individuals and groups with their different ideologies and tribal identities fight it out; at best, music is a laissez-faire collection of musical communities, cultures, or homes, each of which must be accepted on its own terms.[16] Music education involves helping children explore and imaginatively identify with other people and their music. In that sense, the new multiculturalism is dedicated to developing a wider sense of community. This is potentially empowering, but in the absence of criticism it is difficult to imagine how students are to make qualitative distinctions and thereby gain some modicum of intelligent control over their sonic environments, let alone understand other people's music and the political or practical implications thereof. Nor can students assume responsibility for their choices and actions, including the ways their beliefs and practices affect others. Multiculturalism becomes just another form of absolutism to be imposed on children.[17]

The current confusion about musical criticism is really one of values and standards. Many music educators continue to believe that the western musical canon represents the high-water mark of human musical achievement and should be used as a yardstick or set of preestablished, objective, and permanent standards for judging all music. Others hold the equally extreme view that no objective judgments are possible, that all music and performances thereof are valid and "equally worthy of consideration" in music education and music education research.[18] Corollary to this is the claim that "Judgments of the quality or 'seriousness' of particular pieces, composers, or styles can only be made according to the aesthetic standards appropriate to the particular sociocultural context in which that music is experienced."[19] Some academics even contend that western classical and popular music have no connection. They seem to want us to believe that all musical cultures and subcultures are essentially different and independent rather than overlapping and interdependent.[20]

But if all music and performances are equally valid or merely relative or subjective—if we live in a world in which no qualitative musical distinctions can be made—then none of it really matters to society. If music is truly only subjective, or only intelligible to members of a particular social or cultural group, then there can be no conversations about musical and educational values, only monologues leading to cultural imposition, increased social fragmentation, and a retreat from the wider world and its problems. This kind of absolutist and expressly ideological thinking "isolates us in our own skins and equates culture to racial or ethnic identity."[21] Students can only accept or learn about different cultures but not engage in intelligent conversation with anyone. A fairly typical example of this kind of laissez-faire thinking can be found in the recent Music Educators National Conference document *Vision 2020,* in which Jane Walters exclaims, "If we can learn to deal with choice, if we can learn to deal with each other as equals, . . . accepting and understanding the joy of everyone's music . . . we are getting closer to the ideals we are setting for 2020."[22] This is just sentimentalism, a form of thinking that Dewey said is "next to deadness and dullness, formalism, and routine" with respect to its potential for stifling growth.[23] I doubt, for example, that Walters truly believes that Marilyn Manson's "AntiChrist Superstar" (1996) is joyful or life-affirming. But then whoever said that music should always be pretty and uplifting and never dark or disturbing?[24] Much music is, after all, intended as social protest. Its social function, as conceived by Manson but also by many other rock artists and even some twentieth-century avant-garde composers and musicians, is to disturb or disrupt middle-class complacency. When followed to its logical conclusion, Dewey cautioned, the kinds of extreme relativistic and laissez-faire thinking such as are found in the *Vision 2020* document result in a "medley of irrelevancies."[25] In the absence of criticism and without at least the possibility of dissent, there can be no freedom of musical expression and no real understanding or productive change, just sentimentalism, self-indulgence, dogma, passive acceptance, or complacency.[26]

Were he alive today, Dewey's response would be that both objectivist and relativist positions are wrong: the objectivist because it confuses quantitative measurement with what is essentially qualitative judgment about values, and the relativist because it ignores music's material and public existence as sound.[27] Music does in fact have objective or discernible qualities that can be subjected to critical and public analysis. The difference, I wish to suggest, is that musical criticism should first be concerned with judging those qualities in relation to the particular cultural contexts in which they arise or whose values their structural organization or performances thereof are meant to represent: whether, to what extent, or in what ways they are representative of a particular culture's or group's beliefs and values. Individual cultural and musical communities have their own musical beliefs, values, and practices that evolve over time and with experience and through praxis—their own criteria for musical excellence. In that sense music should indeed be judged on its own terms, or according to prescribed practice within a community, and not according to supposedly fixed, abstract, and universal musical standards. This, I would argue, is a matter of respect. One engages in criticism not so as to compare and compete for superiority but to understand.[28]

Once that understanding has been obtained, however, the music in question ought to be subjected to further criticism through inclusion in progressively wider and open public conversations leading, perhaps inexorably, to some sort of hybridization of musical values. This may sound threatening to those wishing to protect and preserve, or to conserve, their own particular musical and cultural values and identities from the hegemony and homogenization of mainstream culture. However, all cultural values and identities are by definition "radically, quintessentially hybrid," meaning that they are shaped by social conditions and through experience and interaction with others and are thus overlapping, entangled, encumbered, and constantly evolving.[29] Change is inevitable. The only real or serious questions for any society have to do with whether, how, to what extent, and by whom intelligent control can be exerted over conditions and thus over the nature, direction, and rates of particular musical or other changes. And in democratic societies, as opposed to authoritarian ones, the moral authority and responsibility for making judgments about changes affecting all of society (such as ones involving media censorship, identity politics, cultural values, or public education) ultimately rests with an involved public. Only by actively and publicly participating as mature and responsible citizens in effecting or ameliorating change can individuals and groups hope to protect their own musical freedoms and identities while also contributing to the improvement of conditions.[30] This presupposes knowledge of possible alternatives—as Dewey said, only through "knowledge of a wide range of traditions" can the critic make intelligent judgments—but also of how values are constructed, by whom, with what means, and to what ends.[31] Contrary to what critics of democracy suggest, however, this does not mean that we are doomed to ever greater cultural homogeneity ultimately resulting in a universal cultural blandness. That would be wrong on at least two counts: first because it would be confusing globalism and capitalism with democracy, and second because the idea of democracy contributing to a reduction in diversity is a contradiction in terms. As already stated, democracy depends on the desirability and possibility of difference and dissent leading, we hope, to positive change.

As Dewey reminds us, "We are criticizing, not for its own sake, but for the sake of instituting and perpetuating more enduring and extensive values."[32] Criticism, because it implies awareness of antecedents and consequences, means and ends, is essential to understanding and personal and civic responsibility. And in democratic society we are all responsible and accountable to each other.[33] The social purpose of public criticism is the pursuit of the common or greater good. This, as Amy Gutmann explains, involves "connecting the democratic value of diversity . . . with the value of expanding the cultural, the intellectual, and spiritual horizons of all individuals, enriching our world by exposing us to differing cultural and intellectual perspectives, and thereby increasing our possibilities for intellectual and spiritual growth, exploration, and enlightenment."[34] Criticism seeks to transcend ideology, naked greed, and mere self, class, or cultural interest.[35] Individuals and groups are obliged to contribute their own ideas to democratic culture, but, in so doing, they must leave themselves open to criticism and consideration of alternative possibilities. As a result, they themselves may be changed, although this does not mean that individuals and groups must surrender their own personal or collective authority and integrity—their identities—to mainstream or any other culture. Thus, in democratic society, different cultures may be deserving of respect, but nothing is sacrosanct or immutable. Everything is at least potentially subject to criticism and thereby also to change. In Dewey's own words,

"Judgment and belief regarding actions to be performed can never attain more than a precarious probability."[36] Further, once thinkers converse with one another, "no one can wholly predict what will emerge."[37]

Public criticism is thus not equivalent to logic. Logic can be a useful tool when applied to certain kinds of very narrow legal, technical, or philosophical problems, but most of the problems that really matter to us cannot be reduced to final or definitive answers. Logic, because it is purposefully devoid of emotion and empathy, cannot help solve our most pressing social problems by educating us in our humanity. It is a machine language that, when applied to human experience, results in winners or losers, not reconciliation. Criticism is instead a messy and many-sided conversation in which the participants acknowledge the social contingency, complexity, and fallibility of human values while seeking the truth.

The Role of the Intellectual in Democratic Musical Society

The role and moral task of the intellectual or cultural critic in all of this is to prevent closure and to extend open conversation, to help seek the truth while putting things into historical and cultural perspective.[38] Truth is seen as socially contingent, polyvalent, and provisional. This, however, is not to suggest that all musical ideas or truth claims are equally valid or good or that "we have a duty to justify everything."[39] Rather, when deemed necessary, the worth or potential value of musical or other beliefs, ideas, and knowledge in particular situations or contexts ought to be judged with reference to both democratic principles and criteria (such as those identified by Mursell in the 1950s) and practical or social realities.[40] Knowledge serves society, and it is the particular role of the intellectual, as a member of a privileged minority with the luxury of time, facilities, knowledge, and training, to guide people in making informed decisions while also pointing them in potentially fruitful and productive new directions.[41] Intellectuals ought to be authoritative, meaning that they possess an abundance of knowledge that can be applied in the service of society, but not authoritarian. They are, in short, public servants and leaders charged with defending the common or democratic faith.[42] Intellectuals are accountable to the public, particularly to the weak and enfeebled, those who for whatever reasons are unable to adequately represent themselves in public conversations.[43]

Relatively few people outside of academia have the luxury of devoting much time and energy to the pursuit of truth and understanding. That is all the more reason why public intellectuals are needed in democratic society; it is also the reason why those individuals are the first to be censored or imprisoned by totalitarian regimes. The question is whether music teachers, music education majors, and children in democratic society ought to learn how to think and behave as public intellectuals, particularly in music and music teacher education classes. The case for music teachers and undergraduate music education majors is perhaps self-evident, since they are by definition present or future leaders of children.[44] One would hope that teachers would be interested in developing and contributing their own ideas to professional and public conversations, of engaging in public criticism about musical and education values and thereby helping to shape informed public opinion. Teachers, after all, must be prepared to champion and explain their educational values to the public if they want to be held accountable for the attainment of realistic goals.[45]

Such appears not to be the case, however, with many music education majors and even experienced music teachers. A growing body of research suggests that many of them are intellectually passive in the sense that they are too accepting of received knowledge, including highly prescriptive methods and the latest fads.[46] Perhaps worse, there seems to be impatience among them and perhaps among teachers in general with things intellectual. Many music education majors and teachers narrowly conceive themselves as performers and performance teachers—as practitioners charged with acquiring and replicating traditional performance and teaching methods—and not intellectuals in the sense of being politically aware and disposed to question and challenge the professional status quo. Nor are they disposed to engage in public criticism of wider educational, social, and political values.[47] As is explained in chapter 4, this leaves them at a decided disadvantage in the current political climate in which public education is increasingly under attack and subject to defunding by government.

Music teachers are also notoriously conservative, a fact that was recently emphasized in a survey report by Norton York, who concluded that "the typical picture of a secondary school teacher in England and Wales is of a classically trained musician who has entered teaching straight from a traditional music degree."[48] Although popular and ethnic musics are included in the English National Music Curriculum, the majority of the 750 respondents in York's survey clearly felt most comfortable teaching classical music, despite its perceived "demotivational" effects on students. This, York concluded, supports the charge that "school music culture tends to be introverted and avoids looking for models of current practice from the art of music rather than relying on the received knowledge of music education."[49] In short, music education in England and Wales (and probably in North America, too) is out of touch with current school and social realities. But then, adult society and government usually expect teachers to appear "normal" or "conventional" and to conform to traditional middle-class values and established models of professional practice. Nonconformists and those lacking the requisite knowledge of the western musical canon and of established educational practice are not as likely to be accepted into, let alone succeed in, music teacher education programs.[50]

University schools of music and music teacher education programs must thus share at least some of the blame for the intellectual passivity and conservatism of music teachers, since it is they who set the criteria for admission and through whose "narrow portals" undergraduates must pass before gaining admittance to the profession.[51] Those institutions and programs are designed to create professionals and not public intellectuals. As such they are inherently conservative and "intolerant of genuine innovation" and dissent.[52] This is particularly the case in the current utilitarian political climate in which education is increasingly seen as only vocational and subject to the dictates of the global marketplace. Many undergraduates, and not just music education majors, only want "the practical information to acquire jobs."[53] These and other factors have contributed to the preparation of tame and intellectually passive musicians and music teachers who appear incapable of thinking for themselves and coping with real-world problems and situations involving uncertainty, uniqueness, and value conflict.[54] York's music teachers, for example, while acknowledging that they are out of touch with their students' interests and needing to learn more about contemporary popular musical culture, appear incapable of helping themselves. Although willing to learn more about other musical styles and genres if opportunities present themselves, those teachers appear to be passively waiting for someone else to initiate change through professional development.[55]

Even more disturbing is the relative lack of conversation between York's music teachers and students with respect to their obviously conflicting musical beliefs and values. Some teachers use popular music as a stepping-stone to the classics, while many grudgingly acknowledge that it ought to be taught for reasons of national pride or because it represents a huge industry providing pleasure to a multitude of people, especially the young. Others believe that it ought to be taught because it is something that students can enjoy.[56] The situation is arguably not much better in North America, where many music educators are said to regard popular music "as a vast wasteland of musical mindlessness."[57] Popular music is mentioned in the United States National Standards for Music Education and may actually be prevalent in many American and Canadian school music programs, but there is little acknowledgment that it should be taught for its own sake as something warranting serious scrutiny and criticism. Besides, and despite their willingness to incorporate popular music into the curriculum, North American music teachers, like their English counterparts, are still at heart classically trained musicians. Even when popular music instruction is included in school curricula, it is apt to be based on principles "abstracted" from the western musical and peda-gogical canon (see chapter 6 for several suggestions for teaching popular and so-called world music).[58]

Many of students' most cherished beliefs and values, however, are learned through popular, and not "high," culture.[59] Yet, although high culture has been the subject of increasing debate and deserved criticism among aca-demics, pop culture remains largely uncritically examined by music educa-tors. And while there are obviously exceptions, students clearly reject the mu-sical values of previous generations inherent in the classics. As Allan Bloom declared in *The Closing of the American Mind,* "Classical music is dead among the young."[60] So what we have are two generational groups with their re-spective musical belief systems living side by side, in the same classroom, in splendid cultural isolation. There is perhaps some intergenerational and cultural sharing of factual knowledge and information, a certain amount of tolerance or passive acceptance, but little evidence of musical conversation, of the mutual curiosity, respect, and criticism that philosophers like Dewey thought essential to liberal education and thus to social amelioration and the growth and improvement of community. There appears to be little meeting of musical minds.[61]

Music Performance Reconsidered

Given these observations about the intellectual passivity and conservatism among music teachers and their lack of engagement in intellectual conver-sation with their pupils, Elliott's pursuit of happiness, enjoyment, and self-growth through performance seems self-indulgent and of only secondary importance.[62] Performance is obviously important to society, but in the ab-sence of intellectualizing and public conversation about the nature and role of music and music education therein, performance and skills-based approaches can lead to the continued isolation and marginalization of music education from the educational and social mainstreams.[63]

John Ralston Saul goes even further, arguing that the splintering of educa-tion into so many specialties controlled by a multitude of expert gatekeepers makes the kind of serious, integrated debate necessary for the defense of democracy virtually impossible. There is a sense in which the citizenry feel "that they have been abandoned by their thinkers; a sense of being betrayed by an intelligentsia which does not take the humanist experience seriously, particularly not the drama of the citizen-based democracy."[64] Composers of so-called serious music are particularly faulted for abdicating their re-sponsibilities as public intellectuals. During the latter half of the twentieth century, they "turned . . . toward an arid, mechanistic rationalism" that left "the field of public engagement in contemporary music . . . wide open to the propagandists."[65] With the notable exception of individuals like R. Murray Schafer (many of whose works were actually intended as social criticism), contemporary composers have simply and deliberately abandoned the public sphere altogether, self-indulgently composing esoteric works organized mathematically with minimal public appeal. Much the same criticism has been made of younger conservatory and university-trained musicians, who are said to value technique over musicality and interpretive ability. In consequence, "few have found a way to play that reaches the souls of today's audience."[66] Today's composers and classically trained performers speak a private language that for the most part is only understood by, or of interest to, fellow composers, musicians, and academics, and not by the remote and distant public. Composers and classically trained performers have a serious communication problem.[67]

When not subscribing to the authoritarianism of the western musical and pedagogical canons, teachers may have gone too far in the other direction, giving children and their parents what they want or resorting to spectacle and bombast when they ought to be helping them to intelligently explore the musical world while exercising self-restraint. Henry Giroux and other cultural critics reveal how easy it is to use bombast and spectacle to dismiss, mask, or distort politics, history, and culture. The emotional content, spectacle, and sheer volume associated with the performance of some music, particularly that utilized in movie theaters, television advertisements, sports events, rock concerts, religious ceremonies, political rallies, and the like, can overwhelm students' and auditors' critical faculties, leaving them even more susceptible to rhetoric and propaganda while making conversation impossible.[68]

Rhetoric is formalized or received knowledge that only imitates intelligence while masking or obscuring reality. It is formalized propaganda in the service of ideology and special interest groups whose intent is to manipulate and, possibly, deceive.[69] Today's propagandists, particularly corporate advertisers and politicians, are adept at using popular music and art, coupled with communications media, to discourage critical examination among their target populations. Although the commodification of popular music is often associated with liberty and democracy, in reality it has nothing to do with, and may even be inimical to, the pursuit of freedom.[70]

As is also explained in chapter 4, the ubiquitous commercial music piped into retail stores, offices, and even into our schools and homes and marketed around the world under the rubric of global free trade is intended to be used like Muzak to entice, develop, control, and manipulate consumers.[71] Companies like the Cyber Music and Consumer Experience Company in Britain are now going beyond Muzak to provide customized sound environments to companies wishing to more aggressively influence customer purchasing behaviors. The music is provided by these companies via satellite and computer and can be tailored according to customer demographics such as age or purchasing habits or according to other variables such as store traffic.[72] Other companies, such as AEI Music Network, are offering customized "signature" soundtracks to companies including Red Lobster, Starbucks, Nike, and Banana Republic in hopes that customers, like Pavlov's dog or Skinner's rats, will associate particular tunes and genres with their products and stores.

This branding of music is nothing new. Popular music and musicians have always been important to radio and television advertising. The difference is that popular music is no longer just background or accompaniment to corporate advertising. Rather, it has become a focal point of media advertising as corporations resort to ever more subtle and sophisticated ways of insinuating themselves and their products into consumers' psyches and lifestyles. Popular music is now the brand essence of companies including Volkswagen, Molson Breweries, and clothing designer Tommy Hilfiger, while popular musicians such as the Rolling Stones are no longer just entertainers: They are "live-action-advertising."[73] Their role in broadcasting and corporate-sponsored festivals and concert tours is to propagandize and to render consumers silent "before the spectacle of commodities."[74]

Similarly, in the political realm, popular music is used by governments and opposition parties as the "Trojan Horse for policy proclamation and indoctrination."[75] One of the most glaring examples of this misuse of music by a political party is in Russia, where supporters of ultranationalist Vladimir Zhirinovsky have opened Zhirinovsky's Rock Store to entice young rock music fans to his Liberal Democratic Party, which is hardly democratic.[76] Yet another example of how popular music can be used to mask a political agenda is found in Australia, where the right-wing national government recently utilized the music of rock musician and social activist Joe Cocker as part of its multimillion-dollar publicity campaign promoting radical tax reform. "Far from resisting the abuses of popular music," writes R. Murray Schafer, "our politicians endorse it at every opportunity."[77] And whereas in the past tyrants were visible and publicly recognized, "the new masters are invisible, and sing a siren song of markets in which the name of liberty is invoked in every chorus."[78]

Music might lack literal meaning, and it might not be especially conducive to the expression and communication of intellectual ideas, but it can titillate and appeal to the emotions.[79] Music can be used to celebrate love, sex, religion, or patriotism, but it can just as easily be used to silence opposition or to stoke excessive patriotic, nationalistic, religious, or sexual fervor and thus channel, distort, or wipe out thought. It can even be used as a weapon of humiliation and torture, such as happened during the U.S. invasion of Panama in 1989, when marines bombarded the Vatican embassy with the music of AC/DC as a means of forcing the surrender of General Manuel Noriega, in the former Yugoslavia where Croat prisoners were reportedly forced to sing Serb songs while enduring other indignities, or, most recently, in Guantanamo Bay, Cuba, and in postwar Iraq, where American soldiers have been subjecting suspected Al Qaeda prisoners to continuous rock music and other culturally offensive music as means of breaking down their resistance to interrogation.[80]

These, I think, are among the most compelling reasons of all why music ought to be subjected to critical scrutiny in the home, school, and public sphere. For leaving aside the difficult and probably insuperable question of whether its content has moral value, music can be used for good or for ill. It can be used or abused. It can be used to provoke self-examination and growth by challenging individuals and groups to confront their own preconceptions, limitations, and moral failings. But it can just as easily be used as an instrument of torture or as decoration to distract, mislead, or pervert, lulling children and adults into a false sense of identity and security while discouraging them from becoming intellectually involved in the world.[81]

Music teachers need to be careful lest they contribute to the musical disfranchisement of children by failing to address the ethics of professional and public practice, including issues of musical rhetoric, propaganda, and commodification. While I am not accusing them of deliberately or intentionally manipulating children and their audiences, music teachers are by no means blameless with regard to the musical disfranchisement of children. The historical roots of traditional school concert bands, orchestras, and choirs are after all to be found in autocratic institutions such as the military, church, or aristocracy, and not in parliamentary or other democratic institutions. One still hears orchestras described as operating under the "military discipline of the conductor," and music teachers are thought by some critics to be overly controlling.[82]

MENC has also recently been implicated in questionable business partnerships and practices with major corporations including Disney, Yamaha, Texaco, and PepsiCo that may effectively place corporate interests over those of children and society. It has also collaborated with Disney in the production of promotional movies such as *Mr. Holland's Opus* and *Music from the Heart*, which some argue are sexist or racist.[83] Indeed, to the extent that music teachers depend on these and other major corporations for their promotional propaganda or educational music and supplies, relying on the latest arrangements from Disney movies or musicals such as *Aladdin, Pocahontas,* or *The Lion King,* they may be helping indoctrinate children to middle-class consumer culture (more about this in chapter 4). This may especially be the case in performance-based programs in which music is taught for its own sake and without taking into account larger political, cultural, and other considerations affecting its presentation and reception. Much the same criticism applies to musical participation in highly commercialized spectacles like sporting events or in certain kinds of religious services or political rallies when leaders, musicians, or teachers resort to bombast and spectacle to distract, overwhelm, or entertain rather than to elucidate and educate.

As Dewey cautioned, there needs to be a "marriage of emotion with intelligence.... Emotions not fused with intelligence are blind."[84] Obviously some kind of balance or fusion of the two is needed if music and music education are to appeal to children and the public while also contributing to their growth. An imbalance in either direction, on intellectualism or emotional content, and to the extent that the public interest and welfare are ignored, may also represent an abdication of personal and civic responsibility and authority on the parts of composers, musicians, and music teachers alike. An overemphasis on intellectualism, skill, or talent may contribute to elitism and the further isolation of so-called serious musicians and music teachers from the political and cultural mainstreams, while an overemphasis on emotion, spectacle, ritual, or musical commodification may also contribute to the undermining of democratic culture by failing to adequately prepare children to intelligently participate in public musical life. Either approach may contribute to the disfranchisement of children when music teachers ought to be providing more musical leadership with respect to increasing the breadth, depth, and vitality of students' musical experiences so that they can contribute to the democratization of musical culture.[85]

Music educators, it should also be acknowledged, have their own rhetoric and propaganda. Witness, for example, the rhetoric and sloganism evident in so many music education advocacy arguments and the almost religious zeal with which particular pedagogies and methodologies are proselytized and taught. Music education advocates and proponents of particular music pedagogies make all sorts of quasi-philosophical and practical claims as to their efficacy and superiority without resorting to reason or much evidence. One is simply expected to accept their dogmatic claims and pronouncements as true. In my own experience there is seldom interest among advocates and pedagogues or their followers in engaging in public conversation about educational ethics or the validity of their philosophical and educational claims, goals, and purposes, let alone the efficacy of their methods in accomplishing those goals.

The situation is particularly difficult in the area of music pedagogy, where criticism is considered heretical, even treasonable. As Estelle Jorgensen writes,

> The fact that instructional methods have been worked out to a high degree of sophistication and defended as dogma is oppressive to teachers. It fosters their dependence on methods and those who promote them and on passivity, timidity, meritocracy, technocratic attitudes and behaviors, and even anti-intellectualism construed as a lack of interest in and reflection about questions that underlie practice.[86]

The etymology of words can often reveal hidden and less desirable shadings of meanings that, while perhaps lost to contemporary consciousness, remain operative. A pedagogue, as the term was originally employed, was a "slave who escorted children to school."[87] The last thing music teachers should want is to remain slaves to overly prescriptive pedagogies and methodologies that may well stifle the thinking and creativity of their students.

Highly prescriptive pedagogies and methodologies are usually convenient and extremely well organized, thus saving teachers preparation time and effort. But if the assumptions underlying them are outdated, flawed, or false, and if those methods stifle the individual creativity and thinking of students and teachers alike, then they serve no one well, except perhaps those wishing to dominate and control. To that extent they may better serve autocratic or totalitarian rather than democratic ends.[88] While not wishing to throw out tradition and pedagogy altogether, as some critics appear to be suggesting, I nevertheless agree with Giroux that in the continued absence of public discussion and scrutiny of musical and educational values and ends, and the relation of means to ends, pedagogical or other claims (e.g., advocacy and repertorial ones) may only amount to dogma, rhetoric, and propaganda masking special or class interests.[89] Pedagogy has all too often been used in the past as a means of controlling students and teachers, rendering them passive receptacles of preordained and merely asserted expert or canonical knowledge. That was what Christopher Small meant when he complained about universities and institutions of "higher" learning breeding intellectual passivity and conservatism in music teachers—that institutional culture, particularly when it emphasizes drill over inquiry, passive acceptance over criticism, and form over content, can all too easily stultify and dehumanize rather than educate.

This is why it is so important that music teachers, parents, and even children learn how to think and behave as public intellectuals and not just passively accept or ignore music and pedagogical practices. As Wayne Bowman admonishes music teachers, "Failure to 'theorize practice,' to reflect critically on the ends to which our musical and instructional practices may lead leaves open the very real possibility that our musical engagements miseducate rather than educate."[90] And as already stated, in the western democracies perhaps the most important educational end of all is political. Education should gradually prepare all children, each according to his or her own abilities, to participate intelligently as mature citizens in public deliberations or conversations about common musical and other social values. Music teachers are as much democratic as musical or educational leaders and are charged with helping children develop, warrant, and defend their own beliefs and ideas—their own values and choices—while simultaneously opening themselves up to the world and to possible criticism. Unless children learn how to do this, they will not be able to understand the issues or exert intelligent control over their own musical lives, much less contribute to the improvement of the human condition. Not all children will learn to do this to the same extent or degree of confidence. After all, as Dewey said, people are not created equal. But if democracy depends on individuals actively participating in the communal shaping of values, ideas, and events, then they had better at least try to engage in public criticism; otherwise, someone else will do it for them.[91]

Music education is thus inevitably political and, owing to its potential for either promoting personal and collective freedom and growth or contributing to the musical disfranchisement of children and future music teachers (by rendering them intellectually passive), it is something that should profoundly matter to society and that should itself be subjected to continuous and close scrutiny.[92] Failure to do this, to criticize practice, politics, and experience, may represent not just an abdication of personal authority and responsibility on the parts of teachers and other citizens. It may also be construed as an act of civil cowardice.[93]

Performance Alone

Elliott knows all this, as he is in fact a liberal of sorts, as evidenced by his frequent references to Dewey, his conviction that music education should provide children with opportunities to "confront beliefs" while looking beyond special interest in pursuit of a wider community of musical interest, and his ardent belief that education should prepare children "for life as a whole."[94] He even acknowledges that "some amount of liberal education is essential for a rational life."[95] However, there is little sense in Elliott's praxial philosophy of children being prepared to eventually participate either musically or verbally in democratic society as political beings and moral agents of musical and social change.[96] Children are expected to engage in self-examination leading to the development of personal responsibility and awareness of "the musical consequences of the beliefs underlying different music cultures," but there is little, if anything, said of the importance of children developing a sense of social responsibility.[97] Music is defined in terms of its "use" within particular communities of expert musicians, but nothing is said of its potential misuse or abuse and, relatedly, of the importance of students and teachers making informed moral choices (such as taking into account whether their own choices or uses of music might impinge on the similar rights of others).[98] And while Elliott acknowledges that music education can contribute to democratic society, it is at best a laissez-faire democracy in which individual musical cultures with their various musical practices are to be simply accepted on their own terms.

A laissez-faire democracy, though, is a contradiction in terms, since individual and collective rights and responsibilities are only protected to the extent that people participate intelligently in public life.[99] In Elliott's philosophy, children are inducted into preexisting musical cultures and communities of musicians, which is said to be humanizing, but there is all too much emphasis on congruence with "authentic," "real," or "genuine" existing traditions and practices.[100] Music teachers are similarly enjoined to identify and replicate "excellent music education curricula" and "excellent music teaching in action."[101] Nowhere, at least that I can find, does he explicitly address the importance of children and teachers publicly criticizing musical or educational values, practices, and standards of excellence; of engaging in meaningful conversation among themselves and with the public about the social consequences of their respective musical and educational beliefs and values, of the ethics or morality of their actions. The pursuit of musical excellence, personal enjoyment, and self-fulfillment can, after all, be detrimental to others, such as often happens when children are excluded from performing ensembles because they don't measure up, expert musicians colonize, caricature, or parody other people's music, girls or boys or minorities are marginalized or excluded from practice and public deliberation altogether, children are pressured to conform to particular gender role identities, or indigenous or other music is abstracted from its original cultural contexts against the wishes of its creators or simply distorted and misrepresented.[102]

A Fanfare for the Common Man and Woman

As for the question of whether performance is essential to musical understanding and participation, and, by extension, that children should emulate professional or expert praxis, performance-based curricula can work to disfranchise those labeled as less talented or "nonmusicians" by rendering them passive or subservient to experts or by simply excluding them from conversation altogether. Ethnographic studies of conservatory and university-trained music and music education majors in both the United States and Canada suggest that students identified by their teachers and peers as less talented may be inhibited in their development. In one ethnographic study of the social world of Canadian university schools of music, for example, it was reported that social status within the institution was afforded music education majors (N = 116) based on their perceived level of performing expertise and not on their teaching ability or educational knowledge. Many felt stigmatized by being labeled music education majors, a condition that was hypothesized as potentially leading to a reduction in motivation and professional commitment.[103] Similarly, nonmusic majors participating in a longitudinal study in England (N = 10) testified that they were rendered passive during the primary music teaching internship by feelings of musical inadequacy. Although the majority had studied music during their own schooling, including university courses in music, art, dance, and drama in preparation for teaching the English National Curriculum, they nevertheless believed that teaching music—even in primary schools—demanded an abundance of performance expertise. No such precondition was assumed with the teaching of other arts classes, such as drama and dance. Music, it seems, is viewed by at least some nonmusic majors and future classroom teachers as a "special specialism."[104]

Both Dewey and Noam Chomsky long ago cautioned against relying on experts or specialists "for insights into fundamental human values." The cult of the expert, wrote Chomsky, was both "self-serving" and, "for those who propound it, . . . fraudulent."[105] Chomsky was writing about the role of the behavioral and social sciences during the Vietnam War and the technical rationalist claim by experts to specialized knowledge. But the parallel with music, as revealed in the following quotation, is striking: "To anyone who has any familiarity with the social and behavioral sciences (or the 'policy sciences'), the claim that there are certain considerations too deep for the outsider to comprehend is simply an absurdity, unworthy of comment."[106] While acknowledging that it is important to listen to experts, in our case expert musicians and music teachers, decisions about fundamental human values like music ought not to be left to the experts. Small perhaps says it best:

> Our lives at every turn have become the property of experts, through whom our experience is to be mediated. We have experts to tell us we are sick, and to tell us when we are well again, . . . how to educate our young, experts to paint our pictures and compose and perform our music for us, and finally experts to tell us which of the products of the composing or performing experts we should be listening to.[107]

Elliott is hardly a technical rationalist. In fact, he specifically cautions against such approaches. Music education is conceived by him as a form of social interaction, or conversation of a sort, between experts and their acolytes in which the latter gain increasing personal authority by formulating their own musical interpretations relative to past and present practice.[108] The problem, I think, is one of confusion of ends. That is, while students are inducted into communities of practitioners in which knowledge is constructed through praxis, those communities are too hierarchical, narrow, and exclusive. Those communities are not particularly, or even necessarily, democratic ones. In Elliott's ideal community of musicians and music educators, expert musicians and music teachers possess all of the knowledge that really matters. Students encounter expert and foreign beliefs, but there is little sense of a true exchange, interplay, and cross-fertilization of beliefs, values, and ideas. Nor is there necessarily an attitude of mutual respect. Less expert musicians and teachers are marginalized while nonmusicians and other "outsiders" are excluded on the pretext that they are incapable of understanding and appreciating the issues.[109]

This is obviously elitist. It also is not true. As Kivy explains, and despite his own valorization of the classics, music and music education are shaped through complex social interaction involving all manner of people, including expert musicians, composers, critics, audience members, the media, and the public at large. All have some say in the shaping of musical values and standards. In the end, though, as Kivy reluctantly admits, and as orchestras throughout the western world have belatedly discovered to their dismay, the audience has the final say, at least in democratic society.[110] Audiences and the public show their understanding and appreciation or lack thereof and thus also influence the shaping of musical values in all sorts of ways.

Ordinary people, it also needs to be said, have long been sources of inspiration and materials for musical experts. Witness, for example, the indebtedness of the western classical tradition to folk and nineteenth-century popular music or the cultural appropriation or sampling of rap music virtuosi.[111] Jazz and professional folk artists, too, colonize and capitalize on the music of ordinary people, taking their songs and dressing them up to suit more sophisticated tastes. Yet ordinary people are seldom acknowledged for their musical opinions or paid for their contributions. Music teachers, too, are in the business of exchanging knowledge for money, which begs the ethical question, "Who should make money off of whose music?"[112] If anything, ordinary people tend to be disdainfully treated as passive recipients and worshipers of expert musical and educational knowledge when they ought to be viewed instead as allies of musicians and music teachers in pursuit of a more open, democratic musical community.[113] Besides, whatever their personal limitations, individuals are nevertheless entitled to contribute to public deliberation if for no other reason than that the decisions made may affect the quality of their lives.

Everyone affected by social institutions and programs should have some say in their governance. As Dewey expressed it in "Democracy and Educational Administration" (1937),

> Others who are supposed to be wiser and who in any case have more power decide the question for them and also decide the methods and means by which subjects may arrive at the enjoyment of what is good for them. This form of coercion and suppression is more subtle and more effective than are overt intimidation and restraint. . . . The individuals of the submerged mass might not be very wise. But there is one thing they are wiser about than anybody else can be, and that is where the shoe pinches, the trouble they suffer from.[114]

No one has a monopoly on truth and understanding, while individuals, including nonmusicians and children, are entitled to decide their own tastes and to participate in public deliberations about musical and other values (although all of us can certainly profit from guidance and advice from those with more experience and knowledge).

The current lack of public support for orchestras and classical music, and for music education in public schools, may in significant part be a consequence of past elitist and exclusionary performance and teaching practices (or treating music education as "just" entertainment) and our general failure as a profession to respectfully engage with the public through performance, certainly, but just as importantly through the spoken and written word. As Saul writes, highly specialized artistic dialects are often "purposefully impenetrable to the non-expert."[115] Having been excluded from decision making and intelligent conversation about what and how musical values ought to be represented in the concert hall, university, and school, the public has simply and perhaps understandably withdrawn its moral and financial support.[116] In the days when musicians and music teachers enjoyed the patronage of the rich and powerful, they could afford to ignore the public. Today, as that patronage continues to evaporate, musicians and music educators ignore the public at their peril.

Musicians and music teachers would do well to remember Chomsky's admonition to experts in *Equality and Social Policy* (1978):

> In discussion of freedom and equality, it is very difficult to disentangle questions of fact from judgments of value. We should try to do so, pursuing factual inquiry where it may lead without dogmatic preconception, but not ignoring the consequences of what we do. We must never forget that what we do is tainted and distorted, inevitably, by the awe of expertise that is induced by social institutions as one device for enforcing passivity and obedience. What we do as scientists, as scholars, [as musicians, as music teachers,] as advocates, has consequences, just as our refusal to speak

or act has definite consequences. We cannot escape this condition in a society based on concentration of power and privilege. There is a heavy responsibility that the scientist or scholar [or musician or music teacher] would not have to bear in a decent society, in which individuals would not relegate to authorities decisions over their lives or their beliefs. We may and should recommend the simple virtues: honesty and truthfulness, responsibility and concern. But to live by these precepts is often no simple matter.[117]

This is a worthy creed for musicians and music teachers. There is nothing wrong with professing the acquisition of performance expertise as a worthwhile end in itself, provided it is recognized as but one part of an inclusive, liberal education in which moral, ethical, cultural, and political issues come to the fore and in which there is a serious effort made to reengage and reconnect with the public in pursuit of reconciliation, mutual understanding, and respect.[118] That, declared Dewey, is the only intelligent thing to do. Intelligence is a matter of faith in humanity's potential for social progress. It is an act of loving concern for humanity and its problems.[119] As such it ought to be defined and judged in humanitarian terms and not just with reference to skills and abilities or narrow personal or professional goals. Rather than being innate or fixed, intelligence is something that needs to be nurtured and developed in children through provision of the right kinds of environments and conditions. In short, it is a search for identity, not so much in the sense proposed by Kivy, in which music is a form of ritual that socializes us into our tribal identity, but in terms of the development of moral character and personal integrity.

The challenge for democracy as the expression and attempted realization of this common faith is to find ways to "harmonize the development of each individual with the maintenance of a social state in which the activities of one will contribute to the good of all the others."[120] Only by preparing students to intelligently participate as mature citizens in the democratic shaping of their world through the pursuit of humane values and social amelioration, whether through music or other subject areas, can parents and teachers work to secure the future. This, as Dewey cautioned, "is not to assert that intelligence will ever dominate the course of events; it is not even to imply that it will save from ruin and destruction."[121] Rather, and given our own abilities, limitations, and circumstances, it is to make the best and most socially responsible choices in an uncertain world. Performance can obviously contribute to that project because it can motivate conversation. It can also be viewed as a sort of ethical deliberation, albeit of a very limited kind.[122] But even when coupled with certain critical abilities and an abundance of musical knowledge, the pursuit of performing expertise or any other kind of knowledge alone and for its own sake is hardly going to contribute significantly to democratic culture. Performance alone, particularly when divorced from a democratic interest, does not qualify as intelligent action, or at least not significantly so. It is simply too narrow.

Worth remembering, too, is that professional musicians, music teachers, music education majors, and children all need to be prepared for a life beyond music. A liberal education of the kind suggested above is probably necessary to intelligent functioning and happiness in a democratic society in that it can help individuals define and understand their relationships with others and their respective places, roles, responsibilities, and potential contributions to the common good. A liberal education can help individuals, including musicians and music teachers, lead more fulfilling personal and professional lives while also allowing them greater flexibility in the pursuit of life and social goals. And finally, as I attempt to show in chapter 3, a liberal approach to problems in music education philosophy and practice may contribute to the resolution of some of the profession's most persistent and debilitating internal problems by fostering a wider sense of community.

Living in a Postmusical Age

Reclaiming the Concept of Abstract Reason

3 In *Postmodern Theologies: The Challenge of Religious Diversity,* Terrence Tilley writes that the present era is stamped with a peculiar prefix. We live in a post-age, with contemporary theorists variously proclaiming it to be postmodern, poststructural, postmoral, postauthorial, postliberal, etc.[1] Many music education philosophers and theorists believe that we live in a postmusical world in which music as a conceptual paradigm or autonomous domain has ceased to exist. Wayne Bowman, for example, argues that it is useless to try to define music in terms of structure and qualities of sounds. He and other scholars contend that any musical criticism must be socially grounded.[2] It is this call for the recognition of and accounting for the social and cultural contexts of music in education that distinguishes much contemporary music education theory from so-called traditional or aesthetic theory. To a growing number of music education critics, we live in a postaesthetic world in which notions of beauty and universality and transcendence of time, culture, place, and biology are passé.

Postmodernism can be understood as an intellectual reaction to modernist assumptions about nature and the structure of knowledge.[3] Many postmodernists believe that everything is a complete and total social fabrication and thus amenable to contestation and change. Everything is also political, for if truth is only relative and history is nothing more than a contest among competing narrative constructions over which individuals have no control, then all that remains is political struggle. Musical culture becomes nothing more than a battleground in which competing groups with their different ideologies and "versions of social reality fight it out."[4]

Paradoxically, however, postmodernists also think that individuals and groups are virtually incapable of transcending the musical and other narratives and ideologies to which they are subjected. As S. J. Wilsmore writes in relation to deconstruction, which, although now passé, continues to provide the philosophical underpinning for much of what is called postmodernism, "the idea is that the individual is himself constructed out of language [or music, etc.], so that as subject he does not exist; he therefore cannot be said to be *responsible* for what is written."[5] Educating children to think for themselves, which implies that they should mean what they say and do and be held accountable for it, is a form of intentionalist fallacy. Instead, students are enjoined to engage in a cynical game of deconstructive attack against tradition, the status quo, and the western metaphysics embedded in our forms of language.[6]

Postmodernists seek to unmask the desire and will to knowledge and power that permeate language (and music), as in the sense of the "word of God" or "of reason." Thus, when postmodernists and other critics disparage the western musical canon, and by extension aesthetic theory, what they are really questioning or challenging is the concept of abstract reason upon which they are based. The more fundamental question in music education philosophy and practice, then, is not whether aesthetic theorists or their critics are right or wrong, or whether the western musical canon is authoritarian and anachronistic, but what is the nature of reason as it applies to music and music education? This is properly an epistemological question and concerns how we are to ground our musical and educational truth claims (e.g., that one genre of music or a particular performance, methodology, or philosophy is as good as, or better than, another). It is also a political question, for the concept of abstract reason has long served as a philosophical cornerstone for notions of democracy and justice.[7]

An attempt is made in this chapter to explain and justify the concept of abstract reason on the grounds that, in a democratic and multicultural musical society, some set of intellectual and social rules of engagement is required if individuals and groups are to transcend or bridge differences and ideologies in pursuit of social amelioration, or if they are to defend themselves from the vicissitudes of change and the hegemony of mainstream culture. This is preliminary to showing that the definition of abstract reason that postmodernists and other music education critics are fond of stigmatizing and using as a foil for their own musical and political agendas is reductive and needlessly divisive. Relatedly, it is argued that the strategy of savaging aesthetic theory is misguided, even counterproductive, when it comes to solving some of the music education profession's gravest ills.

Finally, after having furnished a more extensive and inclusive definition of reason, an attempt is made to apply that concept to music education philosophy in hopes of fostering a climate of reconciliation. As is shown, implicit in the concept of abstract reason are consensus building and a sense of democratic community—of reaching out to, connecting, and empathizing with others—but also a sense of continuity with tradition and the past. Rather than being synonymous with logic or instrumentalism, reason, as defined herein, is a tool of understanding that intellectuals employ in their ongoing conversation as to the nature of truth, beauty, freedom, and justice. Viewed this way, postmodern and other contemporary music education critics have not finally gotten it right, having proven aesthetic and other so-called traditional theory falsely edifying. Although obviously important to contemporary intellectual conversations, postmodernist and other critics of the status quo are not the only ones needing to be heard. Aesthetic and other theorists must be included in debates as to the nature and value of music and music education while being accorded the respect they deserve.

Historicizing Reason

Many radical feminists and postmodernists make a distinction between private and public, or abstract, reason.[8] Women and other marginalized groups have their own private or particular reasons for thinking and acting as they do, although they might not always feel the need to explain or justify themselves publicly. The public realm is often depicted as a predominantly masculine sphere of influence that is hostile to them. Some even charge that the concept of abstract reason is itself Eurocentric and patriarchal; that it merely reflects the interests and "moral norms, values, and virtues" of dead white European males that have been imposed on them as means of making them conform to "malestream culture."[9] Radical feminist Carol Gilligan, for example, argues that women have their own ways of thinking and knowing, their own modes of reasoning, they being historically situated in the home which traditionally has been governed less by rules of justice as by instinct and sympathy. This moral mode of reasoning, Gilligan continues, is based on an ethic of care that is fundamentally incompatible with the concept of abstract or public reason and its corresponding concept of justice.[10]

However, and paradoxically enough, another plank in the radical feminist platform is that the private is public, meaning that private conceptions of difference and subjective hurt, although not necessarily justified in the public realm through abstract reasoning, are nevertheless deserving of recognition. But even a private claim to musical difference or subjective hurt is a claim to truth, if only partial and situated, and thus, if it is to be given credence by others and promoted, it begs public evidence, discussion, and evaluation.[11] Moreover, a call for public recognition effectively places what was previously in the private realm in the public light. Once made public, it is private no longer. In any event, feminists do in fact have good reasons "why women should not be discriminated against."[12] One of the purposes of education, they believe, is to cause male and female students to appreciate those reasons.

Radical liberal musicologist Rose Rosengard Subotnik argues convincingly in support of an abstract or public concept of reason in music for just such a purpose, but also as a guard against those who would effect changes through intimidation.[13] Once in the vanguard of those attacking the abstract concept of reason in music as epitomized by the western musical canon, Subotnik now concedes that some such concept in music is also needed as a check against particularist excesses.[14] Pleading that an abstract ideal of rationality be retained as means of preserving the concept of music itself, although not at the cost of excluding alternatives, Subotnik is proposing that a balance be struck between the universalist and particularist, or the modern and postmodern, agendas. She envisions an ongoing musical dialectic or tension between so-called traditional and poststructural paradigms, the modern and postmodern, each of which is informed and to some extent defined and kept in check by the other. This is only being pragmatic, since no matter what our respective positions toward the construct of music, our "language and thought will continue to preserve it, at least for the foreseeable future."[15]

This strategy of maintaining a healthy tension between the universal and particular has, at first glance, a thoroughly postmodern ring to it, as for example in deconstruction. The purpose of this technique is to decenter meaning or dismantle tradition while still retaining it. But as Wilsmore complains, "It is always clear which side the deconstructionist favors; he is coy in his irony with the one and cutting with the other."[16] Subotnik takes a more impartial and conciliatory approach. While admitting that an uncritical commitment to an abstract concept of reason has led to untold trouble in the past, that, she argues, is no reason for exacting retribution upon the "old" musicology. Besides, alternate modes of reasoning do not necessarily exclude the abstract one. All concepts of reason have something in common.

Much more is at stake here than whether musicians, musicologists, and music educators become more tolerant of their respective differences. A world without some such concept would be an inhumane one in which many of our democratic safeguards with respect to individual and collective liberties would be discarded and in which there would be no possibility of identifying common concerns. As a result, society would become increasingly fragmented and our culture desiccated in a Darwinian struggle among competing musical, academic, and other interest groups.[17]

Some critics would counter that any concept of abstract reason is inevitably prejudicial against those marginalized on the basis of ethnicity, gender, or social standing. However, the fact that a particular power structure makes a false claim to universality does not diminish our stake in identifying universal or shared values.[18] The very notion of social critique of oppressive systems is grounded on the universal belief in the right to freedom and justice for all. Even Jacques Derrida believes that some such right or ideal is necessary if freedom is to be obtained and defended.[19]

Emancipation depends upon a commitment to an ethic or ideal of justice, not to mention standards of truth; otherwise, there would be no possibility of progress. Moreover, within any multicultural and democratic society there must be some bounds of permissible behavior.[20] Some shared intellectual and social framework (including a civil code) is needed if diversity in the postmodern world is to be guaranteed. Rather than legitimating cultural uniformity and oppression, abstract reason, as a foundation of our justice system and civil code, can be used to promote and then safeguard cultural and musical diversity and equality.

The very notion of democracy is founded on a concept of abstract reason. However, if democracy is to be defended and maintained, our society will have to do more than just acknowledge its stake in that construct. As was mentioned in chapter 1, Dewey understood the importance of cultivating in children a democratic ethos, which meant teaching them how to think, or reason, and to participate in public debates about the nature of democratic society. Modern-day liberals agree that the teaching of abstract reason should continue as an important component of education, since individual and collective freedoms depend on active and public participation in the shaping of events. If children and others are to eventually contribute to communal understandings of the nature and value of music and music education, they must, among other things, learn how to reason.

Exorcizing the Cartesian Anxiety

Critics of abstract reason usually describe it as cool, objective, and disembodied. Many radical feminists, for example, treat reason as synonymous with logic, which, by definition, ignores or devalues the emotive, the sensory, and the body.[21] This, though, is a deformed notion of reason that is both needlessly reductive and divisive. Logic functions to clarify and order our thinking, making it more consistent and amenable to communication. As such, it is an important element of reason. But only if we accept an extreme Cartesian version of reason does the schism between radical and so-called traditional concepts remain plausible.

Few philosophers today adhere to the concept of instrumental reason that many contemporary critics are fond of stigmatizing and using as a foil for their own particularist political agendas. Indeed, if there is a consensus emerging in philosophical circles today, it is that rationality is a form of democratic social practice dedicated to the *common* good.[22] Like Dewey, many contemporary philosophers believe that reason inheres as much in the cultivation of a democratic character and ethos as it does in any specific intellectual or musical rules, skills, and abilities or general principles.

Central to this evolving and consensual concept of abstract reason is the making of moral, ethical, and aesthetic distinctions with respect to what is of value to self and society. If these kinds of distinctions are to be made, and if we are to avoid the pitfalls of subjectivism, we need reference to some sets of general principles, standards, and ideals as communal guides to musical thought and action. Some postmodernists and radical feminists counter that it is the obsession with general abstract principles that got us into trouble in the first place. And it is true that liberals, including those in music education (such as Bennett Reimer), have been more interested in identifying general, or universal, principles than in determining how they might be applied in particular cases. However, it does not automatically follow that liberals are heedless of the moral implications of their work or that they care less for others.[23] The prevailing view is that any such principles, standards, and ideals must be applied provisionally and humanely, rather than autocratically, as means of gaining increased insight into and understanding of the relationship between self and others. Those general principles and standards are useful but fallible tools of an understanding that is continually reconstructed through application to lived musical and other experience.

Probably the most important of those general principles and standards is that of objectivity. The Cartesian concept of objectivity has been devastatingly critiqued by numerous philosophers and theorists, including many feminist ones. Recently, however, some feminist theorists have begun calling for a return to a concept of objectivity on the grounds that some yardstick is necessary if feminists and others are to warrant their truth claims and be held responsible and accountable for their actions. While challenging the notion that reason can provide a totally objective foundation for truth claims, they nevertheless acknowledge that feminists must provide "robust facts about the social world which can be used as evidence for the claim that the current social arrangements are oppressive to women and which act as premises for recommendations for change"; they must give "reasons why change is required."[24] This implies that they must conform to some public standard of reason, including some minimal notion of the independently existing, or that which is objective and intersubjectively accessible. The value of objectivity as a general regulatory principle and guide for rational inquiry in music and music education lies in the appeal to standards of truth.

The difference between this and Cartesian definitions is that it is contextual, meaning that truth claims are socially positioned and can only be asserted, understood, and agreed upon if the parties in question already share certain assumptions, interests, beliefs, and values in common. Included among these commonalities, and in addition to a commitment to egalitarianism, is an intersubjectively accessible way of identifying and dealing with problems in light of socially constructed standards and rules of evidence. Abstract reason, thus conceived, is a kind of social contract. It is a means of effecting changes in self and society that is colored and shaped by the constitutive goals, standards, and practices of the democratic societies in question. Included among those constitutive goals, standards, and practices are prior and existing standards of truth, beauty, and justice.

Any notion of progress depends upon individuals having faith in the past; otherwise, they would be disarmed by absolute skepticism from proposing alternatives and rendered passive. No one is advocating rationality as mere means. Ultimately, the aim of education is achieved through criticism of ends, meaning that the individual is mindfully engaged in leading the good life. To Dewey and many other liberals, there is no room in education for destructive polarizations such as between means and ends, thinking and feeling, mind and body, past and present, modern and postmodern, or aesthetic and praxial. Education presupposes the possibility of synonymy, or at least near synonymy, of meaning. Without it, there could be no communication, and the study of history, anthropology, archaeology, and ethnomusicology, to name only a few, would be pointless, as there would be no possibility of reaching mutual understanding.

What liberals are advocating, then, is sensible as opposed to absolute skepticism. Students should be encouraged to question and challenge tradition and the status quo, but if this is to be more than a nihilistic exercise they must have faith in the past and in the possibility of progress. Because deconstruction demands a close reading of the text and the reader considers both what is said and what remains unsaid, it has a certain plausibility. "All good advice," though "scarcely new."[25] For much the same reason, it also has a degree of continuity with the past. But deconstruction was never intended to succeed. Trapped in the mire of metaphysics, Derrida has never been able to bring himself to consider whether the more pernicious aspects of logocentrism could be remedied. He has always assumed the impossibility of progress, of effecting productive change.[26]

It is largely as an antidote to Derrida's pessimism and the quagmire of metaphysics that other contemporary philosophers have returned to democratic theory as a more productive framework for discussions as to the nature of abstract reason. Ultimately, as contemporary philosophers such as Richard Bernstein conceive it, abstract reason is a means of achieving a sense of democratic community. The point of exercising reason is not to impose a normalizing discourse on society or to achieve social or musical superiority. Rather, it is to work toward the establishment and maintenance of dialogical communities dedicated to mutual recognition, solidarity, and participation.[27] Implicit in this definition of abstract reason is a spirit of mutuality and inclusiveness and a commitment to the democratic ideals of independence, equality, and participation.

Postmodernists recognize, and even valorize, the concept of democratic community, although with their emphasis on diversity and plurality they generally prefer to conceive of society as consisting of many different communities. Each of these communities has its own particular political agenda and interests. Postmodernists, however, have yet to satisfactorily address what happens when those groups disagree. Any society, owing to its complexity, must necessarily entertain a plethora of competing and often conflicting claims. Without some minimal notion of public reason, which implies a spirit of mutuality, empathy, tolerance, and civility, but also rules of evidence, claims to oppression become nonfalsifiable and society runs the risk, as happened recently with the Canadian National Action Committee on the Status of Women, of becoming increasingly fragmented and incapable of collective action.[28]

Many contemporary critics try to get around the difficult problem of mediating the confusing welter of competing and conflicting societal claims by locating them within the contexts of class, gender, and other struggles. To their way of thinking, society's institutions, its traditions, and the status quo are oppressive by virtue of the fact that they represent systems of authority and power that are overly restrictive and controlling. Their job is to reveal and then subvert, undermine, or repress those political power structures as means of creating a utopian society in which everyone can "live fully and freely."[29] As E. Louis Lankford writes, postmodernism is "characterized by the critique and rejection of cultural and social hierarchies, followed by the empowerment of previously disenfranchised members of society, including those marginalized on the basis of ethnicity, gender, religion, cultural group affiliation, sexual preference, lifestyle choice, and physical and mental abilities."[30]

All heady stuff, but utopian social agendas inevitably lead to the creation of dystopias, or the creation of small gulags "off to the side for those who fail to live up to the utopia."[31] Leaving aside for the time being the moral question of inclusiveness, of including in debate all potential participants, the point needs to be made that perfect equilibrium is characteristic not of living systems but of artificial and dead ones. Moreover, Foucauldian notions of social system dynamics fail to explain "the kind of truth that can bring down regimes and empower the powerless."[32] Foucault's theory has nothing to say about positive or real freedom. While allowing for sites of resistance to arise, in the end Foucault, like Derrida, claims that all resistance is futile. Foucault has not dismantled determinism. He has only decentralized it, thereby further contributing to the epistemological nihilism of our age. As a result, and while much is made of the current so-called "paradigm shift" in educational philosophy, business continues as usual in the classrooms of the western world. Philosophy in general has become divorced from practice and the world.[33] Music education philosophy, too, has become just another narrow academic specialty divorced from the real world and its problems. Much more is said in the next chapter of this fracture between music education philosophy and practice and between music education and the public sphere.

Habermas and Gadamer on the Nature of Reason

While the German philosopher and neo-Marxist Jürgen Habermas exhibits a similar concern for marginalized peoples, for overcoming systems of power and oppression, and for accounting for the social and contextual nature of thought, he refuses to be labeled "postmodern." In part, this is because that category has already been preempted by antimodernists such as Derrida and Michel Foucault, but even more so because he refuses to abandon the modernist project. Wishing to build on, rather than abandon, the gains of the Enlightenment, Habermas argues that the problem is not with the concept of abstract reason per se, but that its benefits have been enjoyed by only an elite few. What is needed, he contends, "is not the rejection of this freedom, but the extension of emancipation to include all the spheres—personal, social, economic, political—in which humans live and move, and to include all the people—not just western elites—in this emancipatory process."[34]

But while Habermas still has faith in the crucial benefits of reason, he shares with most contemporary theorists, including postmodernists, a certain skepticism with respect to the way it has been instituted in the world. Rejecting monolithic and instrumental definitions because they lead to irrationalism, contradiction, and ideology, he proposes instead, and as an antidote to the ills of modernism, a reduced and interactive notion of reason as communicative action. Consistent with the contractual definition of reason already introduced, Habermas defines it as a means of engaging in the democratic process and reaching consensus on important matters concerning personal and collective freedom. Rather than being transcendent in the sense of transcending time and space, or instrumental in the sense of divorcing means from ends, reason is "in the world." It is colored and shaped by the social, cultural, and economic environments of our respective lifeworlds. Positing that our lifeworlds have become colonized by self-regulating institutions that have become overly controlling and domineering, Habermas calls for the development of "ideal" communities dedicated to communication and a public ethic that will wrest back control for the lifeworld from these oppressive systems. Reason, as Habermas defines it, is a universal moral-political project and form of social praxis dedicated, as Dewey expressed it, to the common good.

One of the premises of his theory of communicative action is that political deliberation is required if people are to be prompted to question, and not continue to be victimized by, authority in the forms of dogma and ideology. Without public deliberation, people will tend only to accept the status quo, thereby remaining susceptible to the false consciousness engendered by ideological and other distortions.[35]

I sympathize with Habermas's project and have much in common with him. However, what Habermas does not make clear is how we are to know when we are subject to a false consciousness; that we, the supposedly enlightened ones, are not similarly deluded by systems of power and oppression. For if our selves are socially and culturally embedded, and Habermas insists that this remains primary in his theory, the question becomes how we are to achieve impartiality when considering the truth claims of others, who are similarly embedded in their own contexts and can only think in those terms. In trying to get around this problem, Habermas resorts to the concept of decentering, or disinterestedness if you prefer, whereby individuals bracket and set aside their personal interests, needs, and prejudices. But is this possible?

Hans Georg Gadamer, Habermas's countryman and archrival, argues that it is not; that all of our thinking is prejudiced in the sense that it can only take place through socially and culturally conditioned ways of thinking which can both obscure and facilitate understanding. While distinguishing between blind and enabling prejudices, he insists that both are constitutive of what we are, that there is no knowledge without prejudice. All so-called facts, forms of knowledge, and beliefs are matters of interpretation because we see and hear through socially and culturally determined prejudices that necessarily limit our understanding. Provided we possess the right kind of attitude, we can apply those prejudices to experience as means of opening ourselves up to the world and thereby gaining increased understanding of that which is seemingly different, foreign, or opaque. We do this, however, not so as to achieve final, conclusive explanations or answers, since this is beyond us, but to achieve a fusion of horizons between our own and someone else's understanding. Viewed this way, reason and understanding are forms of mediation between different but overlapping social, cultural, and historical realities.[36] And we only discover which of our particular prejudices are blind or enabling by risking and testing them through application to lived experience through a "dialogical encounter with what is at once alien to us, makes a claim upon us, and has an affinity with what we are."[37]

An important distinction between Habermas and Gadamer is that Gadamer rejects the dualistic oppositions that have been entrenched in western philosophy "since the Enlightenment—between reason and tradition, reason and prejudice, reason and authority."[38] Rather than being the enemy, tradition, too, is constitutive of what we are. Moreover, Gadamer views Habermas's assertion that reason and authority exist in abstract antithesis as a form of dogma. "Authority," Gadamer contends, "is not always wrong."[39] Habermas's dualistic tendencies and his confidence in our ability to unmask false pretences have been cited by Gadamer and other philosophers as evidence of latent transcendentalism.

Notice how thoroughly postmodern Gadamer sounds. In responding to Habermas's faith in our ability to attain objectivity, Gadamer states that "reality does not happen behind the back of language; it happens rather behind the backs of those who live in the subjective opinion that they have understood the world (or can no longer understand it); that is, reality happens precisely *within* language."[40] However, stating that our understandings are constructed through language is not the same as saying that we are prisoners of the narratives to which we are subjected. The whole thrust of Gadamer's hermeneutics is that, no matter whether different languages or ideologies are incompatible or incommensurable, some increased level of mutual understanding, empathy, respect, and, by extension, concerted action is always possible. All languages and forms of thinking share certain properties in common that make it possible for us to approach and make some degree of sense of them. Implicit in his concept of reason and hermeneutical inquiry is faith in human progress, in our capacity to learn and grow and to effect needed changes in ourselves and society.

And indeed, Habermas, too, believes that all languages share a common purpose. He also acknowledges that there is an important hermeneutical dimension to reason, since the intention of his communicative action is to achieve mutual understanding. The difference is that he thinks Gadamer is not sufficiently "critical" in the sense of providing an adequate basis for social critique. Moreover, because Gadamer takes a more skeptical view with respect to the possibility of attaining Truth with a capital T, he has been accused by Habermas and others of lapsing into relativism with all of its attendant difficulties.

The important distinction I think Gadamer makes is between truth and wisdom, his point being that any claims to truth and the concepts of reason on which they are based, while of practical necessity, are inevitably socially, culturally, and historically situated and thus only partial and tentative. As such, they are inherently fallible. There are no absolute truths.[41] This, however, is not obscurantism. It is not to say that we cannot know anything, that our knowledge cannot be improved, or that truth is arbitrary. It just means that we have to be very careful and circumspect with regard to our own truth claims. We also have to be more tolerant and open-minded, meaning that we have to be willing to open ourselves up to the world and listen to, and learn from, what others with competing truth claims have to say (including those in positions of authority), and to attempt to arrive at some level of mutual understanding and respect.

This precludes any assumptions about systemic oppression. As Robert Holub remonstrates, "We have to avoid . . . recourse to uncriticizable premises such as the cynical, orthodox Marxist proposition that we derive our morality from the class [or gender] struggle—since this has more often than not been the pretext for the abuse of ethics."[42] If we are to avoid, or at least minimize, blind prejudice and the vicissitudes of the politics of blame, we must consider each case on its own terms and not treat propositions as articles of unquestioned faith or dogma. We cannot and should not blithely assume anything.

We academics should be constantly on guard against the hegemony of theory.[43] Critical, radical feminist, and other brands of theory provide useful lenses for examining problems, but they are, after all, only theory and not fact. Moreover, any theory necessarily privileges certain kinds of knowledge and understandings over others. Perhaps the best way to conceive of reason and theory is as tools of understanding that are necessarily limited by human finitude. Thus any insights gained from their application are only provisional, not definitive or absolute. Reason is virtually synonymous with, or at least strongly implicated in, inquiry, which is "hypothetical and never finished, never certain and never unimprovable, that it is a practical activity, that inquiry or the attempt to improve our understanding of things is a legitimate and virtually eternal aspect of human culture, and that it is only within and through cultural activities and products that understanding and truth occur at all."[44] Theory, because it implies a reciprocal relationship with reason, acts as both a guide to rational inquiry and a means of putting the fruits of our inquiry into context.

That said, we need to be careful not to make the arts objects of our own theorizing, meaning that we one-sidedly impose our theories onto them. As Wendell Harris says, we should not use the arts just to illustrate our own theories.[45] But while I agree with Harris that we should not impose our theories onto the arts, or onto others for that matter, I cannot agree with him that we need a complete cleansing of the stables altogether; that we should just throw out theory altogether. As with the concept of reason, we just need to be more humble and circumspect about our claims, particularly those that may have dire implications for others with respect to their democratic musical rights, freedoms, and obligations.

As defined herein, reason and theory are reciprocal elements in our never-ending quest for personal and mutual understanding, truth, and justice. At times that quest might mean attempting to reach consensus on important matters of mutual interest, such as on the nature and value of music and music education, but it can also mean trying to gain a better appreciation of, and asserting, our differences, or simply trying to muddle our way through confusing situations and problems such as we encounter when confronted with the music and customs of cultures other than our own. Reason and democracy are aesthetic as much as practical ideals the nature of which should be "permanently open for examination and discussion."[46]

If reason is a central term of democracy, we had best avoid monolithic definitions and theories of any kind. And, if democracy is the end, we had better also avoid committing ourselves to utopian or perfectionist agendas. As Cahoone insists,

> Democracy is not only non-utopian, it is in principle anti-utopian. Democracy and the humanism that serves as its intellectual base is a radical acceptance of ineradicable imperfection and everlasting conflict. Democratic individualism is the negation of any and all utopian visions, for it bars the state, majority, or collective from politically excising the autonomous individual.[47]

Cahoone, however, is not suggesting that democratic culture is a battleground in which competing individuals and groups with their respective ideologies fight it out. Rather, it implies communication and striving toward common goals. Individuals and groups often disagree, but in a democratic society their intent is also to arrive at some level of mutual understanding and respect.

One of the cornerstones of liberal democratic theory is the notion of the rational, autonomous individual. Postmodernists and other contemporary critics contend that this is just another metaphysical delusion. However, many of them would probably agree that the aim of education in democratic society should be to assist students, regardless of gender, class, ethnicity, or culture, and to the extent that it is possible, to construct their own musical identities or differences free from excessive coercion. This sounds a lot like individualism. Moreover, if music and the other arts were as self-referential as many postmodernists and radical feminists seem to think, they would hardly be appropriate sites in which to explore issues of gender, sexuality, and ethnicity.[48] The fact that many feminists and postmodernists valorize the concept of democratic community while remaining skeptical of arbitrarily imposed authority, and that they generally claim to be interested in emancipation, suggests that they retain a latent faith in the concepts of abstract reason and individualism.[49]

Much of the disagreement between contemporary critics and liberals over the question of individualism can be attributed to misunderstanding and word play. Nowhere in the literature on democratic theory, Saul writes, is "the individual seen as a single ambulatory centre of selfishness. That idea of individualism, dominant today, represents a narrow and superficial deformation of the western idea; a hijacking of the term and—since individualism is a central term—a hijacking of western civilization."[50] Many contemporary critics have simply taken that deformed notion of individualism as selfishness and applied it to the group in the service of ideology. What we have, then, is a "Platonic marriage of reason and ideology"[51] in which the former is treated as the prisoner of the latter, rather than, following the Socratic tradition, a prime means of questioning authority in all of its guises, including the ideology of the group. Then, too, as both Saul and Cahoone remind us, the cynical reduction of society to competing collectivities is a deformation of the democratic principle of participation. Central to the notion of democracy, Cahoone argues, is the "commitment to the intrinsic value of every individual and that individual's cultural contribution."[52]

All of this, however, is academic because while many contemporary critics say one thing—that everything is only ideological—they mean another. The real question is not whether we as individuals exist, but to what extent we can develop personal and collective autonomy, given the social and other impediments confronting us. Even Susan McClary agrees with this, since she states that the purpose of deconstructive attacks on the western musical canon is not so much to disable the master narratives on which it is based as it is to clear a space in which women can develop their own voices.[53]

On Seeking Reconciliation in Music Education Philosophy

What gets many contemporary leftist critics and theorists into trouble, I think, is their monolithic and dogmatic assertion that all authority is arbitrary and therefore suspect; that absolutely everything is socially constructed (Barbara Riebling refers to these as totalitarian theories of truth). A more reasonable proposition is that we are both processes and products of some complex, even chaotic, mix of biological nature and lived experience. But aside from the cultural left's rejection of authority and attempts at social engineering, I see no irreparable gulf, no irreconcilable chasm separating our respective musical and educational agendas.

My purpose herein has been not so much to critique contemporary theory as to simply point out that probably the majority of us within the music education philosophy community share an interest in the same ultimate values, which are equality and freedom, and how they might realistically be achieved. However, we approach those problems in different ways. If, as was suggested, reason is an inherited and ongoing conversation among intellectuals about the nature of truth and understanding, then music educators should listen more closely to one another while avoiding extremes. As Bernstein would say, we need to get beyond our present obsession with proving each other wrong and try to arrive at a closer understanding of our respective philosophical agendas. We need to have more faith in our humanity and respective good intentions coupled with a genuine respect for our philosophical differences.

As a case in point, for the past decade a good deal of criticism has been directed at Bennett Reimer's philosophy of music education as aesthetic education. Reimer's philosophy has been variously described as sexist, racist, elitist, and ideological.[54] I will not deal with the first three of these charges because Reimer has more than adequately defended himself against them. However, I find it interesting to note that his philosophy is said to be overly ideological when, in fact, he has long railed against ideology, literal mindedness, and music teachers' slavish dependence on methods. Aesthetic education, he has claimed, is the "antithesis to methodology and ideology."[55] In essence, his philosophy is based on the idea that we should all of us engage in research and discourse about music and the arts' deepest values and revise our practices accordingly.

We might not always agree with Reimer on the particulars of his philosophy, but I can think of no one else in the field of music education who has as consistently, and for such a sustained period of time, lived up to the principles of his or her own philosophy. For almost forty years he has continued to learn and grow and to change his philosophy in response to new philosophical, psychological, and other developments and understandings. While stung by his critics, and perhaps overly defensive at times, he has nevertheless remained sensitive to their criticisms. Perhaps the best evidence of this is his very recent acknowledgement that our profession now requires a more comprehensive philosophy that takes into account all of our respective philosophical positions without necessarily resolving them. What he is proposing, I think, is just the kind of ideal community of music education philosophers and theorists of which Habermas and Subotnik would approve (provided that Habermas dropped his prejudice against authority and tradition) in which scholars participate in mutual inquiry with a view to building on their respective insights and commonalities and in which all of the various philosophical positions exist in productive tension with one another. Rather than being vilified, I would argue, and because he seems to personify and exemplify many of the democratic values, qualities, and sensibilities alluded to herein that are so necessary to reason (e.g., tolerance and inclusiveness), Reimer should be held up as a model for others wishing to pursue philosophical inquiry in our field.

The sticking point for many of Reimer's critics is that music education as aesthetic education has become institutionalized. His philosophy, so the thinking goes, because it has been adopted by those controlling our institutions, has become overly ideological and patriarchal by virtue of the fact that teachers and students habitually defer to its authority.[56] But while acknowledging that people may tend to do this, I see no reason why Reimer should be blamed for the failings of individual teachers and students to take his teachings to heart and to think for themselves. And indeed, by this standard, radical feminist and other critical theorists on the cultural left, too, are becoming increasingly ideological. It is they who have gained ascendancy in many of our institutions of "higher" learning. At least that seems to be the case in Canadian faculties of education where music and other education students are dogmatically exhorted to politicize everything and where schoolteachers are depicted as the unwitting agents of capitalist interests.[57] Although undertaken with the best intentions (i.e., to encourage students to take more responsibility for initiating productive change), the approach these instructors take seems more indoctrinal than educational.

Many liberals would agree that student teachers should be encouraged to examine their own musical and educational beliefs and ideologies and to become more inclusive with respect to whom and what they eventually teach. However, they would take issue with the presumption that teachers are social engineers charged with ensuring "representation, inclusion, and equity for every member of the class at all times."[58] The danger of perfectionist or utopian educational agendas is that they are by definition unrealistic and repressive. They imply a teacher-centered and authoritarian approach to the training of future music teachers. Ironically, while criticizing teachers for being too controlling and for acting as "enforcers" of the status quo, some contemporary theorists seem to think that they have a monopoly on truth coupled with a moral right to "police" the classroom in order to ensure compliance with their specific social and political agendas. And here is the crux of the matter. The teacher's political agenda and particularist theoretical framework are being imposed on the classroom.

The problem, I hasten to add, is not completely with postmodernism or with critical or radical feminist theory, since any theory or theoretical paradigm is just a tool of understanding. What matters is how it is applied to actual educational practice; whether it is simply imposed on practice as a panacea, or whether it is used intelligently and provisionally as *one* means of gaining increased understanding of each particular and complex educational context and how, within that dynamic social context, individuals and groups might be empowered to participate more actively. Too many contemporary theorists, though, seem to know the answers to their questions before they have been asked, particularly with respect to aesthetic theory, which is assumed to be patriarchal. In this and other respects, contemporary theory and postmodernism have become ideological and formulaic! Proponents of those theories or paradigms simply teach students to identify the powerful and then to deconstruct, and thereby subvert and disable, their philosophical and political agendas as means of achieving equality.

Seldom addressed by those critics, though, is whether, within a democratic community, the authority of those in positions of power is warranted and legitimated by public support. Moreover, as I have said elsewhere in relation to choral pedagogy, the danger of deconstructive attacks on the status quo is that, in the absence of progressive and clearly thought-out alternatives that have been reached by democratic consensus, and without an understanding of what equality means, we might end up with something much worse.[59] In any event, this is all based on a misconception, since Foucault did not mean to suggest that freedom implies an absence of authority.[60]

Much of the invective on the part of contemporary critics against aesthetic education is misguided and needlessly divisive. Those critics wrongly accuse Reimer of Cartesianism while overlooking the fact that liberals such as he share a similar foundational concern with musical democracy and equality. However, the kinds of free-wheeling debates wherein these kinds of communal understandings should be worked out have not yet taken place in our profession or at least not to any significant extent. For example, many contemporary theorists claim to be working to achieve equality, but the fundamental and extremely complex and vexing question of what is musical equality still remains to be addressed. At the very time when we should be working together to develop such communal understandings as part of a cohesive and *reasonably* comprehensive and consensual philosophy of music education in order to help ensure music's place in the schools, we are blinded by our differences and prevented from recognizing our commonalities, including our shared interests, purposes, and philosophical origins! At times we even appear to be working at cross purposes.

Critical and radical feminist theorists are not the only ones who are misguided in savaging aesthetic theory. It should be clear by now that the practice of using aesthetic theory as a foil for sociological theories of music education is wrongheaded, not only because aesthetic theorists and musicologists do in fact recognize and to a certain extent take into account the social contexts of music, but also because the "truth," whether or to what extent musical values are universal or particular, can probably never be resolved. Postmodernists may prefer "heterogeneity and locality to homogeneity, uniformity, and universality,"[61] but if charges of dualism are to be avoided they will also have to recognize and celebrate both our distinctiveness and commonality.

This, of course, is what Reimer and other liberals have been saying all along: that we and our musics are all in some respects both alike and different.

Even more to the point, there exists no unanimity among theorists with respect to what is to be done with the western musical canon. The question has hardly been addressed at all in the academic literature. What we find, instead, are deconstructive attacks on the canon that, in the absence of positive alternatives, fail to bring about productive change. These attacks accomplish nothing with respect to broadening the canon. Then, too, we have yet to consider counterclaims by Richard Rorty and other "radical" postmodernists that the western canon should be retained on the grounds that it is very diverse and yet performs an important function in providing students with a common cultural basis.[62] Rorty, like Subotnik, thinks that we need both unity and diversity in our educational system, which implies a shared culture.

Given the uncertainty of the times, Subotnik's solution to the problem, in which she views the aesthetic and sociological positions—the modern and postmodern—as existing in some sort of tension, seems the most humane, reasonable, and potentially productive approach to problems of music education theory and practice. It is also more inclusive and realistic, given the fact that, to borrow a turn of phrase from Subotnik, no matter what the criticisms of music and aesthetics, our language will continue to preserve some such constructs for the foreseeable future. Besides, as my colleague Harold Fiske has pointed out, no amount of *proving* aesthetic theory *wrong* is going to justify the logical sufficiency of other sets of principles.[63]

Inclusiveness in philosophical and theoretical discourse is no guarantee of truth, but as Harvey Siegel points out, it "may well be an epistemological (methodological) virtue in the sense that the more voices and perspectives are included in theorizing, the more likely it is that epistemically worthy beliefs/hypotheses/theories will be generated and accepted."[64] And remember that Gadamer says that it is only through "a dialogical encounter with what is at once alien to us, makes a claim upon us, and has an affinity with what we are"[65] that we discover whether our particular prejudices are blind or enabling ones. Aesthetic theory makes a claim upon all of us in music education philosophy in the western world and has an affinity with what we are, yet it is sadly underrepresented at some meetings of contemporary music education theorists. It is difficult to imagine how any kind of democratically formed consensus and communal vision for music education theory and practice is ever to be accomplished unless people like Bennett Reimer, and others who disagree, are included in discussions and are accorded the respect they deserve. Doubtless some will insist that aesthetic theories should be excluded from contemporary philosophical debates on the grounds that they are "resolutely nonsociological."[66] Others, however, would respond that differences between Reimer's aesthetic theory and praxial and other more sociological approaches have been overdrawn and that, while the social and cultural contexts of music and music education are obviously important, they are not the whole picture.[67] As Dewey wrote, the social might be the largest whole that we can understand, but it is not *the* whole.[68] But then this is a mute point since, as Gadamer expressed it, we are limited by our human finitude. We can never finally understand.

Music Education and the Culture Wars

4 Previously, I discussed the nature and value of a liberal music education and how the future health of the profession depends on music teachers becoming more intellectually and politically involved in the profession and its problems and in the wider public sphere. I also addressed the nature of abstract reason and intellectual conversations as means of helping resolve debilitating professional problems while contributing to a sense of community and common purpose. If music educators are to be politically successful and effective within the public sphere—if they are to function as public intellectuals and shapers of informed public opinion with respect to musical and educational matters—they will have to develop a social vision and explicit political purpose.

That behooves me to say something now about the current political climate of the public sphere. If music educators are to become more involved in the public sphere, they require a basic familiarity with some of the larger political movements, issues, and agendas shaping public education throughout the West. They require political perspective in order to understand what has been happening to public education of late and, possibly, their own culpability in the societal devaluing of music education. The devaluing of music education is essentially a political problem requiring a political solution.[1] Music educators know that they have a serious problem with respect to low levels of governmental and public support.[2] What they lack, as suggested by the dearth of professional literature and discussion on the topic, is an understanding of the political nature of the problem.

On the Profession's Retreat from the Public Sphere

Regrettably, music teachers long ago abandoned, or were abandoned by, the public sphere, retreating into the relative isolation of their profession while losing touch with the wider political ideals and movements that once inspired them. During the 1950s and 1960s, and especially with the rise of the civil rights and aesthetic education movements in the United States, music teachers passionately believed in, and publicly voiced, the importance of music education for all children.[3] This rallying cry for music teachers was explicitly linked to the democratic principles of equality, universal suffrage, and participation.[4] Where many music educators erred was in assuming that all children everywhere should aspire to and attempt to uniformly replicate "definitive" expert performances of the western "masterworks." Further, and while motivated by democratic intentions and ideals, music teachers failed to develop the philosophical understandings, teaching models, and pedagogical strategies that would help them accomplish their democratic goals.[5] Instead, they reverted to traditional performance-based models, repertories, and pedagogies divorced from the real musical world and its social problems.[6]

Today's music teachers are for the most part no longer, or at least not adequately, represented in public conversations about the nature, value, and purpose of music and music education in democratic society.[7] Sadly, the coupling of democracy with musical culture and education is viewed with deep suspicion and distrust.[8] Some music critics contend that democracy has no place in music or music education. Democracy is just a political process that "has little or nothing to say either about how we should live or about how we should die; still less does democracy provide us, outside the world of political process, with a 'way of life.'"[9] This is a gross misconception, as democratic states are far from anarchical while the concept of democracy implies much more than just a political process. As Dewey reminds us, democracy is no more just a political process or form of government than is a home or a church just a building constructed of bricks and mortar.[10] It is an ethical ideal about a certain way of life, of "moral and spiritual association," of which the political process and public goods such as health care and education are important expressions. They all ought to be viewed as means to that end; of maximizing public participation in the shaping of communal values while contributing to the improvement of the quality of life for all, not just for the rich or elite. I hope that this book will help to clear up some of the conceptual confusion among music teachers and others about the nature of democracy and its relevance to professional practice. As was explained to some extent in chapter 2, democracy implies a loving concern for others and their welfare. If nothing else, the pursuit of a democratic aim or purpose through music education should motivate children to care more about, and thus to become more involved in, the wider musical and social world around them. One would think—hope—that music teachers and parents would applaud any educational or musical initiative that might help to overcome adolescents' apathy and indifference to music other than that which they consider their own.

Many contemporary music teachers, though, consider democracy to be potentially dangerous to practice in that it can undermine their authority while contributing to the degradation of musical and other standards. Dennis Tupman, a music education advocate and past president of the Canadian Music Educators Association, blames the rise of constructivism in education, "with its attendant perceived chaos," for the lack of musical rigor and standards in school music. Bemoaning the current dominance of popular culture in western society, Tupman wistfully muses that music education's salvation may be found in the growing neofundamentalist movement with its claims to possession of absolute truth and values.[11] As was suggested in chapter 2, rather than conversing with children about their respective musical values, music educators like Tupman want to ignore the problem of popular music altogether, passively burying their heads in the sand while waiting for the political climate to change. They view popular music as toxic sludge; classical music is the one true music. Little has changed during the past several decades with respect to music teachers' beliefs and attitudes about their professional role. Despite the public's clear rejection of the classics and their attendant and supposedly absolute musical values, many music teachers still view themselves as "conservers" of tradition and the "masterworks" charged with indoctrinating children to the canon of genius.[12] It is no wonder that most children and members of the public consider music education irrelevant. The very strong conservative and elitist streaks in music teachers contribute in no small way to their estrangement from the public. To some extent, music teachers are probably the authors of their own misfortune.

Many twentieth-century music education researchers also retreated from or abandoned the social world of music by subscribing to the logical positivist belief that music was reducible to the physics of sound and that its structural properties, because they were socially abstract and objective, could and ought to be measured according to empirical and quantitative standards as means of testing for musical intelligence or determining the qualitative value of individual compositions or even entire musical cultures.[13] This confusion between quantitative measurement and qualitative judgment of values was addressed in chapter 2.[14] The thinking at the time was that the identification and application of universal perceptual laws governing all music learning could help students better internalize music, as if the goal were to have them simply copy, and not construct, their musical world. Music cognition was ideally and perversely conceived as a mechanistic process untainted by human values, subjectivity, and intentionality.[15] The aim of such research, when applied to teaching practice, was to strip away children's subjectivity and humanity such that they became more objective and scientific, more machinelike, in their musical judgments. Perhaps even worse, researchers were all too often content addressing trivial problems of no real consequence or interest to music teachers or the public.[16] For the most part, and with perhaps a few exceptions, music education research continues to be ignored by music teachers and the public alike. The lack of perceived relevance of music education research to professional practice and to society, coupled with the continuing standardization and routinization of music education curricula, repertoire, and pedagogy according to traditional or scientific, not democratic or humanistic, principles, has contributed to the increasing stultification of the profession. Music education, I submit, is becoming increasingly stodgy and difficult to justify in democratic society.

The Hijacking of the Public Sphere by the New Right

The abandonment of the public sphere by music teachers and researchers, and the concomitant devaluing of music and other "soft" subjects like art and philosophy, are really part of a much larger social problem: the hijacking of the public sphere and its institutions by the New Right. By "soft" subjects, I am referring to the nineteenth-century notion of "formal discipline,"[17] or the belief that general mental faculties were like muscles that could be strengthened through application to certain difficult or "hard" subjects such as Latin or mathematics. Today's "hard" subjects are language, mathematics, and the sciences—the ones that are most susceptible to quantitative assessment and that are deemed useful in business and the workforce. To many people's utilitarian way of thinking today, and particularly that of the New Right, subjects such as music and philosophy are not sufficiently "concrete" to be of much use to anyone.

The term "New Right" refers to a loose coalition of neoconservatives and Christian fundamentalists who believe that society and its institutions, including the delivery of public goods such as education and healthcare, ought to be subject to the whims and dictates of the market. Committed to the ideologies of free trade, globalism, and rugged individualism, their mantras are deregulation, privatization, and competition.[18] Since the election of Margaret Thatcher in the United Kingdom in 1979, followed by Ronald Reagan and George H. W. Bush in the United States, the public sphere has been steadily privatized as the New Right consolidates its hold on governments throughout the West or pressures incumbent liberal governments to accede to their demands for more and deeper tax cuts, regardless of potential negative consequences to public education and social programs.[19] For more than a decade now, public education at all levels in the West has been consistently defunded while the public everywhere has been subjected to the same political rhetoric and propaganda about the failing state of education.

The media were among the first casualties of the New Right's attack on the public sphere as the public representational apparatus was seized and exploited in a crass but largely successful attempt to convince the public that education was in crisis. As Gregory Jay writes about the United States:

> Trained by well-financed experts in the fields of public opinion and media, the messengers of the Right soon saw their stories reprinted in most of the

major magazines and newspapers and occupying prominent places on the best-seller list. What Michael Bérubé, in his justly famous account, called "the media's big lie" was in fact a product manufactured by new sectors of the right-wing knowledge industry.[20]

The American educational system, it was reported in *A Nation at Risk: The Imperative for Educational Reform* (1983), was responsible for a "rising tide of mediocrity" that threatened the country's commercial and military preeminence.[21] Public schools and universities were blamed by the New Right for regional or national economic reverses because they failed to equip students with the requisite knowledge, skills, and attitudes to allow business to successfully compete in the global marketplace. Seldom, if ever, were those same institutions given credit when the economy was healthy.

The New Right's solution to this manufactured crisis has been to treat public schools and universities as training grounds for business and the workforce. The future of these public institutions, too, these propagandists insist, is to be shaped by the forces of market discipline and Darwinian competition.[22] Thus the New Right's continuing interest in voucher programs, charter schools, and tax incentives to help parents send their children to private schools.[23] The New Right does not really believe in egalitarianism, which they regard as unnatural and an obstacle to the pursuit of excellence.

Missing from the educational rhetoric and propaganda of the New Right is any strong sense of the moral and democratic purpose or obligation of public schools with respect to creating informed and critically engaged citizens with a social conscience and minds of their own. Nor is there an acknowledgment of government's obligation to ensure equality of educational opportunity for all children. Children, and indeed most people, are instead viewed as fundamentally "lazy, fearful, and irrational, more suited to being compelled by their superiors than to being allowed to think and act for themselves."[24] Public schools are accordingly conceived in almost Dickensian terms as operating along the factory model with principals functioning as a managerial class overseeing an assembly-line education in which teacher-workers fashion new student-products to meet the immediate utilitarian needs of business and industry.[25]

The Standards Movement

The standards movement and standardized testing are implicated in this takeover of public education because they provide the wherewithal for "naming and shaming" schools failing to meet arbitrarily imposed standards, but also because they help emasculate administrators, parents, and teachers who no longer have much input or control over matters of curriculum and school governance. Given that the intellectual roots of the New Right are in late-nineteenth-century British utilitarianism, its investment in the standards movement and standardized testing is only natural and expected. Both are expressions of late-nineteenth- and early-twentieth-century industrial planning. During the early twentieth century, interest in standards and standardized testing in education was sparked when educational theorists and psychologists began to apply "proven" industrial manufacturing techniques to public schools to improve educational efficiency.[26]

When simply charged with efficiently delivering and assessing student acquisition of curricular knowledge, though, teachers essentially have only a managerial or assembly-line function and not so much a creative one. Further, the continuing obsession on the part of the New Right with standards and standardized testing contributes to the impoverishment of the curriculum, "reducing 'education' to what can be measured and quantified."[27] As James Beane writes,

> The standards movement is in full swing, as are the national testing schemes. The long lists of facts and skills they entail are mistakenly called a curriculum, and the definition of curriculum planning itself is reduced to the managerial function of aligning standards, tests, lesson plans, and the rest of the authoritarian mechanisms needed to control young people and their teachers. We are led to worship test scores, the false idols of education.[28]

There is nothing inherently wrong with assessing and holding schools accountable to the public. Accountability is, after all, a defining attribute of democracy. Democratically elected leaders and public servants, including teachers, are supposed to be accountable to the public. Nor is there anything wrong with the appropriate use of quantitative measures in educational testing and accountability. But when used exclusively or as the single most important measure of educational success or failure, quantitative assessment distorts the nature of education while disfiguring "the picture of our children, of education, and of our society."[29] If quantitative measurement is to contribute to accurate assessment of schools, programs, and teachers, then it needs to be coupled with qualitative assessment techniques taking into account their uniqueness. Standardized tests and other quantitative measures might be more efficient in the sense that they are relatively easy to administer and grade, but because they are extremely limited with respect to what they can actually assess, when used alone they provide only the illusion of *quality* control.[30] Besides, the factual knowledge and memorization and recognition skills usually assessed in standardized tests are representative of only lower level kinds of thinking that arguably are not very important to anyone, including businesspeople.[31] Yet the quantitative data obtained from these tests continue to be used as the sole measure of educational quality and accountability for students, teachers, and principals. These are high stakes tests indeed!

The music education profession has long been complicit in standardized testing, and for essentially the same reasons as proponents of the New Right, but also to add to music's status as a bona fide curriculum subject.[32] For much of the twentieth century, music educators eagerly embraced and used tests like the *Seashore Measures of Musical Talents* (1919), Wing's *Standardized Tests of Musical Intelligence* (1939), the *Drake Musical Aptitude Tests* (1957), Bentley's *Measures of Musical Abilities* (1966), Edwin Gordon's *Musical Aptitude Profile* (1965), and Richard Colwell's *Music Achievement Tests* (1969–70) to identify the talented or measure student progress as means of achieving greater educational efficiencies.[33] Perhaps because music education philosophy hardly existed until the second half of the century, few thought to ask "efficiency for what or to what ends," let alone whether those ends were morally and ethically justifiable. Efficiency became an end in itself. This can have serious consequences for public life.[34] For example, the practice in the not too distant past of using standardized tests in music education to exclude those lacking "the right stuff" so that teachers could concentrate their energies and limited resources on the "deserving" probably only contributed to the estrangement of music teachers from the public.[35] By choosing to limit themselves to teaching only the talented while ignoring or entertaining the masses, music teachers undermined their own future political legitimacy.

Interest in using standardized tests waned throughout the 1970s and 1980s as music teachers realized the obvious limitations of those "industrial" measures, and many came to view them as being potentially counterproductive to what was then seen as the real aim of music education: the development of personal creativity, expression, and love of music. The growth of interest in humanistic education throughout the 1950s and continuing into the 1970s eventually led to the profession's rejection (or at least deep suspicion) of standardized testing and its underlying mechanistic worldview.[36] More recently, however, and in response to repeated calls by the New Right for a return to standardized curricula, testing, and greater educational accountability, the American Music Educators National Conference (MENC) has collaborated with the Consortium of National Arts Education Associations in developing and publishing *National Standards for Arts Education: What Every Young American Should Know and Be Able to Do in the Arts* (1994).[37] While many view this as a positive step, I suspect that it may be a cynical attempt by the MENC to ingratiate itself with the New Right in hopes of preempting criticism while strengthening music's place in the schools. Critics like art educator Elliott Eisner caution that the move toward greater standardization of curriculum and testing has become too pervasive in contemporary society and may be damaging to democratic culture.

> We need to celebrate diversity and to cultivate the idiosyncratic aptitudes our students possess. Certainly, an array of common learning is appropriate for almost all students in our schools, but the preoccupation with uniform standards, common national goals, curriculums, achievement tests, and report cards rings in a theme that gives me pause.[38]

The title of the MENC document is disturbingly like that of neoliberal (read "conservative") E. D. Hirsch's popular book *Cultural Literacy: What Every American Needs to Know*, which has been widely and roundly criticized for its listing of information to be learned by children and its denial of cultural diversity.[39] The MENC National Standards are deliberately more open-ended while promoting cultural diversity and understanding. However, there is a curious lack of emphasis therein on the importance of criticism and interpretation.[40] In this and other respects, the MENC National Standards appear old-fashioned and, possibly, politically suspect in that they might only contribute to the New Right's political agenda by rendering teachers and students intellectually passive and docile.[41]

The publication of the MENC National Standards has naturally given new impetus to assessment and evaluation in music education.[42] Hopefully this will not prompt a return to an undue emphasis on standardized testing and measurement within the profession. The possibility remains that some states may eventually choose to develop standardized tests or other measures explicitly linked to the MENC National Standards as means of assessing music teachers and programs with respect to their efficacy in "delivering" curriculum. This may sound far-fetched to some American music educators, but the setting of national educational standards presupposes measurement of some sort.[43] Further, there has already been at least one precedent. For almost a decade now, music teachers in England have been subject and accountable to the national School Curriculum and Assessment Authority for delivery of a National Music Curriculum.[44] External school inspectors evaluate music teachers to ensure compliance in meeting curricular goals while the curriculum is said to "have a politically conservative agenda" and to be overly controlling of both teachers and their pupils.[45] Certainly the English music teachers whom I have met are deeply resentful of their government's policing of education. The future for British teachers of all kinds appears very bleak, as they are no longer involved in educational policymaking. Nor, since the

Teachers' Pay and Conditions Act of 1987, do they have any negotiating rights with respect to pay and work conditions.[46] It is no wonder that teachers are in short supply in that country.

The situation for Canadian music teachers is not quite as discouraging as it has been for teachers in England, in part because education remains a provincial and not a federal jurisdiction. Provincial ministers of education sometimes collaborate on curriculum reform, but Canada does not have a government-sanctioned national music curriculum, set of standards, or standardized assessment regime for music education.

Nor is there much interest among music teachers in developing a national curriculum and set of standards along the lines of the MENC National Standards for Music Education. Although subject to many of the same reforms as their American and British counterparts, including at the provincial level an increased reliance on standardized (and often conservative) curricula coupled with a corresponding emphasis on accountability, Canadian music teachers (with the exception of some in the Canadian Band Association) remain wary of the notion of a national music curriculum or set of standards.[47]

The Political Agenda of the New Right

The New Right's move toward privatization and standardization of curricula and testing is really part of a much larger, and hidden, political agenda that may well be both racist and classist and thus inimical to democracy.[48] The real aim of the New Right is to return to a more autocratic, ordered, and structured society controlled by corporate greed. Thus the New Right's interest in controlling the public educational system—as a means of "creating the sort of society in which they believe."[49] The move to the Far Right is in certain key respects a reaction to the complexity, diversity, and confusion of the postmodern world. Motivating the New Right's rhetoric and propaganda is a nostalgic desire to return to the simplicity, certainty, and stability of the "good old days" when society was more rigid and autocratically controlled, to a time when people still had faith in absolute values and deferred to the authority of the church, the state, and the wealthy.[50] A major criticism of New Right governments in Canada, the United States, and the United Kingdom is their lack of recognition of the complexity of many educational issues coupled with their lack of interest in public deliberation. "Deliberation, evidence, argument, and contestation" have been replaced by "ideological assertion and unexamined political prejudice."[51]

Wilfred Carr and Anthony Hartnett explain in *Education and the Struggle for Democracy* that the New Right's attitude toward public education is in large part a reaction against a progressive educational system that "stands for openness, is uncertain and unpredictable, puts an emphasis on respect for difference and variety rather than deference, is difficult to control, and is skeptical of absolute standards."[52] This accounts for the emphasis on the basics, religion, accountability, and so-called traditional values to be found in the educational rhetoric of the New Right and the lack of acknowledgment of the importance of criticism in school curricula, for criticism can undermine authority while contributing to uncertainty.[53]

The Discrediting of Public Schools and Universities

A key element of the New Right's political platform is the discrediting of public schools and universities, those bastions of progressive education. As Jay explains with reference to the situation in the United States,

> In order to bring the representational apparatus of the educational system under tighter ideological control, privatization proponents work to discredit the public image of schools, colleges, and universities. Their campaigns aim to stall efforts to maintain or increase education funding by state legislatures and municipalities already bankrupted by having to pay for programs that the Republican administrations refused to fund.[54]

Given the continued defunding of public education, the introduction of voucher programs and charter schools, and the encouragement given by government to private schools generally, the ranking and shaming of public schools based on standardized test scores alone appears to be done more for expressly ideological than educational reasons. As money is "siphoned off" from the public school system, presumably resulting in a reduction of educational quality, more parents will choose to send their children to private schools.[55] The recent decision by a former Ontario provincial government, for example, to provide educational tax credits for parents with children attending private schools, effectively diverting even more money away from public schools, was probably intended to exacerbate that trend.[56] What we have is a "selling off" of the public trust—and at discount prices—in the name of class interest and corporate greed.

But while proponents of privatization work to discredit public schools, often by pointing to substandard performance on standardized tests, private schools and universities are by definition not subject to the same conditions and standards as public ones. Private schools are by definition "exclusive and excluding."[57] Thus it should come as no surprise if private schools outperform public ones on standardized tests or any other academic measure. This, however, is beside the point, as private schools are not generally required to administer standardized tests to their students, let alone report their scores to the media, government, and public. Nor are they always required to hire certified teachers or follow provincially or state-mandated curricula. As a result, no one knows whether private or charter schools on the whole actually do outperform public ones, as private schools are simply not accountable to the public. Yet the New Right continues to look to private schools as the "gold" standard according to which all other schools are to be judged and after whom they are to model themselves.[58] Most likely, the encouragement of private "niche" or "boutique" schools by New Right governments has more to do with political ideology, self-interest, and the recruitment of an elite, and not the pursuit of higher standards for all.[59] Indeed, failure is built into the current system of ranking schools according to provincial or state averages on standardized tests. As Janice Gross Stein explains,

> Using averages to measure educational performance is a curiously competitive standard. It tells us little about what students actually know, about how proficient they are, and instead assesses only whether they are better or worse than average. In this kind of reporting, some students, schools, and provinces will always be below average, regardless of what the students know. . . . This kind of reporting makes it appear that some students, or schools, or provinces, or countries, are doing terribly, no matter their level of proficiency. It creates the impression that some schools are failing, but the way the results are presented, some schools must always fail.[60]

Carr and Hartnett might be right when they imply that the use of standardized tests, at least as presently used where school test results and rankings are published without acknowledging mitigating social, economic, or cultural factors affecting individual schools and school districts, is more about reproducing social class and power structures than the pursuit of excellence.[61] As they explain,

> At all levels of education—pre-school, primary, secondary, and university—institutional, curricular, and assessment changes in policy have created novel ways to label and differentiate children and young people from each other. . . . Opportunity and choice for an increasing minority of children mean deprivation and exclusion for the rest. . . . Education, on this model, becomes more like housing, under which the "market" allows those with power, status, and wealth to "purchase" what they can afford.[62]

American educational and cultural critic Henry Giroux agrees with this assessment while adding that the defunding, discrediting, and subsequent ghettoization of public education has left it extremely susceptible to commercial exploitation. As privileged and middle-class students abandon public schools, thereby further depriving them of needed tax dollars, those schools become increasingly dependent on business for financial assistance. While some see this as a marriage of convenience and necessity, critics like Giroux charge that it amounts to the deliberate and cynical commercial exploitation of the young. During the 1980s and early 1990s, corporate interests aggressively supported the defunding of public schools by the New Right. Having achieved their goal, they stand to reap huge financial rewards by gaining access, at the cost of a few "crumbs," to a young, impressionable, and captive audience that can be "'trained' as consumers."[63]

Giroux and other critics such as Barber, Jay, and Saul make compelling cases against the collusion of corporate interests and the New Right in the subversion of public education by citing numerous examples of how the former have insinuated themselves into public schools in ways that threaten their democratic purpose.[64] The public education system is becoming increasingly privatized as businesses vie to provide school services and teaching supplies, usually in exchange for advertising privileges or greater market share. As already suggested in chapter 2, popular music is implicated in this takeover of public education, for it provides business the most important means of seducing impressionable young minds through the stoking, deliberate shaping, and satisfying of their wants and desires. Thus the importance of music teachers and parents not just accepting or ignoring popular music but treating it as something warranting serious study and criticism. Children like to think of popular music and culture as their own, as an expression of their collective tastes, but in reality they are literally the property of corporate interests. The commodification of popular music and culture serves the interests of corporations and not children and society. That is one good reason why they ought to be viewed with an appropriate amount of skepticism in both the home and school.

The Illusion of Choice

The New Right's rationale for allowing the commercialization of public schools and for promoting voucher programs and charter and private schools is that parents want more educational choices for their children.[65] Parents are told that they have a right to choice, which is supposed to foster competition resulting in efficiencies of cost while allowing for greater personal autonomy and freedom.

Choice has long been a part of the liberal democratic heritage. But, as Stein notes, "if we are coerced and manipulated, we do not have the capacity to make meaningful choice."[66] Further, freedom without constraint and commitment to others, without regard for the ways our own choices may impinge on others, restricting or limiting their choices and opportunities for pursuing personal autonomy and growth, and particularly those of the less fortunate, is no basis for democratic culture. We hear more and more talk today about the right to choose in contemporary society but far less about the freedom to choose or of the moral obligation to others and their similar right to choice and how the often intractable and sometimes incommensurable values underlying and informing those different choices are to be mediated and accommodated. We hear plenty of talk about rights but little of the conversation, compassion, and willingness to listen, compromise, and make amends that are the foundation of a more just, equitable, and progressive society. Without that kind of open and unhindered public conversation about values, and an educational system that actively supports and promotes it as a public good by preparing all future citizens to intelligently participate therein as moral agents, the right to choose can easily exacerbate social inequities and unrest while favoring incumbent elites. Choice without commitment and responsibility to others, and particularly the less fortunate among us, is hardly intelligent social behavior as it is bound to foster injustice, resentment, and social strife, thereby eventually bringing about the very uncertainty that so frightens those on the political right.[67]

And herein lies the rub as far as the commercialization and privatization of public education is concerned. As Barber explains, "Choosers are made, not born. For free markets to offer real choice, consumers must be educated choosers and programming must proffer real variety rather than just shopping alternatives."[68] Besides, big business, while using the rhetoric of choice, cannot afford to offer real choice. The kinds of advertising strategies that corporate interests employ in schools are not meant to promote critical thinking any more than they are to present children with a range of choices. The last thing that the corporate world really wants is educated and thoughtful consumers who care about things like equality and justice and can see through media shallowness and advertising hype while demanding serious alternatives. The mind-numbing consumerism and titillation of so much of the corporate media's programming, educational products and services, and advertising—the deliberate shaping of desire and satisfaction through music and image in pursuit of profit—are probably antithetical to education and the development of personal and possibly even national autonomy. To quote Barber, "McWorld's strategy for creating global markets depends on a systematic rejection of any genuine consumer autonomy or any costly program variety—deftly coupled, however, with the appearance of infinite variety."[69]

All that corporate interests can offer children is the illusion of choice, for "selling depends on fixed tastes (tastes fixed by sellers) and focused desires (desires focused by merchandisers)." This means that there can be little or no variety, as "variety means at best someone else's product or someone else's profit."[70] Further, the supposedly fixed or absolute tastes and values to which corporate interests and other members of the New Right wish young children to conform in school are white middle-class tastes such as those idealized and proselytized through media and advertising imagery by the Disney Corporation, soft drink bottlers, and, of course, the ubiquitous fast-food chains whose bland products are now globally available.

The issue here is not whether to reject or embrace those values but whether or to what extent individuals, and particularly children, are coerced. Belief in our capacity and freedom to choose can contribute to a sense of personal control over the maelstrom of life. It can provide us with a sense of increased security and stability—of certainty—in an apparently chaotic and often senseless world. But if the options presented us are not real ones, and if the intent of those controlling the media is only to entertain and titillate while selectively channeling and manipulating cultural identity and memory for purposes of propaganda, such as happens in movies in which history is deliberately distorted for patriotic or nationalistic purposes, or children are trained as mindless consumers, then the exercising of choice becomes a chimera to distract us from the real world while helping us forget our own complicity in its problems.[71]

There is more going on here than just mindless consumerism and the shaping of desire and satisfaction. The images, tastes, and values that children encounter in school play a role in the construction of social identities and worldviews.[72] This is too important and potentially influential to entrust to big business, which, after all, is primarily interested in representing consumerism and middle-class culture as things desirable and appropriate for all people everywhere. Not surprisingly, Giroux and others think that this packaging and selling of middle-class culture—the Disneyfication and suburbanization of the world through popular culture—is a form of cultural hegemony, or imperialism if you prefer.[73] Popular movies, art, literature, and music are all used by major corporations as means of rewriting history and collective memory and thereby rationalizing the "authoritarian, normalizing tendencies of the dominant culture."[74] And just when the public needs them most, governments throughout the West have been abdicating their responsibility to "conceive and defend the common good" by defunding, downsizing, and privatizing the public service, including public education, while simultaneously deregulating industry in the name of global free trade.[75] This, coupled with an absence of school curricula emphasizing critical analysis and political awareness, makes public schools and children even more vulnerable to manipulation and control by politicians and corporations whose intent is simply to breed intellectual passivity and not to prepare children for their future role as informed and discerning citizens.[76]

The Invective of the Cultural Left

Giroux, however, is too radical for my own tastes. There is a "ritualistic anti-capitalism" in the academy that probably exacerbates the problem of rampant and uncontrolled consumerism by making it all too easy for the New Right to dismiss their critics while relegating them to the Ivory Tower.[77] By representing democracy as a battleground in which competing self-interest groups with their own particularist and tribal identities fight it out, and not as a culture based on compassion, sharing, and mutual obligation, academics on the left, including musicologists such as Susan McClary, have contributed to the New Right's political success by suggesting that there can be no meeting of minds, no public or common good.[78] In one very important sense, leftist challenges to the status quo can be seen as continuing the democratic tradition of rejecting fixed definitions of the public good while contributing to public deliberations about changing social values. "The difficulty arises," explains Stein, "when by telling our own story, we unfairly and rudely preempt the tales of others."[79] Much the same point was made in chapter 3, in which radical feminists and other members of the cultural Left were criticized for their dogmatism and savaging of aesthetic theory. Nor, as was explained, is leftist scholarship free of problems involving favoritism, abuses of privilege and power, intimidation, intemperate language, and manipulation of choice.[80] As Stein admonishes us,

> Even as we assert our right to tell our own story, we must listen attentively and fairly to the stories of others. What is important is inclusive and reflective public conversation, first about values and only then about choice, first about ends and only then about means, and first about purpose and only then about instruments. And as post-industrial society takes form and shape, as knowledge expands our sense of what is *collectively* possible, we will have to find new ways to bound possibility with commitment. As the one forecloses the other, possibility and commitment are always in tension with one another. The language we use to speak about this tension will test our capacity to provide both the "public" and the "good" in public goods.[81]

In the end, the invective of the cultural Left probably contributes to their marginalization from the public sphere and from other academics and public schoolteachers by discouraging or shutting down conversation altogether. The "ceaseless politicking" and rejection of all authority by the cultural Left has only contributed to the corporate Right's success by making civil conversation about ideas impossible.[82]

Besides, like it or not, virtually all of us in the West, including academics, are consumers and invested in the stock market. Capitalism can be a serious threat to democracy, but it is not always and completely, or even necessarily, bad. It can be a source of inspiration for creativity, for previously unimagined possibility leading to productive change. Business just needs to be closely monitored, regulated, and held accountable by governments so that, when the former is involved in the delivery of public goods (which itself ought to be the subject of considerable public attention and conversation), it adheres to high ethical standards while serving the public interest.[83] That is what Stein means when she states that "the language of possibility needs to be bounded by the language of commitment." Public goods such as education and health care must by definition be available to all citizens, while the role of the state ought to be as a "guarantor of quality" and "trustee of fairness, equity, and justice."[84] Proponents of the New Right are often critical of the managerial role of government, arguing that we need less, not more, government. But if public markets continue to be privatized, then governments must play a more active role in their regulation so as to protect the public interest.[85]

This means that there must be more and not less governmental involvement in overseeing the delivery of public goods, including music education programs. Otherwise business will only look after its own interests, as happened several years ago around London, Ontario, when a prominent national music business was given free rein to operate concert band programs in several publicly funded schools. The company in question had total control of the program to develop its own niche market, renting and selling its own select brand-name instruments and materials and hiring nonunionized music teachers, but was accountable to no one, including any educational authorities. Obviously if government continues to encourage the privatization of school music programs, then it must at the very least reinstate the state, provincial, and local music supervisors and consultants whose positions were eliminated during the past two decades. Those supervisors and consultants traditionally provided much needed professional guidance and leadership to music teachers, thereby helping to improve the quality of music education in the schools. They were also best qualified and positioned to explain and justify music education to government and the public alike.[86] Were these positions to be reinstated, one would hope that these individuals would also be responsible for overseeing any privately owned music programs operating in public schools.

The Need for a Language of Critique and Possibility

Other factors contributing to the marginalization and even exclusion of academics and public schoolteachers from the public sphere include increased workload and the nature of professional training.[87] Since seizing power through domination and control of the media, New Right governments in the West have been subjecting academics and teachers to heavier workloads, leaving them little time and energy for becoming involved in public life beyond their immediate professional responsibilities. In the case of public schoolteachers, this has been accomplished by reducing the size of the workforce, mandating longer hours of instructional time for those remaining, and increasing class sizes. Public universities have fared little better in the face of continued and consistent underfunding, despite frequent pleas for financial assistance for hiring new faculty to replace an aging professoriate. Throughout Canada, for example, the number of full-time professors continues to dwindle despite a burgeoning undergraduate population, while at least one provincial government (British Columbia) has introduced legislation to override terms of hard won collective agreements such as class size and workload provisions.[88] The Spanish government, like other member countries of the European Union, has also moved to curtail the rights and freedoms of its professoriate in the names of privatization and global market economics.[89]

Academics have unfortunately not helped matters much with their apparent inability to communicate effectively with the public and government. The increasingly specialized training of academics and teachers ill prepares them for participation in public conversations. The highly specialized and esoteric language of the academic world is partly at fault. Academics are often rendered impotent in public conversations about educational and other values because they are unable to communicate in ways that ordinary people, and even other academics, can understand.[90] To some extent this may be deliberate, as academics have long held mainstream and popular culture in contempt. Universities have perhaps contributed to the problem by fostering a kind of "idiot savant academic culture" disconnected from the real world and its problems.[91] Academics often don't understand how the real world works. Obviously this has not helped their cause, any more than the eschewing of popular culture by music teachers in school and university has helped further the cause of music education in democratic society.

For public schoolteachers, including music teachers, the situation is somewhat different with respect to language, although the effect is arguably the same. While perhaps having the advantage of increased contact with parents and other members of the public through parent-teacher interactions and school concerts and other activities, teachers lack a language of critique and possibility.[92] Music teachers typically have little training, experience, or practice thinking philosophically and critically about musical, educational, or other values, let alone clearly expressing their own educational values to the public. Then again, music teachers are often impatient with things intellectual. The problem is not so much the use of highly technical and esoteric language as it is a lack of interest in and knowledge of philosophical and political issues and an inability to intelligently engage in public conversations about educational issues and values.

Music teacher education programs in the United States and Canada, and presumably in other western democracies, are designed to create professional practitioners and performance teachers and not public intellectuals. The lack of involvement by music teachers in public intellectual life is doubtless exacerbated by the reality that there is a disconnection or discontinuity in our society between school and university and between educational institutions and their communities that often hinders communication and the sharing of ideas. Many undergraduate music education majors are also profoundly ignorant of the world around them and of the grand political, philosophical, artistic, and social movements that shape their culture. This makes it all the more difficult for them to converse with undergraduates and academics from other disciplines and to relate to the public. In my own experience, few music education majors entering their senior year can distinguish Marxism from capitalism, capitalism from democracy, the political Left from Right, or the modern from the postmodern. Nor do they seem aware or worried about the kinds of political developments affecting public education, some of which can have dire personal consequences for them with respect to their future careers. They possess highly specialized musical knowledge and can categorize western art and popular music according to genres and musical style periods, but they are often at a loss when asked to locate music and music pedagogy within larger artistic, historical, political, and cultural contexts and movements. This, however, is perhaps only to be expected, since music education majors, unlike their counterparts in art and literature, are seldom asked to make connections between their own and other disciplines or to engage in intellectual conversation with so-called nonmusicians. For all too many music education majors, the best policy with respect to intellectual conversation is avoidance. One important and long-term challenge for music academics, including music teacher educators, is thus to find ways to reform and reinvigorate undergraduate music education such that undergraduates *must* engage in meaningful and sustained dialogue with representatives of other disciplines and with the public about the ubiquity and centrality of music in their lives.[93]

Much has already been explained in previous chapters about the need for inclusivity, diversity, and criticism as part of a liberal music education for future music teachers. In the remaining two chapters, I elaborate upon these and other liberal values while making more concrete suggestions for reforming and revitalizing undergraduate music education such that it is seen as more expansive and relevant to the university and wider community. This kind of socially proactive approach, focusing on the ethics of practice, musical citizenship, the development of moral and intellectual character and identity, and the pursuit of a wider and more democratic sense of musical community, is more likely to contribute to the profession's intellectual and political legitimacy in the eyes of the public and government than are any advocacy efforts. The culture wars between the political Left and New Right may for the foreseeable future be a permanent feature of politics in the western democracies. And rather than avoid controversy, music educators need to demonstrate their intellectual vitality by reengaging with individuals and groups across the political spectrum, including those on the Far Right and Left, in defense of the public musical good.

Toward Reclaiming the Public Musical Sphere

Multiculturalism Revisited

5 Music teachers are probably uniquely positioned to help break down or bridge institutional, social, and cultural barriers to the free exchange and cross-fertilization of ideas in the public sphere through their use of an increasing diversity of music in the classroom. One would think that the growth of interest in musical multiculturalism made possible by the civil rights movements would facilitate public conversation while helping to free music education from the straitjackets of overly controlling scientistic or ethnocentric curricula, repertoire, and pedagogy.[1] In part, the current interest in musical multiculturalism can be understood as reactionary to the cultural and patriarchal hegemony that critics like Giroux think are implicit in universalistic and scientistic instructional approaches. There is now greater acknowledgment that it may be "unjust to treat unequals equally."[2] Different musical groups with their respective musical values require, even demand, differential treatment.

The multiculturalism movement has helped diversify and broaden the repertory and pedagogical base somewhat. More than ever before, as evidenced by the MENC National Standards for Music Education, western educational authorities and music teachers now include in their curricula a wider variety of repertoire and pedagogical practices representative of different musical cultures. But while the school repertory has been broadened over the past several decades, the emphasis in music education apparently remains much the same as before—to perform musical works more or less the same way everywhere, according to authentic cultural traditions (as if that were possible or even always desirable).[3] More groups and cultures are represented, but there is too much emphasis on transmission and passive acceptance of cultural values and practices as mere musical facts of life and not enough on musical or social criticism.[4] Children may have a certain amount of room in which to maneuver while visiting particular musical cultures, but in the end they must play by the rules of the group or culture in question, that is, with "musical integrity."[5] There is little recognition that cultural groups are dynamic entities that are constantly changing in response to both local and global pressures and social interactions, that so-called world music has been commodified and sometimes deliberately distorted for commercial purposes, and that these create formidable ethical and practical problems for music educators.[6]

As was noted in chapter 2 in relation to Elliott's performance-based philosophy of music education, when the democratic purpose of music education and multiculturalism is acknowledged at all, it is in terms of a relativistic, laissez-faire cultural democracy and not a citizen-based one.[7] The aim of multicultural music education is usually only to acculturate children to existing cultural and group practices—that is, to develop their musical and cultural literacy—and not to prepare them as individuals who can intelligently participate in the shaping and hybridization of musical values or, in more extreme cases, choose to reject values and practices judged overly restrictive, cruel, or inhumane.[8] Children are supposed to engage in musical border crossing and exploration, which is potentially liberating and mind-expanding. But they are seldom encouraged to criticize music or to exercise "real" choice.[9] If criticism is a dirty word in music education, it is especially so in the areas of multicultural and popular music education where teachers wish to be politically correct while discouraging judgmentalism and racism in students.[10] Political correctness, though, serves no one well, except perhaps those wishing to stifle freedom of speech, choice, and association as means of furthering their own political or cultural agendas, of declaring their own truths and values absolute or sacred and thus inviolable.[11]

Judgmentalism and racism ought to be discouraged in our students, but so too should intolerance, ignorance, and complacency. Some musical and pedagogical practices, such as those denying male or female children access to certain kinds of musical participation, emphasizing slavish imitation over personal creativity, or discouraging them from considering alternative values, may well be inimical to democratic culture.[12] Lucy Green and other music education scholars have written extensively about how negative societal attitudes and gender stereotyping contribute to the musical disfranchisement of children by arbitrarily restricting their involvement in specific kinds of school and community activities.[13] Among the more pernicious negative stereotypes already found in schools are that "boys don't sing" and that "girls shouldn't conduct, compose, or play 'masculine' instruments like drums." Similar cultural restrictions on musical participation and personal creativity abound in other parts of the world. For example, drumming is a male prerogative in some African cultures, while in Japan and Northern India students are expected to defer to their teachers when learning traditional music. "Exact imitation of the teacher is the goal."[14] When imported into western classrooms, these and other nonwestern musical and pedagogical practices should also be carefully scrutinized and held to a democratic standard, which means that they may have to be adapted to suit democratic culture. We in the western democracies should want our students to be careful, thoughtful, and respectful of others and their music but not just learn to passively submit or, as Socrates was told, to simply mind their own business.[15]

Music teachers and teacher educators, though, have yet to have much serious, open, and sustained philosophical debate about the values and pitfalls of multicultural music education and its role in western public schools and democratic culture.[16] To date, there has been relatively little criticism of the sometimes preposterous claims made in support or design of multicultural music curricula, such as the notion that teaching children about the music of another culture will help them understand that culture in toto or that children must literally "live" another musical culture in order to understand it at all.[17] And while sometimes acknowledging the democratic purpose of schooling, music educators have traditionally only paid lip service to what this and multicultural music education mean and entail for them and their students. For all of the reasons articulated in previous chapters relating to esoteric language, the continued prevalence of transmission models in music teaching and music teacher education, teacher attitudes, and the discontinuities among university, school, and society, many music teachers remain largely uninformed about the profound challenges and philosophical issues facing them when making curricular and pedagogical decisions. For some time now, a handful of music education philosophers and teacher educators have been attempting to address some of these issues in their own teaching and professional publications as means of initiating educational reform.[18] Few music teachers, however, bother to read academic journals or other research materials.[19]

Democracy Reconsidered

Even if music teachers read academic literature, the partisan politics and extremism of some of the more radical reforming elites might lead them astray as far as the democratic purpose of music education is concerned. Unfortunately, as art educator Stuart Richmond notes, "It has become fashionable for radical academics to denigrate liberal values while remaining silent about, or appearing to support, cultural practices inimical to the very freedoms that facilitate their own critically autonomous position in society."[20] Members of the cultural Left in music and music education call for acts of "terrorist intervention," the "destruction" of tradition and the status quo (because they are said to be patriarchal), and the "policing" of the music classroom in order to counter the imputed male violence and cultural hegemony of the western musical and pedagogical canons.[21] On the political right we have the equally extreme view that liberal values have no place or role in music and music education and that culture is to be created and perpetuated by elite, "self-selecting and self-sacrificing...guardians of righteousness."[22]

In the wake of the attack on the World Trade Center and the Pentagon in September 2001 and the subsequent retaliation against Afghanistan and Iraq, the cultural Left might want to rethink its choice of language and metaphor, its trashing of the Enlightenment, while those at the other end of the political spectrum, the elite members of the New Right with their belief in salvation through the power of logic, fixed musical and educational standards, and global market economics should realize that those countries most heavily invested in elite power structures usually have the greatest social problems. Both sides in this highly politicized debate, however, need to realize that "power without responsibility is a form of illiteracy or ignorance" that breeds passivity while preventing thought. Radical elites on both sides appear "passively certain" of the inevitability of their being proved right.[23] But if everything is preordained and inevitable, or subject to fixed laws, standards, biology, rules of logic, God, market economics, political correctness, or survival of the fittest, then there can be no real choice. That is why neither the cultural Left nor the New Right is particularly inclined to listen to each other or to anyone else's point of view. Neither, I suspect, is a true friend of democracy.

Some academics even doubt that the linkage of democracy with music education is meaningful or practical.[24] Democracy is to them just an empty concept. This criticism, however, is logically flawed because it mistakes indeterminacy of concept for vacuousness. The concept of democracy is indeterminate, meaning that it cannot once and for all be comprehensively defined, but that is not the same as saying that it is devoid of meaning. Democracy is an open and socially constructed concept and set of principles into which each generation must breathe new life through conversation and application to shared experience. This does not make the pursuit of democratic values in music education meaningless or impractical. It is simply an acknowledgment of the complexity and variability of musical experience. Probably the majority of the concepts that give our lives meaning and hope, including music and education but also love, equality, and religion, are ultimately resistant to final definition. Simply abandoning them because they are difficult, messy, or challenging would be a grave mistake as it would be akin to abandoning the humanist tradition and its quest for liberty and justice and the improvement of the human condition.

This is not to say, however, that democracy is necessarily the only appropriate way of life for people everywhere. It is just, as Rorty expresses it, who we in the West are. Democracy is an expression of our own particular history and inevitable ethnocentrism. "To be ethnocentric," Rorty writes, "is to divide the human race into the people to whom one must justify one's beliefs and the others. The first group—one's *ethnos*—comprises those who share enough of one's beliefs to make fruitful conversations possible. In this sense, everyone is ethnocentric when engaged in actual debate."[25] And the task, at least for pragmatists and liberal intellectuals, including liberal music educators, is "to extend the reference of 'us' as far as we can."[26] We in the western democracies are all accountable and must justify ourselves to each other. That is why nothing in our classrooms and rehearsal rooms should be immune from criticism, including western classical, jazz, and popular music but also world music. The same admonition obviously applies to music education philosophy and pedagogy. To do less than that, to refuse to subject world music or any other kind of music, philosophy, or pedagogical practice to intellectual scrutiny and criticism, and thereby simultaneously open ourselves up to the possibility of criticism and change, would be to deny who "We" are while permanently relegating the music and people in question to the status of unknowable "Other." The refusal to engage in criticism of "other" musical and educational values may well be an expression of our own ignorance and condescension, as if the music, philosophies, and pedagogical practices of other individuals, groups, and cultures really don't matter or ought not to be taken seriously. In democratic society, we simply cannot afford to take a laissez-faire attitude toward people and their beliefs, values, or practices, as that would only benefit the forces of tribalism and globalization by further fragmenting and weakening society.[27] Besides, criticism is a matter of respect.

Today, when democracy is in retreat everywhere,[28] our public institutions have been stripped and privatized in the name of efficiency, and charter and private schools have been established in the name of corporate ideology and the pursuit of narrow class, religious, or cultural interests,[29] we hear only the spurious and utilitarian advocacy claim that "music makes you smarter" with respect to spatial reasoning or other abstract abilities. Few have asked the more important question of "smarter for what?" or "to what end?"[30] Intelligence continues to be equated with abstract mechanical processing, problem-solving speed, or technical ability and not with qualitative judgments and deliberations about the public musical or educational good and the pursuit of larger social and musical problems that really matter. Treated this way, music teaching has more in common with training than with education. Even worse, because mere exposure is supposed to make one smarter, the impression is created that music is something to which individuals must passively submit. Whether in supermarkets, elevators, shopping malls, and concert halls or on television and radio, all music is background and intended to shape mood and behavior. "We are taught to 'tune out,' *not* to pay attention. It is a desensitizing rather than an intensifying and expansive experience."[31]

Conspicuously absent in music teacher rhetoric is the democratic interest and purpose that once inspired so many of us in the 1960s and 1970s to become music teachers. Many of today's music teachers appear much more worried about preserving the status quo at all costs than with truly relating to children and the public by engaging in conversation with them about values. The purpose of so much music education advocacy and sloganism is to convince the public of music's utilitarian value to society, which implies communication of a sort. But while obviously well intended, and possibly in some few cases helpful, advocacy is a poor substitute for conversation. Advocacy is by definition one-sided: it is monologue, not dialogue, and all too often self-serving and "devoid of nuance and uncertainty."[32] In the end, the kinds of unrealistic assertions and promises made and the relentless "hawking" of music education to an already jaded public may only contribute to the profession's continued isolation from the educational mainstream and thus also to its political vulnerability by causing the public and politicians to "tune out."[33] Because they have been too exclusive, inflexible, and condescending to the public, music educators may be the authors of their own misfortune. The political situation with respect to education in today's society is extremely complex, and I am by no means suggesting that music teachers are entirely at fault. The point is that music educators have not helped matters much with their insistence that only they and expert musicians know best.

My own view is that the survival of the profession depends in significant part on music teachers, teacher educators, and researchers becoming much more involved in the wider musical and social worlds, which means being as open-minded and inclusive as possible with respect to whose music is included and how it is performed and utilized in the classroom, in the rehearsal room, or in public. Music educators also have to do a much better job of reaching out to people from all walks of life. This does not mean that there should be no standards at all, that everything is only subjective and thus ought to be passively accepted. Rather, we all need to pay more attention to music while engaging in public conversation and criticism about its imputed nature, uses, and abuses. We need much more conversation about the public musical good, including ethical considerations therein.

To my way of thinking, for example, there is all too much cliché, deliberate cloning, and imposition in the popular music world, as evidenced by the succession of bands and artists who all sound and look alike and by the ways their music is foisted on all of us, even those not interested in popular music, via electronic technology and the spectacle of the ubiquitous popular media. In Milan Kundera's novel *The Unbearable Lightness of Being,* the character Sabina describes how she was subjected at summer camp to the "barbarism" of continuous music from which there was no escape.[34] R. Murray Schafer similarly recounts how he and other older patients in a dentist's office were subjected to continuous commercial radio—despite their protests—and that he once witnessed an entire university campus being subjected to the "imperialistic volume" of a noon-hour rock concert.[35] I, too, often feel oppressed when attending outdoor summer music festivals where musicians compete to capture their audiences' attention through sheer volume and not through artistry or wit. They resort to brutalization rather than persuasion. Nor is there much real criticism of music (or of movies, for that matter) in the popular media, which after all are in the business of selling advertising. Barber was right when he complained that the popular media cannot afford, and have no particular wish, to offer real choice.

From a democratic standpoint, it simply isn't acceptable for anyone to impose his or her musical values on others, such as happens when rock or popular music enthusiasts "crank up the volume" on their home or car sound systems without regard for others nearby and their similar right to musical choice or when businesspeople foist Muzak or any other kind of music on an unsuspecting public. All of us need to be much more considerate of others. The issue is one of civility. Those who listen to or perform music need to be willing to exercise self-restraint; otherwise, we may only foster resentment and tyranny.

Several years ago, while attending an academic music education conference at the University of Exeter, I was pleasantly surprised when teenage rock musicians performing during an after-hours session were reminded by their instructor to take their audience members' sensibilities into account.[36] The teenagers were part of the Rock On Project, an innovative community music program designed to encourage at-risk students to remain in school. The program was intended to foster the development of social skills as much as musical skills. Those few conference participants attending the special session were grateful for the consideration shown them, while the reduction in volume made it easier to hear the music and to intelligently and respectfully converse with the teenagers about their creative decision making. This attitude of respect was reciprocated by the teenagers, who clearly took pride in what they were doing and felt that they were being taken seriously. The kinds of creative considerations and decision-making strategies employed by the group (under adult supervision) were similar to those employed in the traditional school concert band, orchestra, or stage band.

Yet rock and alternative music groups, despite their obvious attraction to at-risk students, are seldom countenanced in schools or acknowledged for their potential for promoting musical development or other growth! In my own experience, when those groups are tolerated in schools, they are usually student-initiated and lacking in adult supervision and instruction.

Students are permitted to use the school's music facilities during lunch or after hours, but they are on their own, which only defeats the school music program's purpose (as I conceive it) of fostering civil conversation leading to mutual respect and growth. Rock and alternative music may be about rebellion and instant gratification, but that is all the more reason why those children, too, require guidance and adult supervision. They have much to learn from adults, including parents, teachers, and experienced musicians, which implies communication and the exercising of self-restraint.

For many years the inclusion of classical music in school and university curricula was justified on the grounds that it was thought to be a civilizing force, acting as a kind of social glue that brought people together while humanizing them, making them into "good" men and women. Probably many music educators still hold to the Platonic belief that music education has a civilizing influence on students and society, that the study and performance of the *right* kind of music can promote the development of good citizenship and moral character. Music pedagogue Shinichi Suzuki certainly thought that way. He believed that, as with the Mozart Effect with respect to intelligence, mere exposure to classical music would make children into better, more loving citizens able to appreciate beauty and thus make a greater contribution to society.[37] This sentiment continues to be echoed in a persistent flyer circulated by music education advocacy groups in which an anonymous author claims that music education makes children more compassionate and civilized. The last stanza of this quasi-poetic statement is worth quoting here for purposes of illustration.

I teach [music] to you so that you will be more human
so that you will recognize beauty
so you will be more sensitive
so that you will be closer to an infinite beyond this world
so you'll have something to cling to
so that you will have more compassion, more gentleness, more goodness,
    and in short so that you will have more life.

This argument was long ago exploded when it was realized that utterly ruthless tyrants such as Adolph Hitler and Joseph Stalin were great lovers of classical music. Both used classical and folk music to propagandize their own warped views of cultural identity and destiny.[38] Some historians even contend that Nazism was an expression of racist attitudes inherent in German analytical philosophy, art, and classical music.[39] To Hitler, aesthetic and political ends were synonymous. He was as much interested in dictating people's tastes for art, literature, music, architecture, and even cars as he was in exerting military control over them.

Any thinking and responsible teacher or parent knows that civility is not something that can be learned through study of books or music alone. Rather, it must be inculcated and developed in children. They require instruction and practice in learning how to behave appropriately. Music instruction alone, without lessons in compassion, humility, self-restraint, and mutual respect, and particularly in the absence of appropriate modeling of those values and virtues by parents and teachers, is no more likely to contribute to the development of good citizenship and humane values in children than is mere exposure to music likely to make them smarter. Like sports or just about any other kind of activity, and when taught inappropriately, without concern for others and their sensibilities and welfare, music education can have decidedly negative social consequences. That is why music education for a democratic society "will include lessons in the intellectual, social, moral, and political dimensions of living with people whose beliefs [tastes, values, and sensibilities] differ sharply from one's own."[40] That may well be the most important lesson of all.

On Essential Virtues

If democracy is the end, then the democratic rights and responsibilities of all concerned ought to be constantly in view in classes, lessons, or rehearsals, as should any democratic principles. Among the most important of those principles, states Jay, are those of "nonrepression, nondiscrimination, equal opportunity, access to representation, toleration, [and] nonviolence."[41] These, he believes, are the essential virtues and goals of education in democratic society. But while in agreement as to the importance of these virtues, I personally find them inadequate for the reason that they sound "cool" and "impersonal." They imply a legal arrangement or contract and not an emotional commitment to others. Missing from Jay's list are the most important virtues of all, the Socratic and Aristotelian ones of friendship, love, neighborliness, or mutual respect, call it what you will, coupled with honesty, self-restraint, courage, and a willingness to compromise for the sake of some greater good. Above all, democracy depends on the existence of good faith and generosity of spirit, of character and love for one's fellow men and women. These kinds of virtues are the glue that can bind us together as a society, for they motivate conversation and the forging of relationships leading to a sense of community. Without these virtues there can be no sense of community, while the pursuit of things like freedom or equality, if pursued for the wrong reasons (e.g., out of pure self-interest or class interest), might only contribute to the further fragmentation of society.

These virtues, however, are difficult to intellectualize and teach because they imply personal experience, emotional content, and knowledge. It is one thing for teachers to intellectualize about tolerance, nondiscrimination, or equal opportunity, but quite another for them to define and explain love or compassion, for these must be modeled and experienced to be understood. In the end, as Louis Menand writes, "The only way to develop curiosity, sympathy, principle, and independence of mind is to practice being curious, sympathetic, principled, and independent. For those of us who are teachers, it isn't what we teach that instills virtue; it's how we teach. We are the books our students read most closely. The most important influence in their liberalism is our liberalism."[42]

I still like Leo Buscaglia's metaphor of life being a banquet or smorgasbord in which most people are starving for want of curiosity, confidence, sense of adventure, and love. Music classrooms and rehearsal rooms are all too often drab and joyless places in which drill prevails over inquiry and in which students' heads are stuffed with "facts." The kinds of musical drill and knowledge to which students are subjected in school seldom have much connection to lived experience. As a result, and perhaps not surprisingly, relatively few graduates of school music programs continue to perform or attend concerts featuring classical music or opera.[43] Music continues to be taught for its own sake or as a means to future employment and not as a means of engaging with the world in search of a more just, inclusive, and humane society. As Buscaglia also said, the only sane or intelligent reason for acquiring knowledge is to give it away out of compassion and love for others.[44]

Much the same thing was said in chapter 2 about criticism, that it is an expression of caring and social responsibility motivated by a democratic interest and love of humanity. Pursuit of a more humane and democratic approach to music teaching and learning (as opposed to vocational training or the pursuit of excellence for its own sake) might be the only intelligent or sane thing for music teachers to do, for anything else might only contribute (as happens all too often) to tyranny, oppression, or indifference.

Probably most if not all music teachers believe that music education should help improve the quality of students' lives, which is a noble cause and one with which I personally agree. The distinction that I have tried to make in this chapter is between music as a drug to which mere exposure or immersion is supposed to make children happier and more civilized (albeit rendered passive) and music and music classes as occasions for the development of musical, intellectual, and moral character. Whereas in the first scheme children are learning about a preexisting musical world over which they have no control, in the second they are actively constructing it—at least to the extent it is possible. They are literally living in the world and attempting to come to grips with its complexities while exercising greater choice and personal and social responsibility.

Music Education as an Occasion for Intelligence

Putting Philosophy into Practice

6 In previous chapters, I explained how music education should be reconceived as a study in social intelligence in which consideration is given not just to the pursuit of musical knowledge and skills but also to inculcating in children and music education majors moral imagination and those kinds of personal skills, dispositions, virtues, and attributes needed to mindfully engage in public criticism of musical values. Music education is in the profoundest sense a search for personal integrity and identity. The word "identity" of late is usually treated as synonymous with ethnicity, gender, or nationalism. These are obviously aspects of identity, but as used here the construction of identity has more to do with the cultivation of moral character than with this or that music or group. Individuals must associate with and commit to various groups as means of "finding themselves" and making sense of musical and educational experience. This, however, should not be at the expense of independence of mind and moral and ethical judgment and responsibility.[1]

Music teachers and music teacher educators wishing to instill liberal values in their students will first need to convince them that music is worldly and deserving of criticism but also that their informed opinions matter. As Beane insists,

> We should ask that the curriculum focus on topics that are of real significance to both young people and the larger society. Justification for the curriculum should be clear. The curriculum should never insult the intelligence of our young people or their capacity to recognize the irrelevant when they see it. We should ask that the curriculum treat students with dignity, as real people who live in the real world and care about its condition and fate. We should ask that the curriculum value the knowledge and experience young people bring with them to school, as well as what they think would be worth pursuing. They should have some say about their own learning experiences, and their say should count for something.[2]

Music is not just entertainment or titillation but, owing to its capacity to liberate, seduce, or overwhelm, something that profoundly matters to society.

Students need to know that music's capacity to insinuate itself into the psyche or to obliterate thought can have both positive and negative consequences for them and society.[3]

Music can "pierce like a painful ray of light directly into the most vulnerable parts of the personality."[4] It can break through our self-defenses in ways that language cannot while helping us to empathize with and learn more about others. In that sense music may be truly liberating. However, music can just as easily be used to cynically manipulate, deceive, or distort (as, for example, when anticapitalist protest music of the Vietnam era is exploited by banks and other businesses for advertising purposes). Perhaps even worse, we are constantly bombarded in our technological society with mind-numbing commercial music that is not meant to be listened to, refused, or resisted—just heard.[5] Muzak is only the most glaring example of music that is intended to deaden and manipulate. No one can attend to everything in his or her sonic environment, but it is obviously important that we should exercise our intelligence by learning how to differentiate between the life-affirming and the malignant and not just ignore problems or passively submit. Unless we attend to our sonic environments, we may be more susceptible to abuse.

This implies teaching children and undergraduates how to exercise careful judgment with respect to what is of musical value while also learning how to express their informed opinions in ways their peers and adults can understand. Music education becomes a public forum in which students practice gaining much needed experience in exploring, critically examining, and sometimes defending their values under adult supervision. Face-to-face conversation is vital to the democratic project because it can enhance learning through mutual feedback and criticism but also because individuals, if they are not to be intimidated and coerced, require practice relating to others as intellectuals.[6] Classroom discussion, personal reflections, and critical papers all ought to stimulate the growth of self-confidence and intellectual and emotional maturity in students through provision of appropriate degrees of freedom of choice balanced by constructive criticism and bounded by loving commitment. If the purpose of education is to help students reclaim their authorship of the world so that they can eventually contribute to democratic society, then the social function of music teachers and music teacher educators is primarily moral and editorial in nature.

The actual content of school and public conversations about musical and other values should obviously vary widely according to the ages, levels of experience, maturity, and interests of those involved. The needs of the particular or local community should also be taken into account, as should any wider regional and national concerns as expressed through mandated curricula.

All of those interests and values, however, must be mediated and subjected to criticism and not just mindlessly accepted as self-evident and permanent truths to be imposed on children or society. Further, no one within this arena, including music teachers and academics, has a monopoly on truth, knowledge, virtue, or understanding. (I am not suggesting, however, that students are necessarily their teachers' intellectual or political equals. One would hope that teachers are more mature and experienced than their pupils and thus have correspondingly greater responsibility and authority.) We can all learn from one another and potentially be challenged to grow in new ways, while the role of the music teacher is that of a guide, facilitator, and mediator of musical beliefs and defender of the democratic musical faith.[7]

Music teachers are charged with balancing the needs of both students and society while simultaneously prompting, monitoring, and guiding school and public conversations (such as parent-teacher conversations) so that they remain open, civil, and helpful to all concerned. While the content of school and public conversations will necessarily vary, they ought to share something of the same character. They ought to be motivated by a democratic interest. This means teaching children, parents, and others not to just mindlessly accept or reject what they experience or to pursue self-interest, but to become progressively more involved in musical and educational decision making while exercising critical judgment and self-restraint.

Teachers will need to model appropriate attitudes, habits, and behaviors. But any rights, responsibilities, and obligations of individuals and groups should be made explicit, as should any democratic principles (e.g., justice, equality, reciprocity) and virtues (e.g., friendship, neighborliness, honesty). Any conversations claiming to be educational ought to be framed in those terms. In addition, those rights, responsibilities, and principles should be made focal points of discussion, critical analysis, and self-examination in particular contexts, such as when encountering new and seemingly strange musical practices and behaviors, discussing politically charged issues having to do with musical rhetoric, censorship, identity politics, media manipulation, or government arts and education policies, or simply choosing and considering the relative merits of selected repertoire for study and performance. Whatever the topic of conversation, students must be constantly reminded of the necessity of becoming intellectually involved while remaining open to new possibilities and ideas—of not shutting conversation down or rejecting things out of hand—and of seeking opportunities for personal and collective growth.

Students in performance classes should also be given frequent opportunities to formulate, clarify, express, and justify their own informed musical understandings and opinions with others through musical sounds, physical gestures (e.g., conducting or dance), and the spoken word. Viewed this way, verbal criticism and music performance are forms of moral and ethical deliberation—of practical intelligence—involving knowledge and consideration of self and others, and potentially leading to some kind of continually evolving and shared vision or collective understanding. Both ought to involve a reciprocal exchange and interplay wherein "persuasion, rather than force or dogma, is in principle (if not always in fact) the rule" and in which there is a sense of obligation and commitment to others.[8]

And given Rorty's call "to extend the reference of 'us' as far as we can," music educators and their students have an obligation to become not just more inclusive but also more proactive, reaching out to all manner of people, including amateur musicians, the poor, senior citizens, and even experts in other fields and disciplines such as religion, education, philosophy, art, science, medicine, and history.[9] All of these people can potentially benefit from music teachers' and students' knowledge and expertise while informing music and music education practice in previously unforeseen ways. The role of the music teacher is thus not to simply give children and the masses what they want or to replicate existing standards or conditions. Rather, it is to foster and guide personal and collective musical growth through shared and cooperative social experience. This means challenging individuals to rethink their own limited, habitual, or assumed musical understandings while in pursuit of a more just, humane, and inclusive society. Music teachers and teacher educators are as much democratic leaders as teachers of children or university students.[10]

This kind of democratic leadership and involvement in a progressively wider sense of musical and intellectual community requires great courage, fortitude, and moral imagination from music teachers.[11] Music teachers are obligated not just to challenge the authority of tradition and the status quo but also to envision, instigate, and guide positive change. People like what they already know and are resistant to change. Nevertheless, music teachers should persist in imaginatively seeking new ways of involving progressively greater numbers of children and adults in musical activities of all kinds. These could include, but should by no means be restricted to, frequent performance opportunities.

One way that music teachers can make their performance programs more inclusive is by continuing to go beyond traditional concert and jazz bands, orchestras, and choirs to offer alternative groups and ensembles that might be more attractive to the general population (e.g., percussion, folk, and world music ensembles, rock and popular music groups of various kinds, glee clubs, and community sing-alongs). Some progress has already been made in this direction, although much more remains to be done in terms of diversifying the curriculum while teaching children how to perform intelligently and responsibly. Currently existing groups and ensembles can also be organized to perform as a public service in local hospitals, public parks, senior citizen homes, or even prisons.

Yet another way of encouraging greater public involvement in music in the school, university, or community is by offering music appreciation classes in which the emphases are on musical inclusivity and criticism, and not as is all too often the case on passive reception and regurgitation of knowledge about the classics or any other kind of music. Students can also be encouraged to research and critically examine the social and musical agendas and techniques of politically active musicians such as Ludwig van Beethoven, Richard Wagner, Pablo Casals, Paul Robeson, Woody Guthrie, John Cage, Harry Partch, Aretha Franklin, Joan Baez, Bob Dylan, R. Murray Schafer, Abbey Lincoln, Frank Zappa (who once spoke to the Senate Commerce Committee against censorship and in defense of rock musicians' rights), Paul Simon, Joni Mitchell, Pink Floyd, Glenn Gould, Wynton Marsalis, Sting, Bono, Daniel Barenboim, Susan McClary, and Marilyn Manson. These are just a few of the legions of socially engaged musicians the study of which can inform and inspire or, if nothing else, serve as cautionary morality tales for students (since political activism sometimes comes at a high personal price). This kind of research and study should include consideration of the ways that folk, rock, punk, rap, and other kinds of social protest music has been co-opted and fetishized by consumer society and thereby also often rendered impotent or made complicit in social problems.[12] And, of course, all of this goes hand in hand with lessons in civility. Regardless of the kind of musical activity pursued, students should be constantly reminded of the necessity of expanding their musical and social horizons while learning how to live with others whose beliefs, tastes, values, and sensibilities differ from their own.

Music teacher educators can also contribute to the democratic project by reinvesting in community music, encouraging undergraduates to perform volunteer work in local schools and hospitals (two of my own undergraduates once led community singing for a semester in the psychiatric ward of a maximum security prison), or by running for political office. They can also organize independent research groups and think tanks to publicly contest government social and educational policy and curriculum. At present there is a real need for public intellectuals in music education who are not afraid to challenge the prevailing neoconservative rhetoric in the public media that is so damaging to music and arts education. By such means they can help raise public awareness about social and educational problems affecting music and arts education, thereby providing the leadership that the profession so desperately needs, while also modeling the kinds of democratic values they would hope to engender in their own students. Professional associations such as the Music Educators National Conference (MENC), the Canadian Music Educators Association (CMEA), and, more recently, the MayDay Group have sought to improve professional practice in music education. The MENC, however, is too eager to curry favor with government and business and is thus often complicit in the kinds of social and educational problems addressed in this book (see, e.g., the discussion in chapter 4 about the U.S. National Standards for Music Education), while the CMEA is somewhat anemic and in need of revitalization.[13] While extremely concerned about sociological issues, the MayDay Group has no mandate to speak to the public. Its members and other elite critics are content to argue among themselves at conferences and in academic journals and appear to be uninterested in the public and its problems. This and the lack of genuine dialogue among music educators are probably signs of the profession's own collective immaturity and insecurity.

Developmental Considerations

Although public school and university students are seldom their teachers' equals in intellectual conversations, one should expect to observe qualitative changes in their thought and behavior reflecting growing independence, maturity, and responsibility. Implied is a developmental trajectory in the quality of students' thinking and maturity while the teacher becomes, in Dewey's words, "a student of the pupil's mind,"[14] tailoring curricular activities to suit students' needs while closely observing their progress.

There are two research-based models of intellectual and ethical development that, taken together, can help us understand how individuals progress in the quality and maturity of their thinking with respect to evaluative and ethical judgment. Although these models are far from conclusive and only describe undergraduate and adult thinking, they can easily be applied to children. The habits of thought that freshmen bring to the university are obviously acquired or instilled in them during childhood. The insights obtained from these models may assist music teachers and teacher educators in curriculum development and assessment while also, when made explicit in the classroom, promoting personal awareness in students. If nothing else, knowledge of these models may help students gauge their own intellectual maturity. It can help them place their own personal development in perspective while pointing them in potentially fruitful new directions. In that sense, these hypothetical schemes of intellectual and ethical development are loosely prescriptive.

The models or schemes in question, by Harvard psychologist William Perry and feminist psychologists Mary Field Belenky, Blythe McViker Clinchy, Nancy Rule Goldberger, and Jill Mattuck Tarule, identify various intellectual stances that undergraduates and adults assume with respect to ethical judging as they mature in their thinking. Perry's model applies to male undergraduates, while Belenky et al. are interested in women's experiences and ways of thinking and knowing. The implication is that intellectual development is closely tied to issues of intellectual freedom and personal identity. The feminist psychologists' work is intended to be proactive and remedial in the sense they are interested not just in understanding how women evolve in their thinking over time and with experience but also in raising women's consciousness with respect to social impediments to their intellectual development. Their primary interest is in women's "struggle to claim the power of their own minds."[15] In my opinion, however, much of their developmental scheme and many of their insights apply equally to males.

Essentially, and conflating the two schemes for present purposes, as individuals mature they progress through various qualitative shifts in the ways they perceive the world and make value judgments. The first and most debilitating stance or way of knowing is labeled "Silence" by Belenky et al. and is characterized by a lack of confidence and self-worth coupled with complete reliance on external authorities. Raised in "profound isolation under the most demeaning circumstance," these children and adults fear authority while seeing themselves as "deaf and dumb," as having no knowledge, identity, or voices of their own.[16] One can all too easily imagine a domineering and abusive parent or teacher terrorizing a child into abject submission.

The second phase of intellectual and ethical development is characterized by the recognition by individuals that they already possess knowledge and that they have the potential to learn, albeit still only from experts and authority figures. Often, in women, this is provoked by childbirth and the realization of the need for additional knowledge. Belenky et al. label this stance "Received Knowledge" because there is still an overreliance on external authority. Nevertheless, this is a positive step in intellectual development in that it represents a first, albeit still tentative, reaching out to the world for assistance and support leading to personal growth. Similarly, Perry's male undergraduates at this point in their development were absolutist and dualistic in their thinking, judging the world in categorical black-and-white terms and viewing uncertainty as an error. Teachers and other external authorities were expected to "know it all," and students were upset and disillusioned when informed otherwise.[17]

Perhaps in response to this disillusionment, Perry's undergraduates went to the opposite extreme of rejecting all authority. Whereas they previously viewed the world in absolutist and dualistic terms, they now took the stance that everything was "only" subjective. All opinions and beliefs were equally valid. While obviously extremely problematic, and especially so if there is no growth beyond this point, Belenky et al. see this as a turning point in intellectual development because there is now a sense of self, of personal worth and identity, although still vague and ill-defined. However, if everything is subjective, there can be no conversation and thus no communication or sharing of knowledge. While perhaps gaining some measure of personal confidence, these individuals still have no public voice or personal authority.[18] Perry labels this stance "Multiplicity." Belenky et al. call it "Subjective Knowing."

Fortunately, with experience and increased maturity, some individuals eventually form an appreciation of the complexity of human thought and behavior and realize that some arguments, opinions, or beliefs are better supported or more reasonable than others. They realize that "what is 'true,' 'good,' or 'effective' depends on the context in which it is being considered."[19] At this third phase in Perry's developmental scheme, labeled "Relativism," undergraduates are more mature in their thinking because they begin thinking more critically and taking greater responsibility for pursuing their own interests. Of the few undergraduate students who reach this point of development, however, most are in their senior year.

Belenky et al. refer to this stance as "Procedural Knowledge" because the individuals involved are committed to pursuing higher education as means of expanding knowledge and personal horizons while learning *how* to think like authority figures. Theirs is the voice of reason, of impartiality, objectivity, and mastery of language and subject matter. Implied is a certain amount of intellectual distance between the knower and the known. Significantly, most of the women identified by Belenky and her colleagues as being at this penultimate stage in their intellectual development were "privileged, bright, white, and young."[20] Many had benefited from growing up in homes and schools in which dialogue and debate were encouraged. Individuals assuming this intellectual stance have a considerable advantage over those who think that everything is only subjective. Many at this stage in their development, however, still lack a sense of commitment to others and thus also a clearly defined sense of personal identity (as Ernst Cassirer said, people can only find themselves in groups), whereas others appear more interested in forming personal and existential relationships with their objects of study. Belenky et al. refer to these two kinds of knowing as "Separate" and "Connected Knowing." Both are, of course, necessary to the pursuit of the good life. Individuals should be able to form personal relationships with others while retaining a measure of independence. This integration of separate and connected knowing characterizes the next and most mature stance in intellectual and ethical development.[21]

This last phase of intellectual and ethical development in Perry's scheme, labeled "Commitment with Relativism," is seldom attained by undergraduate students or, possibly, by many adults. At this point in intellectual development there is an integration of personal and public knowledge, as individuals commit to some belief system, group, lifestyle, or career as means of defining the self or making sense of the world and of their place in it. Recognizing that the world is a confusing and often chaotic place, they begin organizing and prioritizing their beliefs and values as means of simplifying and clarifying experience. However, while placing a premium on consistency of thought and behavior, they remain open to new challenges and to conversing with others about their respective beliefs and values. While consciously and deliberately committing to some musical worldview, perspective, philosophy, or methodology, they remain open to learning about and understanding what others have to say (although this should not be interpreted to mean that they must always accept or embrace other people's values). Belenky et al. label this stance "Constructed Knowledge" because the individuals in question have come to the realization that knowledge is socially constructed and that they can contribute to public deliberation and thus also to the shaping of the world. They have voices of their own and feel empowered to contribute to public life and culture while remaining open to conversation and criticism. In short, they have developed both personal integrity and a social conscience.

The development of intellectual maturity and identity based on personal integrity and moral character should be a primary goal of all education, including music education, in democratic society. Parents and teachers can work to secure the future by preparing students to participate as mature citizens in musical and other kinds of public deliberations. This is not to claim that education of this or any other kind can guarantee the safety and security of society. Rather, it is to prepare children and undergraduates to make the best possible choices in an uncertain world.

Music teachers and teacher educators wishing to stimulate students' intellectual and ethical development should probably first attempt to raise their consciousness with respect to existing or potential obstructions to freedom of musical and educational thought and association. This could include discussion and illustration of many of the kinds of problems addressed in this book, including but not limited to consideration of the dangers of musical and educational absolutism versus subjectivism, musical commodification, social and cultural isolation, xenophobia, orthodoxy, and dogmatism, and the attendant problems of musical ideology, rhetoric, propaganda, and censorship.

Maturational factors should also be taken into account. These are among the kinds of problems that should be addressed in school and university curricula since, taken collectively, they constitute a moral and ethical framework for discussion about musical freedom, responsibility, and commitment. Yet, in my own experience, these kinds of issues are seldom addressed in school or university music programs or in state curricular documents. Critical thinking is often emphasized in music curricular documents, which is supposed to develop independence of mind, but this is almost always equated with the development and application of abstract thinking skills and abilities divorced from social, moral, ethical, or political considerations. Few music teachers realize that this separation of mind and matter is a perversion of what Dewey, one of the fathers of the contemporary critical thinking movement, intended.[22]

Teachers and students like to think that they are free. But the fact is that most of life just happens to us.[23] In the end we are presented with few opportunities for making real choices, for making a positive difference to the course of our own lives and of those around us, which is a good reason for not squandering those opportunities through unthinking and habitual commitment to ideology, sheer mental laziness, passivity, ignorance, or lack of curiosity. Typically, though, undergraduates lack a sense of history and awareness of the myriad personal, social, and political problems affecting them and society. Nor does it usually occur to them that there are problems of gender, ethnicity, and class in music education, that some of them (including males) have been effectively silenced by overly domineering parents or teachers, that they may be either dualistic or overly subjective in their thinking, or that they may lack a sense of professional commitment or direction. It is only when prompted to look around them that they realize, for example, that there are serious imbalances with respect to the numbers of males and females entering the profession, that institutional policies and evaluation procedures are representative of white, middle-class norms and values, or that they and experienced music teachers tend to be very conservative. Few question the social relevance of the music studied or realize that nonconformity within the university and in the wider society is usually actively discouraged. If left to their own resources, probably few students would notice or grapple with these kinds of issues, let alone engage in self-examination.

The Virtue of Uncertainty

School and university students and even experienced teachers obviously require assistance if they are to notice and attend to these and other pressing problems while realizing that they are not as free as they previously believed; that the worlds of music, education, and politics are not organized in categorical black-and-white terms; or that "anything goes" in professional practice. Beginning in high school, if not before, students need to be explicitly informed that knowledge and values are socially constructed. This means abandoning as delusional and inhumane the therapeutic search for certainty, for absolute truths and values, while accepting the social contingency and thus also the variability, uncertainty, and fragility of the human condition. Dewey linked the pursuit of absolutist and simplistic answers in human affairs with the need for control and security. While understandable, arising out of fear of the unknown, the quest for certainty is delusional for the reason that the world and our existence are inherently uncertain. We can never establish complete control over events, which is why the fruits of any inquiry ought to be considered at best only provisional and subject to debate. "The virtue of uncertainty," as Saul also reminds us, "is not a comfortable idea, but then a citizen-based democracy is built upon participation, which is the very expression of permanent discomfort."[24] That is the price of civic consciousness and responsibility, and the best that we can do, at least in democratic society, is to use our intelligence for "unsparing social appraisal" in pursuit of the best possible solutions to current problems.[25]

Music teachers would do well to remember R. Murray Schafer's admonition, made during the 1970s, to "always teach provisionally," for no one knows for certain how to teach or, I would add, perform.[26] In the end, there can be no final or definitive musical conception of the "good," no performances, philosophies, or methodologies that will guarantee success as measured by absolute and permanent standards. Probably the best that we can do, whether as musicians, music teachers, or students, is to be both realistic and pragmatic, exploring and attempting to come to grips with current problems that really matter and not, as is all too often the case, burying our heads in the sand or diverting ourselves and our students with the trivial and mundane. For many of the same reasons, proposed solutions to common problems such as those identified in this book ought to be viewed as only tentative and local, applicable in our own time and place but not necessarily for everyone elsewhere and for all time. Context is not everything, but it does matter.

Apologia

Some readers are probably disturbed by my contention that nothing in music education philosophy and practice should be considered sacrosanct or immutable—that everything ought to be considered as only tentative and at least potentially subject to criticism—and that we should just try to make the best of things. No doubt someone is also going to accuse me of being overly negative in my own criticisms and assessment of the music education profession. In response, I will only say that this book is an expression of my own faith in humanity's capacity for self-improvement. "Confronting reality," Saul writes, "no matter how negative or depressing the process, is the first step towards coming to terms with it." This, however, ought to be done not out of self-loathing or misanthropy but out of "delight in mankind."[27] That is the humanist credo, although it need not as some fundamentalists believe entail a rejection of God and religious values.[28] That is a common fallacy that I occasionally hear from undergraduates who have been taught to be "slaves of Christ" (which is a contradiction in terms). There are, of course, many Christian humanists: C. S. Lewis immediately springs to mind. Besides, humanism and Christianity share a common heritage and overlap considerably in their values. They share many values and virtues, including recognition of the importance of honesty, compassion, courage, selflessness, responsibility, humility, and forgiveness. These are human values and aspects of our common faith in humanity's capacity for self-improvement. The challenge for all of us in democratic society, including music educators, is to try to live in accordance with those principles, which is no easy task.

This book represents my own honest appraisal of music education philosophy and practice coupled with some recommendations for possible reforms. Many of the criticisms of music education practice in this book have been made before by other reformers. Anyone familiar with *The New Handbook of Research on Music Teaching and Learning* (2002) knows that there is a considerable degree of consensus among music education philosophers and intellectuals with respect to certain professional problems (like the continued prevalence of technical rationality in music teacher education programs and the attendant conservatism and intellectual passivity of undergraduates and many teachers) and the need for reform so that music education better reflects the postmodern condition. As was mentioned in chapter 3, where music education elites tend to disagree is over issues of power and control with respect to the nature, direction, and rates of change (e.g., whether reforms proposed by me and other liberal music educators are sufficiently radical and representative of minority interests). I have gone to great lengths in this book to explain why these kinds of important decisions affecting the future of the profession and musical society ought not to be left to politicians, businesspeople, an intelligentsia, or professional organizations like the MENC and CMEA. Academics and professional elites obviously can and do play a vital role in recommending, prompting, and sometimes guiding reform. Business can also play a limited role, provided it is properly supervised and adheres to strict ethical standards. The future survival and success of music education in the schools, however, ultimately depends on the involvement of the ordinary or "common" music teacher in professional and community activity and decision making. Like Dewey, I place considerable faith in the intelligence and ability of the common person and teacher, given the right conditions and democratic leadership, to help "generate progressively the knowledge and wisdom needed to guide collective action."[29] My purpose with this book has been to motivate conversation while simultaneously informing music teachers and others about important problems so that they, and not just government, heroic leaders, or elite critics, can help shape the future of music education. As Socrates discovered, people don't always appreciate being disturbed in their complacency. That, for me and other critics, is just the price of personal and civic responsibility.

Probably someone is also going to object to the promotion of democratic values and culture in and through music education on the grounds that, while perhaps laudable, it is not practical. One of the major criticisms of Dewey's own short-lived experimental school at the University of Chicago (1896–1904) was that it prepared children "for life in a society that did not exist, one in which the welfare of all was regarded as the concern of each."[30] Ironically, given his own assertions that there should be no separation between school and society, graduates of his school were apparently ill-prepared to deal with the brute realities of the extremely competitive, capitalistic society in which they lived. This is a legitimate criticism, since "Dewey did not really have much of a strategy for making American schools into institutions working on behalf of radical democracy."[31] My own philosophy, however, is more overtly political than Dewey's. It is also timely, since we live in an age in which capitalism is the new global religion. The whole thrust of my argument has been that teachers and children need to intellectually engage with the world as moral agents of change, which means going beyond criticism of everyday values to include the moral and political implications and ramifications of musical and educational thought and action. Students and their teachers are no longer cloistered in schools where they are coddled and insulated from the "conflicts, divisions, and inequities besetting the larger society," as Dewey's were.[32] They are literally in the world and exercising their own moral authority as future citizens. To a significant extent those "conflicts, divisions, and inequities" *are* the curriculum, and teachers are as much political leaders as instructors of this or that subject area.

Other frequently cited criticisms of Dewey's school and educational philosophy were that his reforms proved expensive to initiate, required exceptional teachers, and were inherently risky. They called for greater risk-taking behavior among teachers and students than would be countenanced in a typical public school. All of these factors, coupled with the complexity of the proposed reforms, lack of clear pedagogical method, and increasing specialization in education, virtually ensured that his ideals would have only limited applicability in the real world of public education.[33] For my own case, I am not as inclined to believe, as Dewey was, in the centrality of occupational training in the curriculum. Much of the expense of his experimental school was incurred through the generous provision of various kinds of equipment, laboratories, and shops for occupational training. But this is really beside the point, since today's neoconservative governments favor vocational training over education for democratic citizenship. Those governments complain about the costs of public education, but they always seem to find the money to provide vocational training or computer equipment for public schools. The issue is thus not so much about financial resources as it is about social and educational values and priorities.

As for the need for exceptional teachers, we live in a different world than Dewey, one in which considerably more is expected of public schoolteachers in terms of subject area knowledge and education in general. Teachers in Dewey's own day possessed only minimal educational qualifications, at least by current standards. Given the years of education required of today's teachers, their own frustration with neoconservative governments, and the popular assumption that schools and universities should serve all of society and not just an elite, it seems only reasonable to expect teachers to become more intellectually engaged in their profession and with the wider world. In so doing they will be modeling the kinds of behaviors, virtues, and democratic character that we would wish to engender in children. Rather than seeking exceptional music teachers, I am actually calling for an *improvement* in professional standards.

An important aim of music education reform should be to attract and develop idealistic and visionary music teachers who see themselves as public intellectuals and democratic leaders of children and not as heroic leaders, dictators, or just employees of the state. Hopefully, those individuals would value substance over form—or personal creativity, integrity, and responsibility over technique and methodology—while pursuing a comprehensive social interest. Although loathe to spell out in explicit detail what this might imply for music teacher education, I think it worth recommending that undergraduates and teachers be encouraged to think of themselves as public servants, even social workers, charged with creatively meeting the needs of all of society and not just the rich and elite among us. For example, during student-teaching practica, undergraduates should be encouraged to work with disadvantaged children as much as or more than with socially advantaged ones. Experienced teachers involved in school and community music programs should also try to reach out to those who are most in need of organized musical and social experience but who can usually least afford it. We hear much nowadays about the social, physical, and psychological benefits of music in lifelong learning, but the reality is that school and adult community musical activities tend to favor the socially advantaged.[34]

Given my above comment about democratically minded music teachers valuing inspiration and substance over form, and my earlier criticisms in chapter 4 of scientistic and highly regimented approaches to music education, readers can safely assume that I am not worried about the prospect of being criticized for lacking a clear pedagogical method. I welcome genuine conversation about the desirability and practicality of pursuing a democratic end for music education. However, I tend to be skeptical of pedagogical and other formal methods, particularly when divorced from ends. Just as thinking is a highly individualistic process whose shape and direction are determined by the personalities of the people involved and the nature and scope of the problem, so too should teaching be conceived as a fluid process that varies according to the nature of the particular kind of music being examined or performed and the interests and personalities of the students and teachers involved. The only constant should be the aforementioned democratic interest and framework. This includes explicit acknowledgment and application of democratic principles as ends in view (they are both means and ends) and consideration of the kinds of social, political, and ethical issues raised in this book.

For example, when teaching popular music performance, rather than drilling students in scales and other kinds of formal technique usually associated with the classical tradition, teachers might incorporate into the classroom or rehearsal room informal learning practices that popular musicians actually use in the real world.[35] This could include rote learning and imitation of recorded performances by musicians of the students' own choosing. Alternatively, it could take the form of jam sessions in which participants consult among themselves and with their teachers or guest artists to establish parameters for group improvisations or compositions. In the Rock On Project, for example, students consulted their instructor and professional rock musicians for guidance and advice about certain civilities and technicalities, but they ultimately made their own compositional and performance decisions. Apprentice models involving community musicians may also be useful and practical with so-called world music, as might simple sing-alongs when introducing children to certain kinds of folk music.[36]

All of these and other practices, however, fail to meet a democratic standard if taught for the wrong reasons (e.g., to further indoctrinate students to popular or other music or to simply entertain or control rather than educate) or if merely imposed without explicit consideration of political and ethical issues affecting the music's reception and production. While by no means suggesting that music teachers politicize everything, they should make frequent attempts to go beyond the music to consider issues of class, power, and control. For example, when using rote learning and apprentice models, teachers should explain to students how and why these pedagogical practices may impinge on their musical freedoms (e.g., to interpret) and to what ends. Similarly, when performing folk or indigenous music in the school or university, students should learn that certain groups might not always appreciate having their music abstracted from its original context and that, further, this kind of activity almost inevitably results in cultural distortion and misrepresentation.

Probably many arrangements and performances of folk songs and so-called world music in today's schools and universities are a far cry from what their creators intended in terms of vocal tone quality, pitches, rhythms, and even sometimes texts. The beloved Newfoundland folk song "She's Like the Swallow," for example, was deliberately altered and distorted over the years by well-meaning but meddling folk song collectors, editors, and publishers in the belief that it needed to be "neatened" and rendered more palatable to middle-class or educated tastes. Words, rhythms, and even entire verses were apparently changed by successive editors and publishers without their ever having acknowledged or admitted those changes in the printed scores.[37] Doubtless similar kinds of changes are made all the time by educational music arrangers as they attempt to adapt popular, folk, aboriginal, and nonwestern music to the traditional school or university band and choir. As a result of these cultural appropriations, music teachers and students are seldom as authentic in their performances as they wish to believe.

This, however, is not to suggest that music teachers and students should altogether abandon performing any particular composition or genre because of problems of authenticity. Nor does it mean that they should necessarily like the music in question or conform to existing practices. Rather, and in addition to doing the usual structural and textual analyses, they should carefully research the ownership and provenance of selected repertoire and performance practices in order to determine whether their creators are being adequately represented and, in certain cases, compensated. This may involve conversations with musical and community groups about the history and ethics of practice or, in the case of ancient or nonwestern music, consulting musicologists or ethnomusicologists for advice about how best to proceed. And rather than just throwing their hands up in frustration or despair when confronted with ethical dilemmas, as teachers may be tempted to do when critics question their assumptions (such as the assumption that white middle-class teachers can appropriately present and represent music from nonwestern cultures), they should engage in conversation with them so as to understand the intellectual bases of their critiques. Only by engaging in conversation with their critics can music teachers and students understand the issues and respond appropriately.[38] If nothing else, this kind of research and approach to music teaching and learning should enable teachers and students to place their own personal problems and creative decisions into a broader perspective by taking into account the intentions and experiences of other people, including previous generations of composers, performers, audiences, and critics. This, I think, has the potential to enrich music study and performance in school or university, for it suggests that regardless of whether performing, composing, listening to, criticizing, or researching music we should all take a longer and wider view, placing things into historical, cultural, *and* political perspectives while considering the ethics of practice.

This more politicized and inclusive approach to music teaching and learning may indeed be risky for both students and teachers, for it implies a shift in power and control within the classroom or rehearsal room. Any increase in student freedom, power, and control is usually at the expense of the teacher, as the latter is no longer the source of all knowledge and authority. This is bound to make some teachers and parents nervous, but it just underscores the importance of communication. When practicing democracy in school, students are by no means masters of their own destinies or in complete control, as that would quickly lead to chaos and tyranny. A little knowledge can be a dangerous thing, and students are seldom ready to deal with musical and moral complexity and uncertainty. They require guidance if they are to learn how to think and behave as mature and socially responsible adults and citizen musicians. Besides, in a truly democratic scheme, any increase in student freedom, power, and control in the music classroom or rehearsal room is always balanced by a corresponding increase in personal and corporate responsibility. Students are free not just to pursue their own interests but to contribute to the life and vitality of the school and community. And while their musical interests, tastes, and informed opinions matter in classroom planning and conversation, students are always accountable to others, including their peers, teachers, and parents. Furthermore, students are ultimately responsible for the development of their own moral character. They are responsible for their own choices and for their growth and evolving sense of personal identity.

Not everyone need have the same risk tolerance level when addressing contentious issues, repertoire, or musical interpretations, or when contemplating needed changes to school and society. They should, however, understand that there is always a cost to political inaction. Passive submission, evasion of politics, and personal or professional inaction with respect to society and its problems all have their own costs. The music education profession's own political inaction and lack of democratic purpose has likely contributed to the stultification of school music and a loss of public interest and support. The cost of personal and educational inaction to students may well be a loss of intelligent control over their own lives.

"Risk" is another one of those words that has a negative connotation for many, but it is important to remember that there can be little or no growth or productive change without risk (and sometimes outright failure). Risk makes life interesting. Rather than something always to be feared and avoided, risk can also be fondly anticipated, prepared for, controlled, and managed (although, again, we can never exert complete control over events). That is all that I have attempted to do in this book: to theorize about related professional and social problems while seeking some middle way between laissez-faire and elitist or autocratic concepts of music education. And while my lack of pedagogical method may frustrate or discourage some, like Dewey, I am not interested in providing teachers with "precise directions about how to run a school."[39] This is simply not that kind of book. Nor do I expect this book to galvanize and revolutionize practice. It remains for music teachers to decide for themselves whether or to what extent this or other democratic visions should be tested through application to their own classes and professional experience.[40] Ultimately, however, they may well have no choice but to take a more democratic approach if music education is to be ensured a place and role in tomorrow's schools. The teaching of democratic citizenship in schools is already considered mandatory by some governments (although neoconservative governments usually equate this with teaching children to passively submit). The coupling of music content with lessons in democratic citizenship in which children are taught to question authority while seeking the truth is one potentially potent means of revitalizing music education while making it more relevant to government and the public.

One's-Self I Sing

One's-self I sing, a simple separate person,
Yet utter the word Democratic, the word En-Masse.
Of physiology from top to toe I sing,
Not physiognomy alone nor brain alone is worthy for the
Muse, I say the Form complete is worthier far,
The Female equally with the Male I sing.
Of Life immense in passion, pulse, and power,
Cheerful, for freest action form'd under the laws divine,
The Modern Man I sing.

—Walt Whitman

NOTES

Preface

1. John Dewey, *Reconstruction in Philosophy*, 3rd ed. (New York: Mentor Books, 1950), 147.
2. Lauri Väkevä, "Interviewing Richard Shusterman," *Finnish Journal of Music Education* 5, nos. 1/2 (2000): 187–95. According to Shusterman, "Pragmatism, as James and Dewey practiced it, seemed to provide the model of how to combine the clear arguments and common sense of analytic philosophy together with the large and socially important issues of continental philosophy" (188). See also Richard Shusterman, *Pragmatist Aesthetics: Living Beauty, Rethinking Art*, 2nd ed. (Lanham, Md.: Rowman and Littlefield, 2000).
3. Wittgenstein and Heidegger are the other two twentieth-century philosophers named by Rorty as being most important. For a discussion of Rorty's views about the contributions of these thinkers to philosophy, see Richard J. Bernstein in *Beyond Objectivism and Relativism: Science, Hermeneutics, and Praxis* (Philadelphia: University of Pennsylvania Press, 1988), 6.
4. Paul G. Woodford, "Development of a Theory of Transfer in Musical Thinking and Learning Based on John Dewey's Conception of Reflective Thinking" (Ph.D. diss., Northwestern University, 1994), 172. For other definitions of critical thinking in music, see Carol P. Richardson and Nancy Whitaker, "Critical Thinking and Music Education," in *Handbook of Research on Music Teaching and Learning*, ed. Richard Colwell (New York: Schirmer, 1992), and Laurel N. Tanner, "The Path Not Taken: Dewey's Model of Inquiry," *Curriculum Inquiry* 18, no. 4 (1988): 471–79.
5. Donald Schön writes that when first introduced to Dewey's writings he considered them to be muddy. The realization that Dewey's thinking was generative came later in Schön's career. See Donald A. Schön, "The Theory of Inquiry: Dewey's Legacy to Education," *Curriculum Inquiry* 22 (1992): 119–39.
6. Janice Gross Stein, *The Cult of Efficiency* (Toronto: House of Anansi Press, 2001), 185.
7. Estelle R. Jorgensen, "Justifying Music Instruction in American Schools: An Historical Perspective," *Bulletin of the Council for Research in Music Education* 120 (Spring 1994): 26. The democratic philosophies of Dewey and Maxine Greene are mentioned as being particularly relevant because they explain the role of education and the arts in fostering democracy and individual and corporate freedom.
8. Stein, *The Cult of Efficiency*, 122, 185.
9. Max Kaplan, *Foundations and Frontiers of Music Education* (New York: Holt, Rinehart and Winston, 1966), 17.
10. Gregory S. Jay, ed., *American Literature and the Culture Wars* (Ithaca, N.Y.: Cornell University Press, 1997), 49.
11. John Dewey, *The Quest for Certainty: A Study of the Relation of Knowledge and Action* (New York: Minton, Balch, 1929), reprinted in Dewey, *Intelligence in the Modern World: John Dewey's Philosophy*, ed. Joseph Ratner (New York: Modern Library, 1939), 793.

12. Dewey writes in *A Common Faith* (New Haven, Conn.: Yale University Press, 1934): "Human beings have impulses toward affection, compassion and justice, equality and freedom. It remains to weld all these things together" (81). The challenge for democracy as the expression and attempted realization of this common faith is to find ways to "harmonize the development of each individual with the maintenance of a social state in which the activities of the one will contribute to the good of all the others." John Dewey, *Ethics* (1932), in *John Dewey: The Later Works, 1925–1953* (Carbondale: Southern Illinois University Press, 1981–91), 7:350. Quoted in Robert B. Westbrook, *John Dewey and American Democracy* (Ithaca, N.Y.: Cornell University Press, 1991), 428.

13. Samuel Lipman, *Arguing for Music, Arguing for Culture* (Boston: Godine, 1990), 429. Lipman thinks that democracy refers only to a system of government and should have nothing to do with culture.

14. Jay, *American Literature and the Culture Wars*, 28.

15. Martha C. Nussbaum, *Poetic Justice: The Literary Imagination and Public Life* (Boston: Beacon Press, 1995), 6.

16. Ibid., xiv.

17. Jay, *American Literature and the Culture Wars*, 56.

18. Alfred North Whitehead, *The Aims of Education and Other Essays* (New York: Macmillan, 1929; reprint, New York: Free Press, 1967), 2.

19. Benjamin R. Barber, *Jihad vs. McWorld: How Globalism and Tribalism Are Reshaping the World* (New York: Ballantine Books, 1996), 6–7.

20. Jean Bethke Elshtain, *Democracy on Trial* (Concord, Ont.: House of Anansi Press, 1993), 139–40.

21. Lawrence E. Cahoone, *The Dilemma of Modernity: Philosophy, Culture, and Anti-Culture* (Albany: State University of New York Press, 1988), 231.

22. Robert C. Holub, *Crossing Borders: Reception Theory, Poststructuralism, Deconstruction* (Madison: University of Wisconsin Press, 1992), 193–94.

1. Intelligence in the World

1. John Dewey, *The School and Society* (1900; reprint, Chicago: University of Chicago Press, 1990), 7.

2. John Dewey, "Democracy and Educational Administration" (1937), in Dewey, *Intelligence in the Modern World*, 404. Intelligence is defined by Dewey as the purposeful use of foresight to control and guide present activity. See John Dewey, "What Is Freedom?" in *John Dewey on Education: Selected Writings*, ed. Reginald D. Archambault (New York: Random House, 1964), 88. Further, as Dewey wrote in *Experience and Education* (London: Collier Books, 1969), freedom implies self-control. Freedom from external control means nothing unless one is also free from the dictates of immediate and personal whim and caprice. "A person whose conduct is controlled in this way has at most only the illusion of freedom. Actually he is directed by forces over which he has no command" (64–65).

3. John Dewey, "Ethics of Democracy" (1888), in *John Dewey: The Early Works, 1882–1898* (Carbondale: Southern Illinois University Press, 1967–72), 1:228–30. Cited in Westbrook, *John Dewey and American Democracy*, 41.

4. John Dewey and James H. Tufts, *Ethics*, rev. ed. (New York: Henry Holt, 1932), reprinted in Dewey, *Intelligence in the Modern World*, 761.

5. Dewey, *Reconstruction in Philosophy*, 155.

6. Dewey, "Democracy and Educational Administration," 400.

7. Ibid., 402. See also Dewey's *Logic: The Theory of Inquiry* (London: George Allen and Unwin, 1938). Dewey explains how this collective intellectual action can change culture. Culture, defined as shared beliefs, meanings, forms of knowledge, and habits of thought that are built up through discourse using symbols and symbol systems, performs a regulative and normative function over human thinking. It is "common sense." Reflective thinking has the potential to organize and enrich common sense by turning thought back upon itself, by making tacit beliefs and forms of knowledge explicit so that they may be critically examined in light of evidence. This process can empower the individual, and potentially society as a whole, to revise common sense as needed (76).

8. Dewey, "Democracy and Educational Administration," 403.

9. Dewey and Tufts, *Ethics*, 766.

10. Dewey, *The School and Society*, 29.

11. Westbrook, *John Dewey and American Democracy*, 433.

12. Ibid., 437.

13. Peter S. Hlebowitsh, "Critical Theory versus Curriculum Theory: Reconsidering the Dialogue on Dewey," *Educational Theory* 42 (Winter 1992): 80.

14. James T. Kloppenberg, "Cosmopolitan Pragmatism: Deliberative Democracy and Higher Education," in *Education and Democracy: Re-imagining Liberal Learning in America*, ed. Robert Orrill (New York: College Entrance Examination Board, 1997), 89–90.

15. Hans Georg Gadamer, *Philosophical Hermeneutics*, trans. and ed. D. Linge (Berkeley: University of California Press, 1976), 95.

16. Dewey quoted in Kloppenberg, "Cosmopolitan Pragmatism," 90.

17. Ibid., 89–90.

18. Ibid., 91.

19. Ibid., 92.

20. Dewey, "Need for a Recovery of Philosophy" (1917), in *John Dewey: The Middle Works, 1899–1924* (Carbondale: Southern Illinois University Press, 1976–83), 10:38, 46. Cited in Westbrook, *John Dewey and American Democracy*, 138–40.

21. Dewey, *Reconstruction in Philosophy*, 108.

22. Dewey, *How We Think* (1910), in *John Dewey: The Middle Works*, 6:185. Quoted in Westbrook, *John Dewey and American Democracy*, 141–42.

23. Dewey, *Ethics*, 359. Quoted in Westbrook, *John Dewey and American Democracy*, 161.

24. Hlebowitsh, "Critical Theory," 75.

25. Westbrook, *John Dewey and American Democracy*, 107, 169.

26. Dewey's classic text, *How We Think*, first published in 1910 and revised in 1933, was written for elementary school teachers. See John Dewey, *How We Think* in *John Dewey: The Later Works, 1925–1953*, vol. 8, ed. Jo Ann Boydston (Carbondale: Southern Illinois University Press, 1989). This text was the inspiration and foundation for my own doctoral dissertation at Northwestern University.

27. John Dewey, "Educators and the Class Struggle," from *The Social Frontier*, May 1936, reprinted in Dewey, *Intelligence in the Modern World*, 699.

28. Ibid., 702.

29. Westbrook, *John Dewey and American Democracy*, 107.

108   NOTES TO PAGES 6–10

30. Dewey, *The School and Society*, in Dewey, *Intelligence in the Modern World*, 717.
31. Ibid., 718–19.
32. John Dewey, "Democracy in Education," in *John Dewey: The Middle Works*, 3:232–33. Quoted in Westbrook, *John Dewey and American Education*, 107. Dewey's Laboratory School lasted until 1904, when it was closed because of bureaucratic infighting leading to his resignation from the University of Chicago and his employment the following year at Columbia University (110–13).
33. Dewey, *The School and Society*, 29.
34. John Dewey, *Democracy and Education: An Introduction to the Philosophy of Education* (New York: Macmillan, 1921), 373–74.
35. Schön, "Dewey's Legacy to Education," 121.
36. Dewey, *The School and Society*, 78.
37. Ibid., 79.
38. Ibid., 92.
39. Marie McCarthy, "The Foundations of Sociology in American Music Education (1900–1935)," in *On the Sociology of Music Education*, ed. Roger Rideout (Norman: University of Oklahoma School of Music, 1997), 73–74. Charles Leonhard and Robert House, in *Foundations and Principles of Music Education*, 2nd ed. (New York: McGraw-Hill, 1972), were of the similar opinion that many of the profession's problems in the United States during the third quarter of the twentieth century were attributable to a loss of democratic purpose among music teachers (75).
40. McCarthy, "American Music Education," 74.
41. John Dewey, *Art as Experience* (1934; reprint, New York: Perigee Books, 1980), 11.
42. Ibid., 12.
43. McCarthy, "American Music Education," 74.
44. Dewey, *Art as Experience*, 11. Dewey's project with respect to the arts was to recover "the continuity of esthetic experience with normal processes of living" (10).
45. Kloppenberg, "Cosmopolitan Pragmatism," 91.
46. For discussion of the difference between values and standards, and the role of intelligent judgment in inquiry, see Dewey, *Art as Experience*, 298–315. The danger of relying upon authoritative standards and precedents to judge new perspectives or endeavors is one of conservatism. New ideas arise out of some dissatisfaction with older ones, yet are judged in those terms. Unless one possesses an attitude of open-mindedness to new ideas, those ideas are likely to be misjudged (306).
47. For a discussion of Rorty's opinions with respect to Dewey, see Bernstein, *Beyond Objectivism and Relativism*, and Kloppenberg, "Cosmopolitan Pragmatism." Other prominent contemporary philosophers influenced by Dewey's pragmatism include Jürgen Habermas and Richard Shusterman.
48. John Dewey, *Essays in Experimental Logic* (Chicago: University of Chicago Press, 1917), reprinted in Dewey, *Intelligence in the Modern World*, 274.
49. Dewey, *The Public and Its Problems* (New York: Henry Holt, 1927), reprinted in *Intelligence in the Modern World*, 399. See also *Art as Experience*, 10.
50. Dewey referred to imagination as the "chief instrument of the good." The occurrence and judgment of new musical ideas are dependent upon the individual's ability to empathize with others or "to put himself imaginatively in their place." Dewey, *Art as Experience*, 348.
51. Dewey, *Democracy and Education*, 279.
52. McCarthy, "American Music Education," 75.

53. Ibid., 76.
54. Edward Bailey Birge, *History of Public School Music in the United States* (1928; reprint, Washington, D.C.: Music Educators National Conference, 1966), 226.
55. McCarthy, "American Music Education," 79.
56. Kaplan, *Foundations and Frontiers of Music Education,* 8.
57. James Mursell, *Music Education: Principles and Programs* (Morristown, N.J.: Silver Burdett, 1956), 61.
58. Ibid., 63.
59. Ibid., 62.
60. Ibid., 121.
61. Ibid., 65.
62. Ibid., 120, 130.
63. Ibid., 132, 310–11.
64. McCarthy, "American Music Education," 80. Dewey said much the same thing in *Democracy and Education.* Social reorganization depends upon educational reconstruction (373).
65. Roger Rideout and Allan Feldman, in their chapter "Research in Music Student Teaching" in *The New Handbook of Research on Music Teaching and Learning,* ed. Richard Colwell and Carol P. Richardson (New York: Oxford University Press, 2002), observe that there has only been one attempt to develop a model of student teaching supervision along democratic lines in which all participants "shared an equal voice [in] assessment and evaluation" (883). See L. Drafall, "The Use of Developmental Clinical Supervision with Student Teachers in Secondary Choral Music: Two Case Studies" (Ph.D. diss., University of Illinois at Urbana-Champaign, 1991).
66. Allen P. Britton, "Music Education: An American Specialty," in *Perspectives in Music: Source Book III,* ed. Bonnie C. Kowall (Washington, D.C.: Music Educators National Conference, 1966), 15–28.
67. Ibid., 18.
68. Julie Kailin, "How White Teachers Perceive the Problem of Racism in Their Schools: A Case Study in 'Liberal' Lakeview," *Teachers College Record* 100, no. 4 (Summer 1999): 728.
69. For example, as Jay observes in *American Literature and the Culture Wars,* critical theorists sound deterministic with their explanations of the role of the structure of language in understanding art, history, and politics, and their consequent emphasis on the group, as against Enlightenment individualism. In giving preference to the group, they may do harm to the individual (42).
70. Some radicals believe that the Enlightenment is to be "circumvented or knocked aside in the pursuit of the reformation of society in accordance with collective (class-conscious or racial-nationalist) ideas." Cahoone, *The Dilemma of Modernity,* 268.
71. Jay, *American Literature and the Culture Wars,* 43.

2. Intelligence in the Musical World

1. Leon Botstein, "The Training of Musicians," *Musical Quarterly* 85, no. 3 (Fall 2000): 328. Mursell expressed this idea thusly in *Principles of Democratic Education* (New York: Norton, 1955): "The governing purpose of education in a democratic society is to support, perpetuate, enlarge, and strengthen the democratic way

of life . . . which means that it [democracy] must determine the whole practical operation of education" (3). See also Bruce A. Kimball, "Naming Pragmatic Liberal Education," in *Education and Democracy*, 45–67. Kimball views liberalism as a philosophy of education permeating all of the professional disciplines (64). See also John Ralston Saul, *The Unconscious Civilization* (Concord, Ont.: House of Anansi Press, 1995).

2. David J. Elliott, *Music Matters: A New Philosophy of Music Education* (New York: Oxford University Press, 1995), 307.

3. Ibid., 308.

4. Bennett, as described by David Frum in *Dead Right* (New York: Basic Books, 1994), is in fact a conservative (12; 42–43). See also William Bennett, *Reclaiming a Legacy* (Washington, D.C.: National Endowment for the Humanities, 1984); Allan Bloom, *The Closing of the American Mind: How Higher Education Has Failed Democracy and Impoverished the Souls of Today's Students* (New York: Simon and Schuster, 1987); and E. D. Hirsch Jr., *Cultural Literacy: What Every American Needs to Know* (Boston: Houghton Mifflin, 1987). Amy Gutmann, in her introduction to Charles Taylor's *Multiculturalism and "The Politics of Recognition"* (Princeton, N.J.: Princeton University Press, 1992), labels this an essentialist view of liberal education. "Essentialists honor and invoke the great books as the critical standard for judging 'lesser' works and societies" (16). For a critique of the educational agendas of E. D. Hirsch and Allan Bloom, see Howard Gardner, *The Unschooled Mind: How Children Think and How Schools Should Teach* (New York: Basic Books, 1991), 188–91.

5. Peter Kivy, "Music and the Liberal Education," *Journal of Aesthetic Education* 25, no. 3 (Fall 1991): 83.

6. Gutmann, in the introduction to Taylor's *Multiculturalism*, 16.

7. Elliott and Kivy agree on at least two major points: first, that music can lead to humanistic or self-knowledge, and second, that one must be able to perform music in order to understand it. As Kivy states, "At the risk of some exaggeration, to listen to music without having performed it at some level, as a singer or player, is like seeing *Romeo and Juliet* without ever having been in love." Kivy, "Music and the Liberal Education," 90.

8. Elshtain, *Democracy on Trial*, 89. See also Saul, *The Unconscious Civilization*, 163, 168; Stein, *The Cult of Efficiency*, 58, 225.

9. *The Oxford Companion to Philosophy*, 1995 ed., s.v. "liberalism." For a more extended discussion of liberalism compared with other contemporary political philosophies, see Will Kymlicka, *Contemporary Political Philosophy: An Introduction* (Oxford: Oxford University Press, 1990).

10. Gutmann, in the introduction to Taylor's *Multiculturalism*, 17. Liberalism, with its idea of the autonomous individual, has been associated with, and blamed for, the rise of capitalism and free market economics. Saul, however, says that this idea of the "unattached" and selfish individual is both a myth and distortion of liberal philosophy. Saul, *The Unconscious Civilization*, 2. Today, as explained in *The Oxford Companion to Philosophy*, s.v. "liberalism," "most liberals . . . accept that justice requires regulating the market to ensure equality of opportunity, or even equality of resources. Those who continue to defend free markets . . . are now called classical liberals or libertarians as opposed to welfare liberals or liberal egalitarians." As used in North America, the term *liberal* is usually associated with

egalitarianism. Classical liberals are called "conservatives" (or in Europe "neoliberals"). For further explanation of the distinction between these two conceptions of liberalism, see Thomas Nagel, "Rawls and Liberalism," in *The Cambridge Companion to Rawls*, ed. Samuel Freeman (Cambridge: Cambridge University Press, 2003), 62.

11. Richard Rorty, "Solidarity or Objectivity?" in *From Modernism to Postmodernism: An Anthology*, ed. Lawrence Cahoone (Cambridge, Mass.: Blackwell, 1996), 582.

12. Gutmann, introduction to Taylor's *Multiculturalism*, 14. Louis Menand writes that the rise of postmodernism in the latter part of the twentieth century led to "almost rote skepticism among academics about the value of the sorts of texts typically taught in core courses." In a sense, this too is part of the liberal tradition of education, albeit carried to extremes. "Skepticism about the tradition is, after all, part of the tradition. That is one of the attitudes the 'great books' teach; and to the extent that discussing the classics skeptically induces students to raise questions, later in life, about appeals to the 'classics,' or to the authority of 'tradition,' this is entirely in keeping with the spirit of liberal education." Menand, "Re-imagining Liberal Education," in *Education and Democracy*, 7.

13. Dewey, *Essays in Experimental Logic*, reprinted in *Intelligence in the Modern World*, 273.

14. Ibid.

15. Ibid., 274.

16. Susan McClary, *Feminine Endings: Music, Gender, and Sexuality* (Minneapolis: University of Minnesota Press, 1991), 29.

17. Elshtain, *Democracy on Trial*, 81.

18. Christopher Small, in *Musicking: The Meanings of Performing and Listening* (Hanover, N.H.: Wesleyan University Press, 1998), argues that all music is valid (13). The claim that all music is "equally worthy of consideration" in music education research is made by Adrian C. North, David J. Hargreaves, and Mark Tarrant in their chapter "Social Psychology and Music Education," in *The New Handbook of Research on Music Teaching and Learning*, 618.

19. North et al., "Social Psychology and Music Education," 618.

20. Joseph A. Labuta and Deborah A. Smith make this absolutist mistake in their book, *Music Education: Historical Contexts and Perspectives* (Upper Saddle River, N.J.: Prentice Hall, 1997). While acknowledging some of the difficulties involved when western music teachers utilize nonwestern music in the classroom or rehearsal room, they assume that various cultural groups are "essentially different" (145).

21. Elshtain, *Democracy on Trial*, 81.

22. Jane Walters, "Response to Paul Lehman's 'How Can the Skills and Knowledge Called For in the National Standards Best Be Taught?'" in *Vision 2020: The Housewright Symposium on the Future of Music Education*, ed. Clifford K. Madsen (Reston, Va.: Music Educators National Conference, 2000), 107.

23. John Dewey, *My Pedagogic Creed* (1897), quoted in Jerome Bruner, *On Knowing: Essays for the Left Hand* (New York: Atheneum, 1970), 115.

24. For a revealing analysis of Marilyn Manson's personal philosophies, see Robert Wright, "'I'd Sell You Suicide': Pop Music and Moral Panic in the Age of Marilyn Manson," *Popular Music* 19, no. 3 (October 2000): 365–85. Wright contends that Mason is misunderstood and wrongly vilified by neoconservatives and others

who would censure or ban his music; that he is in fact engaging in social criticism of "some of North America's most sacred cows" (378–79).

25. Dewey, *Art as Experience*, 304.
26. Philosopher John Stuart Mill long ago observed that criticism is essential to understanding. For a discussion on this point, see Peter Kivy, *Authenticities: Philosophical Reflections on Musical Performance* (Ithaca, N.Y.: Cornell University Press, 1995), 175. For more about Mill's political philosophy, read John Stuart Mill, *On Liberty*, ed. David Spitz (New York: W. W. Norton, 1975).
27. Stein says the same thing when observing that quantitative measurement can create the simplistic and erroneous impression that incommensurable and fundamental human values can be compared and reduced to some common denominator. This, she argues, creates the false promise that intractable value conflicts can be easily resolved. Stein, *The Cult of Efficiency*, 217.
28. As Dewey stated in *Art as Experience*, "Nowhere are comparisons so odious as in fine art" (308).
29. According to Edward W. Said in *Culture and Imperialism* (New York: Vintage Books, 1994), "Cultural experience or indeed every cultural form is radically, quintessentially hybrid" (58). Said concluded, "Contamination is the wrong word . . . , but some notion of literature and indeed all culture as hybrid . . . and encumbered, or entangled and overlapping with what used to be regarded as extraneous elements–this strikes me as *the* essential idea for the revolutionary realities today, in which the contests of the secular world so provocatively inform the texts we both read and write" (317, italics in original). For a discussion of the problems and social benefits of cultural musical hybridization, see Kenneth Dorter, "Multiculturalism and Cultural Diversity in Music," *Proceedings for Music and Cross-Cultural Understanding Colloquium*, 26–28, Twenty-fifth Annual Richard R. Baker Philosophy Colloquium, sponsored by the Departments of Philosophy and Music, University of Dayton, 25–27 September 1997.
30. Cahoone explains in *The Dilemma of Modernity* that in democratic society individuals and groups cannot simply withdraw from public life into the safety and security of private life, whether of the mind, home, or institution, for "if one is free only in privacy then one is not free. Freedom in public and freedom in private are inseparable" (273).
31. Dewey, *Art as Experience*, 311–12.
32. Dewey, *Essays in Experimental Logic*, 268.
33. Stein, *The Cult of Efficiency*, 168. In her introduction to Taylor's *Multiculturalism*, Gutmann observes that "public officials and institutions that make cultural choices are democratically accountable, not only in principle but also in practice" (11).
34. Gutmann, *Multiculturalism*, 9.
35. Saul, *The Unconscious Civilization*, 89. Saul refers to this transcendence of self-interest as "disinterestedness." For obvious reasons (i.e., the negative connotation attached to this word), I prefer the term "democratic interest." This is what Saul really means. We don't want disinterested citizens. We want citizens who are interested in the good of musical society and can rise above their own selfishness.
36. Dewey, *The Quest for Certainty*, reprinted in Dewey, *Intelligence in the Modern World*, 278.

37. Dewey, *Intelligence in the Modern World*, v.
38. Chomsky declares, "It is the responsibility of the intellectual to insist upon the truth; it is also his duty to see events in their historical perspective." Noam Chomsky, "The Responsibility of Intellectuals," in *The Chomsky Reader*, ed. James Peck (New York: Pantheon Books, 1987), 71–72. First published in Noam Chomsky, *American Power and the New Mandarins* (New York: Pantheon Books, 1967), 78. Richard Bernstein summarizes Rorty's position thusly: "The moral task of the philosopher or the cultural critic is to defend the openness of human conversation against all those temptations and real threats that seek closure. And for Rorty, too, this theme is universalized, in the sense that he is concerned not only with European intellectuals' form of life but with extending conversation and dialogue to all of humanity." Bernstein, *Beyond Objectivism and Relativism*, 205.
39. Rorty, "Solidarity or Objectivity?" 582.
40. Mursell, *Music Education: Principles and Programs*. Mursell's principles outline the role and purpose of education in democratic society, including the function of schools in developing moral character and promoting personal growth in students so that they can "make responsible, wise, and right choices about the problems of daily living" (250). The principles outlined by him are essentially elaborations on the following articles of faith: all individuals are fundamentally equal, possess certain inalienable rights, and are deserving of respect. They ought to be conceived and treated as free moral agents who are "governed by reason and conscience" (14–16).
41. Chomsky expressed it as follows in "The Responsibility of Intellectuals": "For a privileged minority, western democracy provides the leisure, the facilities, the training to seek the truth lying hidden behind the veil of distortion and misrepresentation, ideology, and class interest through which the events of current history are presented to us" (60). Edward Said similarly argued that "the job facing the cultural critic is ... not to accept the politics of identity as given, but to show how all representations are constructed, for what purpose, by whom, and with what components." See *Culture and Imperialism*, 314.
42. Democracy, as Elshtain observes in *Democracy on Trial*, "is the political form that permits and requires human freedom, not as an act of self-overcoming, nor pure reason, but in service to others in one's own time and place" (89).
43. Accountability, however, works both ways. Government and society must offer intellectuals the necessary resources and support to protect the public interest; otherwise, efforts at accountability become meaningless or even politically exploitative. Stein, *The Cult of Efficiency*, 161.
44. Abraham A. Schwadron, in *Aesthetics: Dimensions for Music Education* (Washington, D.C.: Music Educators National Conference, 1967), contended that "the educator's role in the development of aesthetic understanding is that of a musical and democratic expert.... Preparation for democratic leadership in musical understanding must become the keystone for the education of the [music] teacher" (106–107).
45. Stein, *The Cult of Efficiency*, 185.
46. Several studies suggest that undergraduate music education majors, having been socialized to professional practice through countless hours of instruction and observation during elementary school and high school, are subsequently resistant to change after they enter the university. Failing to see the relation between

theory and practice, they ignore their academic music education faculty while modeling themselves and their sense of professional identity after performance faculty or former high school music teachers. For a review of this literature, see my chapter "The Social Construction of Music Teacher Identity in Undergraduate Music Education Majors," in *The New Handbook of Research on Music Teaching and Learning*, 675–94.

47. In a qualitative study of occupational identity among undergraduate music education majors at five Canadian universities (N = 116), Brian Roberts found that music education majors lacked any sense of teacher identity at all "except in the form of 'musician' as 'teacher.'" See Brian A. Roberts, "Music Teacher Education as Identity Construction," *International Journal of Music Education* 18 (1991): 34; see also Roberts, "Gatekeepers and the Reproduction of Institutional Realities: The Case of Music Education in Canadian Universities," *Musical Performance* 2, no. 3 (2000): 63–80, and *A Place to Play: The Social World of University Schools of Music* (St. John's: Memorial University of Newfoundland, 1991). For literature about teachers in general, see Michael Apple, *Education and Power* (Boston: Routledge, 1982); Deborah P. Britzman, *Practice Makes Practice* (Albany: State University of New York Press, 1991); and Henry A. Giroux, *Disturbing Pleasures: Learning Popular Culture* (New York: Routledge, 1994).

48. Norton York, "Valuing School Music: A Report on School Music" (London: University of Westminster and Rockschool, 2001), 6. Malcolm Ross, in "What's Wrong with School Music?" *British Journal of Music Education* 12, no. 3 (November 1995): 185–201, acknowledges that there are problems with music teachers and their "training," particularly in terms of their conservative tastes and reliance on conventional performance skills, which have "left them at sea with much of the progressive thinking initiated by . . . reformers" (189). Carol Beynon similarly observes that the teaching profession in general tends to be conservative. The profession tends to attract and admit to its ranks conservative individuals, or those already assimilated to white, middle-class values, while rewarding conformist behavior. Carol A. Beynon, "From Music Student to Music Teacher: Negotiating an Identity." In *Critical Thinking in Music: Theory and Practice*, ed. Paul Woodford, *Studies in Music from the University of Western Ontario* 17 (1998): 86.

49. York, "Valuing School Music," 6.

50. Beynon, "From Music Student to Music Teacher," 86.

51. Brian A. Roberts, "Editorial," *International Journal of Music Education* 32 (1998): 2.

52. Christopher Small, *Music of the Common Tongue: Survival and Celebration in Afro-American Music* (London: John Calder, 1987), 176. Botstein, in "The Training of Musicians," complains that there is an "institutionalized conservative bias in the [conservatory and university music] curriculum (e.g., Vienna and Leipzig) against innovation in composition and an explicit emphasis on re-creation of historic established repertoire" (329). Even in conservatories like the renowned Juilliard School of Music "there is all too much imitation and conformism among our best instrumentalists" (330). Other critics in our own field have similarly complained that music education majors and teachers are too accepting of pedagogical knowledge. See, for example, Bennett Reimer, *A Philosophy of Music Education*, 2nd ed. (Englewood Cliffs, N.J.: Prentice Hall, 1989), and Patricia O'Toole, "I Sing in a Choir but I Have 'No Voice'!" *Quarterly Journal of Music Teaching and Learning* 4, no. 4 (Winter/Spring 1993/1994): 65–76.

53. Peter C. Emberley, *Zero Tolerance: Hot Button Politics in Canada's Universities* (Toronto: Penguin Books, 1996), 22. Emberley claims that intellectual passivity and conservatism are commonplace in universities. Owing to factors such as increasing professional specialization and political correctness within the academy, coupled with the defunding and privatization of public educational institutions, universities are for the most part no longer places in which public deliberation about important social and other values is fostered and encouraged. For further discussion on these points, see Michael Bérubé and Cary Nelson, eds., *Higher Education under Fire: Politics, Economics, and the Crisis of the Humanities* (New York: Routledge, 1995), 25.

54. Donald Schön's concept of reflective practice, for example, is based on the assumption that professional schools fail to train professionals to cope with real-world problems and situations because they adhere to an epistemology of technical rationality and transmission models of educational practice. Donald A. Schön, *Educating the Reflective Practitioner* (San Francisco: Jossey-Bass, 1987), 119–21. Schön, however, is more concerned with design and personal creativity within professional practice than with any political considerations. His concept of reflective practice does not go far enough in addressing fundamental issues and problems having to do with freedom, identity, and moral choice. It should be acknowledged, however, that thus far there is little evidence as to the efficacy of reflective and critical pedagogies in accomplishing their emancipatory goals. For one critique of critical theory, see Elizabeth Ellsworth, "Why Doesn't This Feel Empowering? Working through the Repressive Myths of Critical Pedagogy," *Harvard Education Review* 59, no. 3 (August 1989): 297–324.

55. As is stated by York in "Valuing School Music," "Overall there seems to be a genuine willingness by teachers to find solutions to their problems *if* they are *given* the necessary and correct support in terms of initial teacher training and in-service professional development" (7, emphasis mine).

56. In a 1998 questionnaire survey of sixty-one music teachers in England, Lucy Green found that proportionately more of them were "accepting" of popular music than in a survey conducted in 1982. See Green, "From the Western Classics to the World: Secondary Music Teachers' Changing Attitudes in England, 1982 and 1998," *British Journal of Music Education* 19, no. 1 (March 2002): 5–30.

57. Bennett Reimer writes, "For many American music educators the best policy in regard to pop music is benign neglect, with an occasional inclusion of an example or two to demonstrate open-mindedness. Seldom is popular music, in any of its diverse manifestations, represented in school programs with anything like the presence and seriousness of western classical music, or even jazz and, now, various cultural musics." Bennett Reimer, "Viewing Music Education in the United States through Irish Eyes," *College Music Symposium* 38 (1998): 77.

58. Ross, "What's Wrong with School Music?" 189–90. Reporting on a comparative analysis of English and Ontario music curricula in the 1980s, sociologists John Shepherd and Graham Vulliamy found that even when a more populist approach to music curriculum was taken, instruction was "conceived and managed according to criteria abstracted from the tradition of the established western canon." See Shepherd and Vulliamy, "The Struggle for Culture: A Sociological Case Study of the Development of a National Music Curriculum," *British Journal of Sociology of Education* 15, no. 1 (1994): 28.

59. Giroux, *Disturbing Pleasures*, x.

60. Bloom, *The Closing of the American Mind*. While acknowledging that classical music is still alive and well in universities, in the end, as Bloom observes, only about 5 to 10 percent of university students are involved in classical music (69). Don Cusic, in *Music in the Market* (Bowling Green, Ohio: Bowling Green State University Popular Press, 1996), confirms that sales of classical music today represent only "approximately 5 percent of recorded music sold" (121).

61. Ross refers in "What's Wrong with School Music?" to several surveys of students' and former students' attitudes toward music education in Britain, the first in the late 1960s and the other two in 1992 and 1995, showing that school music is viewed by many (more than half of those surveyed) as being uncreative or unimaginative. "Among vast numbers of girls and boys music in school is a massive turn-off" (186).

62. Elliott's educational aim is to induct children into communities of expert or leading musicians possessing superior knowledge of musical standards and practices. This knowledge, coupled with certain critical abilities, makes it possible for them to generate and develop their own ideas (i.e., musical interpretations) in light of past and present musical practice. David J. Elliott, "Music as Knowledge," *Journal of Aesthetic Education* 25, no. 3 (Fall 1991): 29.

63. Botstein, in "The Training of Musicians," calls for the creation of an institutional culture and curriculum that will expand music students' intellectual horizons while helping them "to resist and overcome the tendency to relegate the making of music to the margins of culture or to the realms of decoration, distraction, and entertainment" (328). In addition to their usual professional training, students require a more liberal and expansive education in which connections are made between music and other subjects like language, philosophy, literature, and film. This, he believes, should give them the breadth and depth required to "create and reach an audience" (329).

64. Saul, *The Unconscious Civilization*, 178–79.

65. Ibid., 66.

66. Botstein, "The Training of Musicians," 329. For similar complaints, see also Cusic, *Music in the Market*, 122–23; and Henry O. Kingsbury, *Music, Talent, and Performance: A Conservatory Cultural System* (Philadelphia: Temple University Press, 1988). Roberts makes much the same observation about music education majors valuing technique over musicality in *A Place to Play*.

67. Hugo Cole, *The Changing Face of Music* (London: Victor Gollancz, 1978). Cole writes that composers speak a private language intended for each other "rather than the remote, hypothetical listener on the far end of the line" (122–23). As he continues, "The age seems to 'select' composers of high intellect and convoluted modes of thought; and perhaps a convoluted puzzle-music is appropriate to the time we live in" (123). Musicologist Richard Taruskin similarly complains that the performance of classical music is becoming increasingly stodgy. This stodginess is attributed to a conservative institutional culture and attitudes among classically trained musicians. See Richard Taruskin, *Text and Act: Essays on Music and Performance* (New York: Oxford University Press, 1995). This, it is suggested, has been a contributing factor in the general decline in audience attendance at symphony concerts. For a similar view, see John Shepherd, "Music and the Last Intellectual," *Journal of Aesthetic Education* 25, no. 3 (Fall 1991): 96–99.

68. Giroux, *Disturbing Pleasures,* 36. For one analysis of how spectacle can be used to discourage or overwhelm thought, see Douglas Rushkoff's *Coercion: Why We Listen to What "They" Say* (New York: Riverhead Books, 1999), 99–130, 140.

69. Saul, *The Unconscious Civilization,* 64.

70. "Profit," as Barber writes in *Jihad vs. McWorld,* "is . . . the only judge" of the popular music industry (111). For a more extended, and welcome, discussion of the social uses of music, including in the retail sector, see Tia DeNora, *Music in Everyday Life* (Cambridge: Cambridge University Press, 2000).

71. Stephen H. Barnes, *Muzak: The Hidden Messages in Music* (Lewiston, N.Y.: Edwin Mellen Press, 1988), 5, 9. For a brief review of research investigating the role and effectiveness of music in television advertising, see North, Hargreaves, and Tarrant, "Social Psychology and Music Education," 604–25. See also Anne H. Rosenfeld, "The Sound of Selling," *Psychology Today* (December 1985): 56; and Barber, *Jihad vs. McWorld,* 108.

72. Rushkoff, *Coercion,* 87.

73. Naomi Klein, *No Logo: Taking Aim at the Brand Bullies* (Toronto: Vintage Books, 2000). Clothing designer Tommy Hilfiger, for example, not only sponsored the Rolling Stones' 1997 Bridges to Babylon tour but arranged to have Mick Jagger and Sheryl Crow actually model his Rock 'n' Roll Collection (47).

74. Jacques Attali, *Noise: The Political Economy of Music,* trans. Brian Massumi (Minneapolis: University of Minnesota Press, 1985), 112. R. Murray Schafer makes the same observation in *Voices of Tyranny: Temples of Silence* (Indian River, Ont.: Arcana, 1993), 152.

75. Martin Cloonan and Bruce Johnson, "Killing Me Softly with His Song: An Initial Investigation into the Use of Popular Music as a Tool of Oppression," *Popular Music* 21, no. 1 (January 2002): 37.

76. Barber, *Jihad vs. McWorld,* 108.

77. Schafer, *Voices of Tyranny,* 152.

78. Barber, *Jihad vs. McWorld,* 108.

79. Saul, *The Unconscious Civilization,* 65.

80. Cloonan and Johnson, "Killing Me Softly," 35. For more about the use of culturally offensive music as an interrogation strategy, see the British Broadcasting Corporation's report "Sesame Street Breaks Iraqi POWS," at http://news.bbc.co.uk, accessed 12 November 2003. I wish to thank my student Linda Cicero for bringing this BBC report to my attention.

81. For a discussion on this point, see Neil Postman's *Amusing Ourselves to Death: Public Discourse in the Age of Show Business* (New York: Penguin Books, 1985).

82. Kivy, "Music and the Liberal Education," 90. See also O'Toole, "I Sing in a Choir but I Have 'No Voice'!"; and Paul Woodford, "A Critique of Fundamentalism in Singing: Musical Authenticity, Authority, and Practice," in *Sharing the Voices: The Phenomenon of Singing,* ed. Brian A. Roberts (St. John's: Memorial University of Newfoundland), 269–78.

83. Julia Eklund Koza, "A Realm without Angels: MENC's Partnerships with Disney and Other Major Corporations," *Philosophy of Music Education Review* 10, no. 2 (Fall 2002): 72–79. See also Koza, "Corporate Profit at Equity's Expense: Codified Standards and High-Stakes Assessment in Music Teacher Preparation," *Bulletin of the Council for Research in Music Education* 152 (Spring 2002): 1–16.

84. Dewey, *A Common Faith*, 80. Nussbaum assigns a "carefully demarcated cognitive role" to the emotions. The emotions, particularly empathy, ought to play an important role in public deliberation and ethical reasoning, albeit carefully circumscribed, for the reason that they "contain a powerful, if partial, vision of social justice and provide powerful motives for just conduct." Nussbaum, *Poetic Justice*, xvi.

85. Elliott, in *Music Matters*, observes that "some teachers act more like political dictators than reflective coaches and mentors" (3). For further discussion on this point, see Kivy, "Music and the Liberal Education," 90; O'Toole, "I Sing in a Choir but I Have 'No Voice'!"; and Woodford, "A Critique of Fundamentalism in Singing."

86. Estelle R. Jorgensen, *In Search of Music Education* (Urbana: University of Illinois Press, 1997), 91.

87. *Merriam-Webster's Collegiate Dictionary*, s.v. "pedagogue."

88. Jorgensen, *In Search of Music Education*, 56.

89. Giroux states in *Disturbing Pleasures* that he no longer believes "that pedagogy is a discipline. On the contrary,...pedagogy is about the creation of a public sphere, one that brings people together in a variety of sites to talk, exchange information, listen, feel their desires, and expand their capacities for joy, love, solidarity, and struggle" (x).

90. Wayne D. Bowman, "Educating Musically," in *The New Handbook of Research on Music Teaching and Learning*, 64. Although Bowman's admonition is made with reference to performance-based programs, it can be applied to any kind of educational activity, including the teaching of music history and theory. See also Bowman, "Music as Ethical Encounter," *Bulletin of the Council for Research in Music Education* 151 (Winter 2001): 11–20.

91. Dewey, *Democracy and Educational Administration*, reprinted in *Intelligence in the Modern World*, 401.

92. As Bowman states in "Universals, Relativism, and Music Education," *Bulletin of the Council for Research in Music Education* 135 (Winter 1998): 9, "The realm where musical values are distinct from political and moral ones is, like the realm of utter objectivity, one without human inhabitants." Tia DeNora, in *Music in Everyday Life*, similarly observes that music is inevitably political and "a powerful medium of social order" (163).

93. Giroux, in *Disturbing Pleasures*, charges that any pedagogy that teaches children to mindlessly accept the conservative political and educational status quo is an expression of "civil cowardice" (163).

94. David J. Elliott, "Music as Culture: Toward a Multicultural Concept of Arts Education," *Journal of Aesthetic Education* 24, no. 1 (Spring 1990): 163.

95. Elliott, *Music Matters*, 307.

96. Jorgensen, in "Justifying Music Instruction in American Public Schools," notes that Elliott and other praxialists like Philip Alperson have attempted to justify music education "mainly in musical terms and they have yet to address other pertinent educational, social, political, and cultural concerns beyond the purview of music" (22).

97. Elliott explains in *Music Matters* that confronting foreign beliefs can provoke self-examination while encouraging "students to examine the musical consequences of the beliefs underlying different music cultures." This, he believes, can help

"minimize the tendency to superimpose a universal belief system on all music everywhere" (293). Charlene Morton, however, takes Elliott to task for ignoring ethical issues in multicultural music education. See Morton, "Boom Diddy Boom Boom: Critical Multiculturalism in Music Education," *Philosophy of Music Education Review* 9, no. 1 (Spring 2001): 36.

98. R. A. Goodrich, "Kivy on Justifying Music in Liberal Education," *Journal of Aesthetic Education* 36, no. 1 (Spring 2002): 50–59. Defining music in terms of its use within a community, however, tells us nothing about "how to distinguish the criterion or criteria for separating relevant from irrelevant uses, odd from normal uses, central from peripheral ones" (58).

99. Dewey cautioned that "the fundamental root of the laissez faire idea is denial (more often implicit than express) of the possibility of radical intervention of intelligence in the conduct of human life" and the "depreciation of intelligence and the resources of natural knowledge and understanding, and conscious and organized effort to turn the use of these means from narrow ends, personal and class, to larger human purposes." Dewey, *A Common Faith*, 80, 82.

100. Elliott, *Music Matters*, 286–87.

101. Ibid., 306.

102. Andrea Rose proposes that indigenous music be included in formal music education at the university level, for example, in instrumental and vocal secondary classes. See Andrea M. Rose, "A Place for Indigenous Music in Formal Music Education," *International Journal of Music Education* 26 (1995): 39–54. This, however, presents some ethical problems. See Timothy Rice, "Ethical Issues for Music Educators in Multicultural Societies," *Canadian Music Educator* 39, no. 2 (Winter 1998): 8.

103. Roberts, "Music Teacher Education as Identity Construction," 36; see also Roberts's *A Place to Play*, 71, 94. For a similar American study, albeit on a smaller scale, see Henry O. Kingsbury, "Music as Cultural System: Structure and Process in an American Conservatory" (Ph.D. diss., Indiana University, 1984).

104. Sarah Hennessey, "Overcoming the Red-Feeling: The Development of Confidence to Teach Music in Primary School amongst Student Teachers," *British Journal of Music Education* 17, no. 2 (2000): 183–96. According to Hennessey, prior negative experiences with their own music education in secondary school "seemed to have left many of them [9 out of 10] with feelings of inadequacy and a strong belief that in order to teach music one had to be an accomplished performer" (188). Music teachers and music education majors apparently agree that teaching is a function of musicianship. See Roberts, "Music Teacher Education as Identity Construction," 32.

105. Chomsky, "The Responsibility of Intellectuals," 71–72. For a devastating critique of the cult of the expert and instrumental reason, see John Ralston Saul, *Voltaire's Bastards: The Dictatorship of Reason in the West* (Toronto: Penguin Books, 1993).

106. One of the parallels between music and the policy sciences is the continued lack of "a body of theory, well-tested and verified, that applies to the conduct of foreign affairs or the resolution of domestic or international conflict." Chomsky, "The Responsibility of Intellectuals," 72.

107. Christopher Small, *Music, Society, Education* (London: John Calder, 1980), 90.

108. Elliott, *Music Matters*, 289.

109. Intelligent participation (including listening and composing) within a musical community, states Elliott, "depends on learning how to make music well." Ibid., 174.
110. Kivy, *Authenticities*, 184.
111. For discussion of the qualities of rap music as art, see Shusterman, *Pragmatist Aesthetics*. Shusterman not only admits liking rap music but thinks that it "satisfies the most crucial conventional criteria for aesthetic legitimacy" (202).
112. Rice, "Ethical Issues for Music Educators in Multicultural Societies," 7–8.
113. Paulo Freire attributes this belief among experts and the intelligentsia that ordinary people have no texts or voices of their own to intellectualist and class prejudices. See *Cultural Action for Freedom* (Cambridge, Mass.: Harvard Educational Review and Center for the Study of Development and Social Change, 1974), 25. There are several obvious parallels here with folksong collecting in the early twentieth century. Simon Frith, in *Performing Rites: On the Value of Popular Music* (Cambridge: Harvard University Press, 1996), writes that popular music and other performers grow to disdain their audiences. Performers' values lead "inevitably . . . to a sense of alienation from the audience which becomes, in turn, a kind of contempt for it" (53). See also Ian Watson's *Song and Democratic Culture in Britain: An Approach to Popular Culture in Social Movements* (London: Croom Helm, 1983).
114. Dewey, "Democracy and Educational Administration," reprinted in Dewey, *Intelligence in the Modern World*, 401.
115. Saul, *The Unconscious Civilization*, 49.
116. Bennett Reimer believes that the current low levels of public support for music in the school and concert hall are attributable to the music education profession's continuing obsession with performance to the detriment of other kinds of musical involvements, such as listening, composing, evaluating, and so on, that are more relevant to the majority of future audience members. Reimer, "Viewing Music Education in the United States through Irish Eyes," 78.
117. Noam Chomsky, "Equality: Language, Development, Human Intelligence, and Social Organization," in *The Chomsky Reader*, ed. James Peck (New York: Pantheon Books, 1987), 202. First published in Noam Chomsky, *Equality and Social Policy* (Urbana: University of Illinois Press, 1978).
118. Wilfred Carr and Anthony Hartnett, in *Education and the Struggle for Democracy: The Politics of Educational Ideas* (Buckingham: Open University Press, 1996), argue that "liberal" and "vocational" educational agendas need not, indeed should not, be mutually exclusive. "The democratic challenge is to move towards a form of 'liberal vocationalism'" (194). Dewey said much the same thing. For a discussion of this point, see John Knight, "Fading Poststructuralisms: Post-Ford, Posthuman, Posteducation?" in *After Postmodernism: Education. Politics, and Identity*, ed. Richard Smith and Philip Wexler (London: Falmer Press, 1995), 29.
119. According to Dewey, "The things in civilization we most prize are not of ourselves. They exist by grace of the doings and sufferings of the continuous human community in which we are a link" (*A Common Faith*, 87). James A. Beane, in "Reclaiming a Democratic Purpose for Education," *Educational Leadership* 56, no. 2 (October 1998), writes that, to Dewey, "Human dignity, equity, justice, and caring were to serve as both means and ends in our political, economic, and social relations" (8). And Saul, in *The Unconscious Civilization*, complains

that increasing specialization in education, coupled with a narrow emphasis on expertise, "feeds our elites across the political spectrum" (168).

120. Dewey, *Ethics*, 350.

121. Dewey, *Essays in Experimental Logic*, reprinted in *Intelligence in the Modern World*, 273.

122. Eleanor Stubley writes of how performance, properly conceived, involves "a moral or ethical tension" between the composer's intentions, as indicated in the score, and the performer's own judgment and personal musical integrity. I would include the audience in that scheme. Composers and performers should also feel that they have an obligation to their audiences. See Eleanor V. Stubley, "The Performer, the Score, the Work: Musical Performance and Transactional Reading," *Journal of Aesthetic Education* 29, no. 3 (Fall 1995): 64. Somewhat similarly, Ross, in "What's Wrong with Music Education?" recommends that music teachers treat instruction like a "language game" and form of play in which the object is genuine conversation. The teacher is a partner and celebrant in this process of meaning making (198–99).

3. Living in a Postmusical Age

This essay, with a slightly different title, was originally published in the *Philosophy of Music Education Review* 7, no. 1 (Spring 1999): 3–18 and is reprinted with permission.

1. Terrence W. Tilley, ed., *Postmodern Theologies: The Challenge of Religious Diversity* (Maryknoll, N.Y.: Orbis Books, 1995), vi.

2. Wayne Bowman, "Sound, Sociality, and Music," *Quarterly Journal of Music Teaching and Learning* 5, no. 3 (Fall 1994): 53.

3. Art educator David K. Holt observes that "postmodernism was created as an antithesis to the modernist emphasis on aesthetics." See Holt, "Postmodernism: Anomaly in Art-Critical Theory," *Journal of Aesthetic Education* 29, no. 1 (Spring 1995): 85.

4. McClary, *Feminine Endings*, 29.

5. S. J. Wilsmore, "Against Deconstructing Rationality in Education," *Journal of Aesthetic Education* 25, no. 4 (Winter 1991): 104.

6. Ibid., 104–105.

7. Mursell, *Principles of Democratic Education*, 15.

8. There are, of course, many feminisms. Following Judith Grant's lead, I define radical feminists as those employing the theoretical construct of patriarchal authority to explain many social problems besetting women. Grant points out that radicals have been the primary builders of feminist theory. This, she says, can be attributed to the rise of the New Left during the 1960s and the belief that theory was essential to politics. But while radical feminism had its origins in leftist politics, many feminists became dissatisfied with Marxism for the reason that it failed to acknowledge that all women, even socially privileged ones, were oppressed by virtue of being women. It was the need "to define oppression differently" that provided the impetus for developing the theoretical construct of patriarchal authority. See Judith Grant, *Fundamental Feminism: Contesting the Core Concepts of Feminist Theory* (New York: Routledge, 1993), 29–30.

9. Kymlicka, *Contemporary Political Philosophy*, 263.

10. Carol Gilligan, *In a Different Voice: Psychological Theory and Women's Development* (Cambridge, Mass.: Harvard University Press, 1982), 173–74.

11. Stephen Miles, "Critical Musicology and the Problem of Mediation," *Notes: Quarterly Journal of the Music Library Association* 53, no. 3 (March 1997): 742.

12. Wilsmore, "Against Deconstructing Rationality," 106.

13. As E. Louis Lankford writes, relying too much on works of the western canon in art classes, or teaching with reference to modernist principles, can lead to charges of "cultural hegemony," "colonialism," and "elitism." The charge of elitism, Lankford continues, is "peculiarly ironic given the exclusivity inherent in the language of most postmodern literature and the ideological superiority presumed by postmodern critics." See E. Louis Lankford, "Aesthetic Experience in a Postmodern Age: Recovering the Aesthetics of E. F. Kaelin," *Journal of Aesthetic Education* 32, no. 1 (Spring 1998): 25.

14. Rose Rosengard Subotnik, *Deconstructive Variations: Music and Reason in Western Society* (Minneapolis: University of Minnesota Press, 1996), xliv.

15. Ibid., xxvii.

16. Wilsmore, "Against Deconstructing Rationality," 106.

17. Cahoone, *The Dilemma of Modernity,* 272.

18. Steven Connor, *Postmodernist Culture: An Introduction to Theories of the Contemporary* (Oxford: Basil Blackwell, 1989), 243.

19. Simon Critchley, "Derrida: Private Ironist or Public Liberal," in *Deconstruction and Pragmatism,* ed. Chantal Mouffe (London: Routledge, 1996), 35.

20. Stuart Richmond, "Liberalism, Multiculturalism, and Art Education," *Journal of Aesthetic Education* 29, no. 3 (Fall 1995): 19.

21. Music educator and feminist Charlene Morton, for example, attributes the resurgence of interest in critical thinking (which she equates with reason) as yet further evidence of "the western tradition's epistemological bias for pure intellection," a bias that serves to devalue those experiences, including emotive and musical ones, that cannot easily be rendered into words and that are not part of "mental" culture. Charlene Morton, "Critical Thinking and Music Education: Nondiscursive Experience and Discursive Rationality as Musical Friends," in *Critical Thinking in Music: Theory and Practice,* ed. Paul Woodford, *Studies in Music from the University of Western Ontario* 17 (1998): 63.

22. Paul Woodford and Robert E. Dunn, "Beyond Objectivism and Relativism in Music," in *Critical Thinking in Music: Theory and Practice,* ed. Paul Woodford, *Studies in Music from the University of Western Ontario* 17 (1998): 55.

23. Kymlicka, *Contemporary Political Philosophy,* 265.

24. Ismay Barwell, "Towards a Defense of Objectivity," in *Knowing the Difference: Feminist Perspectives in Epistemology,* ed. Kathleen Lennon and Margaret Whitford (London: Routledge, 1994), 82.

25. Wilsmore, "Against Deconstructing Rationality," 103.

26. Alexander J. Argyros, *A Blessed Rage for Order: Deconstruction, Evolution, and Chaos* (Ann Arbor: University of Michigan Press, 1991), 4.

27. Bernstein, *Beyond Objectivism and Relativism,* 231.

28. Emberley, *Zero Tolerance,* 227. Emberley refers to a battle raging in the National Action Committee, having to do with identity politics, that led to the association withdrawing from a recent Royal Commission into New Reproductive Technologies and a panel on violence against women.

29. bell hooks, "Feminism: A Transformational Politic," in *Talking Back* (Boston: South End Press, 1989), 26–27.

30. Lankford, "Recovering the Aesthetics of E. F. Kaelin," 25.

31. Cahoone, *The Dilemma of Modernity*, 272.

32. Barbara Riebling, "Remodelling Truth, Power, and Society: Implications of Chaos Theory, Nonequilibrium Dynamics, and Systems Science for the Study of Politics and Literature," in *After Poststructuralism: Interdisciplinarity and Literary Theory*, ed. Nancy Easterlin and Barbara Riebling (Evanston, Ill.: Northwestern University Press, 1993), 178.

33. Rorty specifically cautions against overly elaborate, self-indulgent theorizing divorced from the real world and its problems. Questioning Derrida's political utility, Rorty states that "over-philosophication has helped create in the universities of the US and Britain (where Derrida's, Laclau's, and Chantal Mouffe's books are very widely read and admired) a self-involved academic left which has become increasingly irrelevant to substantive political discussion." Rorty, "Response to Ernesto Laclau," 69. See also Jay, *American Literature and the Culture Wars*, 32.

34. Tilley, *Postmodern Theologies*, 9.

35. Kymlicka, *Contemporary Political Philosophy*, 221–22.

36. Gadamer, *Philosophical Hermeneutics*, xvi.

37. Bernstein, *Beyond Objectivism and Relativism*, 129.

38. Ibid., 37.

39. Gadamer, *Philosophical Hermeneutics*, 32–33.

40. Ibid., 35.

41. William Casement, "Unity, Diversity, and Leftist Support for the Canon," *Journal of Aesthetic Education* 27, no. 3 (Fall 1993): 38. Casement paraphrases Richard Rorty on this same point, that "timeless truths" do not exist.

42. Holub, *Crossing Borders*, 195.

43. Gary Thomas, "What's the Use of Theory?" *Harvard Educational Review* 67, no. 1 (Spring 1997): 75–104. See also Hilary E. Davis, "The Temptations and Limitations of a Feminist Deaesthetic," *Journal of Aesthetic Education* 27, no. 1 (Spring 1993): 99–105. As Davis observes, the feminist proclivity to privilege "the social and political importance of a text . . . causes the reader's or spectator's experience of a text to be overshadowed or dismissed" (103).

44. Cahoone, *The Dilemma of Modernity*, 229.

45. Wendell V. Harris, ed., *Beyond Poststructuralism: The Speculations of Theory and the Experience of Reading* (University Park: Pennsylvania State University Press, 1996), xiii.

46. Saul, *The Unconscious Civilization*, 188. Subotnik says something very similar in *Deconstructive Variations*. While acknowledging that any attempt at defining abstract reason is "fraught with epistemological as well as moral difficulties. . . . and at best can be neither tidy nor definitive," she nevertheless believes that some such ideal is needed to check particularist excesses. As she continues, "Experience as well as reflection persuades me that left unchallenged by an abstract ideal, particularist viewpoints suffer from the same disease they criticize in the old universalistic ones: they want to be the only opinion in the world–and they don't know where to stop" (xliv).

47. Cahoone, *The Dilemma of Modernity*, 272.

48. Harris, *Beyond Poststructuralism*, xii. Holub, too, in *Crossing Borders*, observes that the women's and other civil rights movements appear almost old-fashioned with their claims to individual autonomy and subjectivity. Holub's own view is that "the Enlightenment heritage is not antithetical to progressive politics, but the very code of any meaningful political movement. Enlightenment, conceived in its widest sense, entails emancipation from imposed hegemony, whether this hegemony appears in the form of a church, a state, linguistic structure, or discourse" (200).

49. Robin Usher and Richard Edwards point out that radical feminists have never been willing to abandon completely the modernist claim to abstract reason as a grounding for truth. "In committing themselves to a political programme of changing society which privileges the masculine, they are defending one of the foundations of modernism; the rational, self-directing individual who freely seeks her rights through emancipatory political action." While claiming allegiance to postmodernism, radical feminism remains rooted in modernist assumptions about the nature of truth and knowledge. See Robin Usher and Richard Edwards, *Postmodernism and Education* (London: Routledge, 1994), 22.

50. Saul, *The Unconscious Civilization*, 2.

51. Ibid., 104.

52. Cahoone, *The Dilemma of Modernity*, 272.

53. McClary, *Feminine Endings*, 123.

54. Woodford and Dunn, "Beyond Objectivism and Relativism in Music," 56.

55. Bennett Reimer, "Music Education as Aesthetic Education: Past and Present," *Music Educators Journal* 75, no. 6 (February 1989): 26.

56. Thomas A. Regelski, "Critical Theory as a Foundation for Critical Thinking in Music Education," in *Critical Thinking in Music: Theory and Practice*, ed. Paul Woodford, *Studies in Music from the University of Western Ontario* 17 (1998): 3.

57. Beynon, "From Music Student to Music Teacher," 98.

58. Ibid., 98–99.

59. Woodford, "A Critique of Fundamentalism in Singing," 274.

60. Andrew Barry, Thomas Osborne, and Nikolas Rose, eds., *Foucault and Political Reason: Liberalism, Neo-Liberalism, and Rationalities of Government* (Chicago: University of Chicago Press, 1996), 8.

61. Wayne D. Bowman, *Philosophical Perspectives on Music* (New York: Oxford University Press, 1998), 396.

62. Casement, "Unity," 38. See also Rorty's "Solidarity or Objectivity?"

63. Harold Fiske, Review of *Music Matters: A New Philosophy of Music Education*, by David J. Elliott, *Notes: Quarterly Journal of the Music Library Association* 53, no. 3 (March 1997): 770–73.

64. Harvey Siegel, "Is Inclusion an Epistemic Virtue," *Philosophy of Education Yearbook, 1997*, ed. Susan Laird (Urbana, Ill.: Philosophy of Education Society, 1997), 97–99.

65. Bernstein, *Beyond Objectivism and Relativism*, 129.

66. Bowman, "Sound, Sociality, and Music," 65.

67. Maria B. Spychiger, "Aesthetic and Praxial Philosophies of Music Education Compared: A Semiotic Consideration," *Philosophy of Music Education Review* 5, no. 1 (Spring 1997): 33–41.

68. John Dewey, *Philosophy and Civilization* (New York: Minton, Balch, 1931), 92.

4. Music Education and the Culture Wars

1. Jorgensen, "Justifying Music Instruction in American Public Schools," 23.
2. Dennis F. Tupman, "A Rant about Elementary Music Education—Whither Goest Thou?" *Canadian Music Educator* 43, no. 4 (Summer 2002): 43–44. See also in the same volume Malcim V. Edwards, "Music Education as a Conserving Activity," 14–17.
3. See, for example, Leonhard and House, *Foundations and Principles of Music Education*, 7, and Schwadron, *Aesthetics*, 30.
4. Leonhard and House, *Foundations and Principles of Music Education*, 75.
5. Rideout and Feldman, "Research in Music Student Teaching," 883. See also Michael L. Mark, *Contemporary Music Education*, 2nd ed. (New York: Schirmer Books, 1986), 71.
6. Schwadron's *Aesthetics* and the first edition of Reimer's *Philosophy of Music Education* (Englewood Cliffs, N.J.: Prentice Hall, 1970) were among the first books to address philosophical problems in music education while providing professional leadership and vision. Of the two, Schwadron's book more explicitly acknowledges the democratic purpose of music education in western society.
7. In the United States, James L. Mursell (1893–1963) was perhaps music education's greatest representative in wider educational debates. Mursell, in his roles as psychologist and philosopher, spoke to all educators, not just music educators. See, for example, his books *Human Values in Education* (New York: Silver Burdett, 1934) and *Principles of Democratic Education*. See also Bennett Reimer, "Music Education Philosophy and Psychology after Mursell," in *Basic Concepts in Music Education, II,* ed. Richard J. Colwell (Niwot: University Press of Colorado, 1991), 130–56.
8. Beane writes that it is personally and professionally risky to call for a return to a democratic purpose for education. Beane, "Reclaiming a Democratic Purpose for Education," 11.
9. Lipman, *Arguing for Music*, 431.
10. Dewey, "Ethics of Democracy," quoted in Westbrook, *John Dewey and American Democracy*, 41.
11. Tupman, "A Rant about Elementary Music Education," 44. Tupman says that he is not against constructivism per se, only when it is carried to extremes. I fail to see, however, how constructivism can be reconciled with neofundamentalism.
12. Edwards, "Music Education as a Conserving Activity," 14–17. See also Lois Choksy, *The Kodály Method II: Folksong to Masterwork* (Upper Saddle River, N.J.: Prentice Hall, 1999).
13. See *The Oxford Companion to Philosophy*, s.v. "positivism." Michael Mark writes of how, during the early twentieth century, music education researchers became convinced that the application of scientific principles and methods to instruction could improve practice. Michael L. Mark, "A History of Music Education Research," in *Handbook of Research on Music Teaching and Learning*, 50–52.
14. For more about the confusion between quantitative measurement and qualitative judgment of musical or other values, many of which may be incommensurable or incapable of being compared and judged according to a single standard, see Stein, *The Cult of Efficiency*, 217.
15. Thomas A. Regelski, "Scientism in Experimental Music Research," *Philosophy of Music Education Review* 4, no. 1 (1996): 3–19. See also his essay "Critical Education,

Culturalism, and Multiculturalism," *Finnish Journal of Music Education* 5, nos. 1/2 (2000): 141. Betty Hanley and Janet Montgomery provide an excellent critique of the "scientific," "top down" Tylerian model for curriculum design, implementation, and research in their chapter "Contemporary Curriculum Practices and Their Theoretical Bases," in *The New Handbook of Research on Music Teaching and Learning*, 113–43. The Tylerian model has provided the theoretical underpinning for education in North America throughout much of the past half century. For a description and explanation of Tyler's model, see Ralph Tyler, *Basic Principles of Curriculum and Instruction* (Chicago: University of Chicago Press, 1949).

16. Mark notes in his "History of Music Education Research" that music education researchers have long been faulted for their lack of creativity and interest in significant professional and practical problems. The tendency has been to emphasize research design and quantitative methodology over creativity. Music teachers, for their part, continue to ignore music education research. The problem of music teachers ignoring research is an old and persistent one (50). See also Hanley and Montgomery, "Contemporary Curriculum Practices," 119.

17. For more about formal discipline, see Mark K. Singley and John R. Anderson, *The Transfer of Cognitive Skill* (Cambridge, Mass.: Harvard University Press, 1989), 229.

18. Peter H. Marshall, *Demanding the Impossible: A History of Anarchism* (London: HarperCollins, 1992). Specific groups identified by Jay in *American Literature and the Culture Wars* as belonging to the New Right Coalition include "the Moral Majority, the Christian Coalition, the Heritage Foundation, the American Enterprise Institute, the Olin Foundation, and so on" (44). Frum, in *Dead Right*, describes the Heritage Foundation as a "heterogeneous mass of political forces" dedicated to "restoring America's old moral values" (6–7).

19. Jay, *American Literature and the Culture Wars*, 47.

20. Ibid., 44–45. For a historical look at how the New Right gained political ascendancy in the United Kingdom from 1979 to 1993, see Carr and Hartnett, *Education and the Struggle for Democracy*, 156–71; and Kathleen Jones, *The Making of Social Policy in Britain: From the Poor Law to New Labour*, 3rd ed. (London: Athlone Press, 2000).

21. National Commission on Excellence in Education, *A Nation at Risk: The Imperative for Educational Reform* (Washington, D.C.: National Commission, 1983), 5. For a brief discussion of how this report prompted educational reform, see D. T. Stallings, "A Brief History of the U.S. Department of Education, 1979–2002," *Phi Delta Kappan* 83, no. 9 (May 2002): 677–83.

22. For an excellent discussion and criticism of the New Right's attitude toward public education in the United Kingdom, see Carr and Hartnett, *Education and the Struggle for Democracy*. See also Maxine Greene, "Imagination, Community, and the School," *Review of Education* 15 (1993): 223–31. With respect to the universities, Jay argues in *American Literature and the Culture Wars* that "the towers of academe need to be regularly shaken by genuine controversy, not strangled by the vines of utilitarianism and ideology" (49).

23. Lamar Alexander, "A Horse Trade for K–12 Education," *Phi Delta Kappan* 83, no. 9 (May 2002): 698–99. See also in the same issue Stallings's "A Brief History of the U.S. Department of Education," 680–81.

24. James Laxer, *In Search of a New Left: Canadian Politics after the Neoconservative Assault* (Toronto: Penguin, 1996), 28.

25. Beane, "Reclaiming a Democratic Purpose for Education," 9. See also Saul's *The Unconscious Civilization*, 69, and "Britain: Caning the Teachers," in *Economist*, 23 October 1999.

26. To quote Michael Mark, efficiency "became the key word for educators. They sought ways to make the schools operate at peak efficiency and thus also educate students more effectively. To achieve efficiency it was necessary to have goals and to measure success in achieving them. Thus another term, 'standardization,' found its way into educational jargon. Educators developed standards for many aspects of schooling, including standardization of the curriculum and learning objectives." Mark, "A History of Music Education Research," 49.

27. Carr and Hartnett, *Education and the Struggle for Democracy*, 176.

28. Beane, "Reclaiming a Democratic Purpose for Education," 9.

29. Stein, *The Cult of Efficiency*, 168.

30. Ibid., 217.

31. Saul agrees, referring to politicians and businesspeople advocating a managerial approach to the "delivery" of public goods like education, and relying on standardized tests and curricula, as "false capitalists." While preaching the ideology of capitalism and of the value of initiative and risk taking, they are bureaucratic managers specializing in methodologies and not creative risk takers. *The Unconscious Civilization*, 136.

32. Reimer, in the second edition of his *Philosophy of Music Education*, states that testing and evaluation procedures "will add to our status as a bona fide curriculum and add to our professional expertise. Tests can be abusive, as we know all too well, but they can also be powerful aids in effective education" (172).

33. For a more comprehensive list of standardized music tests, see Mark, "A History of Music Education Research," 50–51.

34. Stein, *The Cult of Efficiency*, 3–4.

35. Greene, "Imagination, Community, and the School," 223. In the second edition of his *Philosophy of Music Education*, Reimer states, "Music education in recent history has focused major effort on developing the musical skills of children with talent" while "entertaining the masses" (25).

36. Joyce Jordan, "Multicultural Music Education in a Pluralistic Society," in the *Handbook of Research on Music Teaching and Learning*, 736. Hanley and Montgomery, in "Contemporary Curriculum Practices," state that "although many music teachers resisted what they considered a mechanistic model [of instruction and evaluation based on the Tylerian rationale] inappropriate to music," music curriculum documents were nevertheless organized along those lines (118). For a now classic argument against standardized testing, see Banesh Hoffmann, *The Tyranny of Testing* (New York: Collier Books, 1962).

37. *National Standards for Arts Education: What Every Young American Should Know and Be Able to Do in the Arts* (Reston, Va.: Music Educators National Conference, 1994).

38. Elliott Eisner, "Why Standards May Not Improve Our Schools," *Recorder* 38, no. 2 (Winter 1996): 64.

39. For one critique of Hirsch's educational agenda by a music educator, see Elliott, "Music as Culture."

40. Ralph Smith, "Recent Trends and Issues in Policy Making," in *The New Handbook of Research on Music Teaching and Learning*, 24.
41. Hanley and Montgomery, in "Contemporary Curriculum Practices," state that there is a need "to examine the politically motivated trend toward national (centralized) curriculum and its implications for music education" (135).
42. For one music education text inspired by and modeled after the MENC National Standards, see Timothy S. Brophy, *Assessing the Developing Child Musician: A Guide for General Music Teachers* (Chicago: GIA Publications, 2000).
43. Catherine M. Schmidt observes, "The very act of establishing national standards presupposes that there is a body of knowledge and/or skills that is identifiable by some authority as true and valuable and that the acquisition of such may be measured." Schmidt, "Who Benefits? Music Education and the National Standards," *Philosophy of Music Education Review* 4, no. 2 (1996): 77.
44. The English National Music Curriculum has been criticized for its "conservative political agenda" and outdated linear and hierarchical nature. The MENC National Standards have thus far been adopted by forty-four states. Hanley and Montgomery, "Contemporary Curriculum Practices," 123.
45. The government's approach at the time was to blame music teachers for any perceived failure of school music while calling for a return to the discipline of the classics. As one witness attests, "What bothered ministers was that there might be too much time wasted on trendy, creative, music-making projects and not enough on getting to know the (White Western, Classical) musical heritage." Ross, "What's Wrong with School Music?" 188.
46. Carr and Hartnett, *Education and the Struggle for Democracy*, 180.
47. Hanley and Montgomery, "Contemporary Curriculum Practices," 124. See also Betty Hanley, "Creating a National Vision for Arts Education in Canada: Pipe-Dream or Possibility?" *Canadian Music Educator* 40, no. 1 (Fall 1998): 9–13. For a comparison of Canadian provincial music curricula, read Vince Rinaldo, "A Fragmentary View of Education," *Canadian Music Educator* 44, no. 3 (Spring 2003): 23–25. The Canadian Band Association has developed its own *National Voluntary Curriculum and Standards for Instrumental Music (Band)*, 2nd ed. (Saskatoon: Saskatchewan Band Association, 2003). This organization, however, has only a very limited membership. Perhaps inevitably, given the subject matter, this document reads more like a technical manual than a true curriculum.
48. Saul, in *The Unconscious Civilization*, complains that throughout the West "we are slipping away from . . . [the] simple principle of high-quality education. And, in doing so, we are further undermining democracy" (68). While proponents of privatization frequently cite shortages of money for cutbacks to public schools, "there is no shortage of funds for those areas of higher education which attract the corporatist elites" (68). In England, some underperforming schools are now being run by the private sector. "Britain: Caning the Teachers," in *Economist*, 23 October 1999.
49. Carr and Hartnett explain in *Education and the Struggle for Democracy* that the New Right has changed the social and political role of education in England "through a combination of managerialism, centralization, and bureaucracy." In so doing they have strengthened "the authority of the state" (180).
50. Stallings reports that educational policy making during Ronald Reagan's term of office was motivated by a "desire to return to the original intent of the Founders." See "A Brief History of the U.S. Department of Education," 679.

51. Carr and Hartnett, *Education and the Struggle for Democracy,* 180.
52. Ibid., 78.
53. Giroux, in *Disturbing Pleasures,* explains that right-wing critics such as E. D. Hirsch Jr., William Bennett, Lynne V. Cheney, and John Silbur blame critical theorists for undermining students' faith in the western educational and artistic canons (110).
54. Jay, *American Literature and the Culture Wars,* 47–48.
55. Saul, *The Unconscious Civilization,* 68.
56. I am referring here to the recently defeated "Progressive" Conservative government of Mike Harris and then Ernie Eves. Their government had downloaded certain forms of taxation to the municipalities, deregulated natural gas, attempted to sell off the provincially owned Ontario Hydro Corporation to private interests, and threatened to deregulate the distribution of electricity. Much of this was done in the belief that increased competition would result in lower costs for consumers. The private school education tax credit has since been rescinded by Dalton McGinty's Liberal government.
57. In *Education and the Struggle for Democracy,* Carr and Hartnett complain that "the most exclusive, and excluding, schools will achieve the highest scores, and this will reinforce the view that they are the 'real' schools" (176). In reality, however, and despite the claim that private and charter schools are to be held accountable by the market, few in the United States "have been closed because they failed to meet academic standards." Stein, *The Cult of Efficiency,* 165.
58. According to Carr and Hartnett, the English "National Curriculum does not apply to elite schools because they themselves both define and represent quality." By the end of the twentieth century, the elite schools in England, which had "insulated themselves from public debate and unwanted state interference, are still the ultimate model for what a school should be like. They are surrounded on their pinnacle of quality, by a sea of legal, ideological, and economic protection which puts them, literally, in another land" (*Education and the Struggle for Democracy,* 178).
59. Saul, *The Unconscious Civilization,* 69–71.
60. Stein, *The Cult of Efficiency,* 161–62. Greene, in "Imagination, Community, and the School," expresses this idea in ironic terms. "We hear constantly that we do not meet 'world-class standards' when it comes to education–a commonly used fiction vaguely understood. We are not, we are reminded, teaching in a manner required of us [in the United States] if we are to insure this nation's technological and military primacy.... And who dares deny that revised modes of assessment, increased rigor, and altered authority structures will guarantee success for us all?" (223).
61. Stacey Ash credits British Prime Minister Margaret Thatcher with initiating educational reform in the English-speaking world. "Thatcher believed standardized testing and curriculum and the ranking of schools would boost student performance.... But after almost 15 years of 'naming and shaming' underachieving schools, 53 percent of 11-year-olds still failed to meet the national standards." Thatcher also made it possible for individual schools to privatize while still receiving full government funding. Stacey Ash, "Globally, Reforms Have Been Drastic," *Toronto Star,* 26 January 2002, A4.
62. Carr and Hartnett, *Education and the Struggle for Democracy,* 177–78. Giroux, in *Disturbing Pleasures,* explains that the early rhetoric of the New Right emphasized both excellence and consumerism. Excellence was equated with mastery of

technique requiring "a return to the authoritarian classroom where transmission, standardization, and control are the defining principles" (49). This is a perversion of the American dream of social equality, and particularly so when coupled with the aggressive marketing of consumer goods and prepackaged curricula by corporate interests.

63. Giroux, *Disturbing Pleasures*, 51–52. Jay makes much the same point in *American Literature and the Culture Wars*, 47–48.

64. One example of corporate meddling in public education involves the introduction of prepackaged curricular materials and technical and media services for schools, all under corporate imprimatur and logos advertising consumer products, but ultimately intended to develop corporate and brand loyalty. Corporations such as McDonald's; Sears, Roebuck; Pepsi-Cola; Nike; and Whittle Communications are particularly singled out by Giroux for their attempts to commercialize schools. See *Disturbing Pleasures*, 50–53.

65. Stein, *The Cult of Efficiency*, 200.

66. Ibid., 204.

67. Ibid., 58. As Stein also explains, increased right to choice must be "balanced, and balanced carefully, against the consequences for those least able to bear the costs of changes in the way public goods are delivered" (225). Saul says much the same thing in *The Unconscious Civilization*. Intellectuals on both the political left and right have been guilty of conceiving individuals as self-absorbed and independent of society, rather than as having a shared role "in the maintenance of the public good" (163).

68. Barber, *Jihad vs. McWorld*, 116.

69. Ibid. Barber also calls for "sharp musicological investigations" of the effects of popular music and culture that will "play havoc with the conscious wishes and willed public policies of traditional nation-states trying to secure the common welfare or to conserve their national cultures" (111).

70. Ibid., 116. Stein expresses more or less the same idea in *The Cult of Efficiency*. The endless shaping of "wants–wants, not needs–through advertising . . . is hardly new." The difference now is the corporate world's capacity to "stoke individual wants and then customize their satisfaction" (200). Saul argues in *The Unconscious Civilization* that the challenge for those concerned about the growing dominance of corporatist interests in western society "is not choosing whether to abolish pleasure or to embrace it" but teaching children to resist mindless conformity to group norms and conventions, including consumer culture (171).

71. Referring to popular culture in general, but especially the Disney Corporation, Giroux writes in *Disturbing Pleasures* that "under the rubric of fun, entertainment, and escape, massive public spheres are being produced which appear too 'innocent' to be worthy of political analyses" (28). Giroux illustrates his claim with critical analyses of the popular Disney movies *Good Morning, Vietnam* and *Pretty Woman*. Music is said to be particularly important in the former, as its producers were eager to appeal to a generation of consumers raised on "the affective energies of high-tech rock" (35). Both movies avoid grappling with political, historical, and ethical considerations while trying to promote a racist, sexist, and/or capitalist worldview (41).

72. Ibid., 50.

73. Lewis Lapham, the controversial editor of *Harper's* magazine, thinks that Americans (and presumably also their allies in the West) have failed to understand the resentment in some parts of the world toward them. He told an interviewer, "We completely mistake why they're angry. We think they're angry because they envy and resent our shopping malls. They [Americans] think everybody else in the world wants the Lexus, and the house in East Hampton and the Armani Suit, and the introduction to Heather Locklear, or whatever success constitutes. But a lot of people in the world don't necessarily want those things. We find that unbelievable" (*Toronto Star*, 23 March 2002, A27). We could add popular music to that list.

74. Giroux, *Disturbing Pleasures*, 31–32.

75. Barber, *Jihad vs. McWorld*, 117.

76. Giroux, *Disturbing Pleasures*, 55. Barber, too, believes that left to itself television "is better at annihilating than at nurturing the critical faculties." *Jihad vs. McWorld*, 116–17.

77. Jay, *American Literature and the Culture Wars*, 34. Jay thinks that the New Right's distrust of academe stems from the belief that academics have been undermining traditional values and institutions, such as the church (31).

78. Speaking about deconstruction, Saul explains in *The Unconscious Civilization* that if people cannot transcend self-interest and the narratives to which they are subjected, then there can be no public good. Deconstruction works in the corporate world's favor by treating people as functionaries rather than as individuals with minds of their own (177). Barber, in *Jihad vs. McWorld*, explains that the re-creation and valorization of particularist and tribal identities, while perhaps only a natural reaction to the creeping globalism of the corporate world and middle-class consumer culture, actually works in concert with the latter to undermine democracy. Neither is a friend to democracy (6).

79. Stein, *The Cult of Efficiency*, 222.

80. Paul G. Woodford, "Music, Reason, Democracy, and the Construction of Gender," *Journal of Aesthetic Education* 35, no. 3 (Fall 2001): 73–86.

81. Stein, *The Cult of Efficiency*, 226 (emphasis mine).

82. Emberley, *Zero Tolerance*, 254–55. For other criticisms of the cultural Left and its perhaps overly combative attitude, see Jay, *American Literature and the Culture Wars*, 46; Holub, *Crossing Borders*, 201; and Elizabeth Sayers, "Deconstructing McClary: Narrative, Feminine Sexuality, and Feminism in Susan McClary's *Feminine Endings*," *College Music Symposium* 33/34 (1993/1994): 41–55. Sayers states that "to oppose or disagree with any of McClary's assertions runs several risks: of ignoring the 'facts,' of being less musical, or less 'in tune' than a five-year-old, of being anti-intellectual, or worst of all, being too much like a man. Thus with her language, McClary tends to discourage any dialogue with her own work (which is perhaps why a critical response has taken so long to occur)" (55).

83. Hanley, while understandably cautious with respect to involving business in public music education, refers to the Canadian Coalition for Music Education as one example of businesspeople and music educators working together in a way that is mutually beneficial while preserving the "integrity of education." Several businesses involved in the coalition contribute money and personnel to help with advocacy efforts. See Hanley, "Creating a National Vision for Arts Education in Canada." 11.

84. Stein, *The Cult of Efficiency*, 216.
85. Ibid., 214. According to neoconservative iconoclast David Frum, in *Dead Right*, American conservatives advocate minimal government in the belief that it will better foster more virtuous citizens who are "self-reliant, competent, canny, and uncomplaining" (202).
86. Jorgensen, "Justifying Music Instruction in American Public Schools," 22.
87. Jay, *American Literature and the Culture Wars*, 45.
88. Paul Bennett, letter to British Columbia premier Gordon Campbell and published in the *Canadian Association of University Teachers Bulletin* 49, no. 3 (March 2002): A2. Bennett is a national official of the University and College Lecturers' Union of the United Kingdom and chairman of the European Higher Education and Research Standing Committee of Educational International. Basing his opinions on similar legislation in the United Kingdom, Bennett predicts that Bill 28 will "set back management/faculty relations by many years." The full title of the British Columbian legislation is Bill 28: Public Education Flexibility and Choice Act.
89. "Dissenters Fight Spain's Reform Law: Mass Protests, Demonstrations, and Strikes in Wake of New Plans to Reform the Country's University System," *Canadian Association of University Teachers Bulletin* 49, no. 3 (March 2002): A3.
90. Jay explains in *American Literature and the Culture Wars* that few academics today have much access to the media or experience dealing with them. Owing to the nature of their highly specialized and esoteric training, they find themselves "incompetent when pulled into the public arena" (45).
91. Bérubé and Nelson, *Higher Education under Fire*, 25.
92. Giroux, *Disturbing Pleasures*, 166.
93. Shepherd, "Music and the Last Intellectual," 113.

5. Toward Reclaiming the Public Musical Sphere

1. For a review of literature and a discussion of the renewed interest in multiculturalism in general education and music education, read Jordan, "Multicultural Music Education in a Pluralistic Society." Richmond, in "Liberalism, Multiculturalism, and Art Education," attributes the recent rise of interest in multiculturalism to a "liberal democratic impulse" (16). According to Labuta and Smith in *Music Education: Historical Contexts and Perspectives*, the current interest in multiculturalism is an outcome of the civil rights movement in the United States (143).
2. Richmond attributes this dictum to Aristotle. See Richmond's "Liberalism, Multiculturalism, and Art Education," 18. See also Connor, *Postmodern Culture*, 243.
3. For example, Labuta and Smith, in *Music Education: Historical Contexts and Perspectives*, emphasize that music teachers ought to be careful not to dilute music from nonwestern cultures such that it loses its "essential" qualities. The implication is that music from different cultures may be essentially different (144). Barbara Reeder Lundquist, in "Music, Culture, Curriculum, and Instruction," in *The New Handbook of Research on Music Teaching and Learning*, also views multicultural music education as the "transmission" of musical culture, preferably by "culture-bearers" (629, 640). Reimer, however, questions whether it is possible to authentically understand the music of another culture and whether music teachers are "sufficiently broad-minded" to teach a multicultural curriculum. Reimer, "Viewing Music Education in the United States through Irish Eyes," 75–76.

4. See Smith, "Recent Trends and Issues in Policy Making," 24–25.

5. Integrity is defined by *Merriam-Webster's Collegiate Dictionary* as "firm adherence to a code of esp. moral or artistic values: incorruptibility, the quality or state of being complete or undivided." Knowledge of what is integral to a particular cultural practice is worth having, provided that it is recognized as only a starting point for further criticism.

6. See Estelle R. Jorgensen, "Musical Multiculturalism Revisited," *Journal of Aesthetic Education* 32, no. 2 (Summer 1998): 77–88; Smith, "Recent Trends and Issues in Policy Making"; and Rice, "Ethical Issues for Music Educators in Multicultural Societies." Jorgensen cautions music teachers against trying to include too many kinds of music in their curricula. It simply isn't possible for them to acquire sufficient knowledge to teach a wide variety of cultural music authoritatively (79).

7. Elliott, "Music as Culture," 164.

8. Keith Swanwick, in *Music, Mind, and Education* (London: Routledge, 1988), takes the view that intercultural music education should open students' minds by exposing them to different musical perspectives and cultures. Saul would probably reply that this is a soft concept of democracy in which individuals are subservient to the group and to experts. See Saul, *The Unconscious Civilization*, 34. More recently, Swanwick has acknowledged worries that teaching for multiculturalism in music education, if handled improperly, might only reinforce tribal practices and boundaries that might needlessly restrict students' freedoms. Keith Swanwick, *Teaching Music Musically* (London: Routledge, 1999).

9. Eisner argues, "What we value in education is not simply teaching children to replicate known answers or to mimic conventional forms. We seek work that displays ingenuity, complexity, and the student's personal signature. In short, we seek work that displays the student's intelligent judgment. Work of this kind requires that we also exercise judgment in appraising its value." Eisner, "Why Standards May Not Improve Our Schools," 62. Smith, referring to the MENC National Standards for Art Education, believes that this evasion of criticism in multicultural music and art education is deliberate, done in "the spirit of fairness, impartiality, and inclusiveness." Smith, "Recent Trends and Issues in Policy Making," 24.

10. Walters, "Response to Paul Lehman's 'How Can the Skills and Knowledge Called For in the National Standards Best Be Taught?'" 106.

11. Political correctness doubtless arises when people identify themselves first as members of groups and not as individual citizens. Saul complains in *The Unconscious Civilization* that in our elite, meritocratic society, individuals are rewarded for their integrative function and not for speaking out or otherwise acting as individual citizens (34). Holub, in *Crossing Borders*, argues that if those on the political left are to contribute positively to the solution of social problems, they must "drop their claim to excessive political correctness" (201).

12. Jordan, in "Multicultural Music Education," cautions against trying to raise nonwestern students' self-esteem and academic achievement by replacing a traditional curriculum with an ethnocentric one. This could be very limiting to those students who would consequently be ill-prepared to participate in the wider cultural world (742). Grant, in *Fundamental Feminism*, makes much the same caveat and argument with respect to university women's studies programs.

13. Lucy Green, "Music, Gender, and Education: A Report on Some Exploratory Research," *British Journal of Music Education* 10, no. 3 (November 1993): 219–53. See also her book *Music, Gender, Education* (Cambridge: Cambridge University Press, 1997). For a review and critique of feminist literature on the problem of authentic female identity, see Woodford, "Music, Reason, Democracy, and the Construction of Gender."

14. Patricia Shehan Campbell, *Lessons from the World: A Cross-Cultural Guide to Music Teaching and Learning* (New York: Schirmer Books, 1991), 124. This specific quotation is made with reference to Japan. A similar description of traditional music learning in Northern India is provided later in the book (127).

15. Saul, *The Unconscious Civilization*, 169.

16. Reimer, "Viewing Music Education in the United States through Irish Eyes," 75–76; Jorgensen, "Musical Multiculturalism Revisited"; Regelski, "Critical Education, Culturalism, and Multiculturalism." Regelski agrees that music teachers are cultural mediators, but he cautions them not to let ethnocentric assumptions go unchallenged (142).

17. In *Music Education: Historical Contexts and Perspectives,* Labuta and Smith state, "People who understand how another culture 'knows' music will also understand how that culture 'knows' most things" (145). In "Music as Culture," Elliott argues that performance is key to musical understanding. By performing music, one lives the culture's beliefs about what counts as music while exploring the relationship between self and other (158). It is not enough just to learn musical styles, however; "one must perceive in full awareness of the socially and historically predetermined concepts and expectations that mediate such perception" (159). I personally doubt, though, that it is possible or practical for students or others to "live" a culture other than their own, except in a very limited and shallow way. I'm not even sure that most people within their own culture have the depth of local knowledge that Elliott thinks is so important to musical understanding.

18. For more about music education reform, including the role and nature of multicultural music education, see Regelski, "Critical Education, Culturalism, and Multiculturalism"; Elliott, "Music as Culture"; Lee Bartel, "Cultural Equity in Music Education," *Recorder* 37, no. 2 (March/April 1995): 51–54; Bennett Reimer, "Can We Understand Music of Foreign Cultures?" in *Musical Connections: Traditions and Change,* ed. Heath Lees (Auckland: International Society for Music Education, 1994), 227–45; Elliott, *Music Matters;* Bowman, *Philosophical Perspectives;* Swanwick, *Teaching Music Musically;* and Ellen Koskoff, "What Do We Want to Teach When We Teach Music? One Apology, Two Short Trips, Three Ethical Dilemmas, and Eighty-two Questions," in *Rethinking Music,* ed. Nicholas Cook and Mark Everist (New York: Oxford University Press, 1999).

19. Michael Mark, "A History of Music Education Research," 50. Music teachers are, of course, not alone in ignoring or even disdaining professional and other literature.

20. Richmond, "Liberalism, Multiculturalism, and Art Education," 22. Richmond also argues that teachers need to be careful not to "engender a passive or accepting attitude in students in response to anything nonwestern" (21). Students should also be reminded that others have similar rights to their own music. "My freedom is your freedom and vice versa. Living together in mutual understanding, learning to appreciate the contribution of cultures besides one's own, being willing to

restrain certain cultural ambitions out of concern for the well-being of the community as a whole, as well as having opportunities to identify with and express one's own culture, is what defines the multicultural promise in a democracy" (20).

21. For example, in "Examining the Political Projects of Four Pedagogies: Progressive, Humanistic, Critical, and Feminist," *Dialogue in Instrumental Music Education* 21, no. 2 (Fall 1997): 126–41, Patricia O'Toole contends, "Patriarchal society is so entrenched in its legal, political, social, and cultural institutions that it cannot be reformed—it must be destroyed for women to become emancipated" (135).

22. Lipman, *Arguing for Music*, 429. See also Bloom's *The Closing of the American Mind.*

23. Saul, *The Unconscious Civilization*, 125.

24. Wayne Bowman, for example, once told me that he considers democracy to be an empty concept devoid of meaning in contemporary society. His reasoning is that it has been defined so many ways that it has for all practical purposes lost any meaning it once had. Conversation with the author 12 June 1998, Dallas, at a meeting of the MayDay Group of music education critics.

25. Rorty, "Solidarity or Objectivity?" 583.

26. Ibid., 575.

27. Barber argues that the ideology of laissez-faire has become the mantra of proponents of globalization seeking to undermine the public good. Barber, *Jihad vs. McWorld*, 276.

28. For a discussion of the growth of intolerance and political correctness in universities and of the abandonment of the public trust and "the idea of a just society," see Emberley, *Zero Tolerance*, 23. Beane, in "Reclaiming a Democratic Purpose for Education," similarly recounts the declining interest in the democratic purpose of public schooling (9).

29. See Labuta and Smith, *Music Education: Historical Contexts and Perspectives,* for a brief mention of the possible damage to hard won civil rights that can result from the move to establish charter and private schools. Even some conservatives have begun to express doubts about encouraging private and charter schools at the expense of public ones (143).

30. See Lee Willingham and Lee Bartel, "'Music Makes You Smarter'—Is There Any Evidence?" *Canadian Music Educator* 43, no. 2 (Winter 2001): 11–12. Music teachers are not alone in their mechanistic view of education as the development of cognitive skills. Emberley, in *Zero Tolerance*, complains that universities all too often imagine "the student as a machine capable of being made clever with knowledge and skills" (24). In *The Unconscious Civilization*, Saul observes that schools often treat children as "inferior" machines (143). For one mechanistic view of cognitive processing in music, see Brophy, *Assessing the Developing Child Musician*. Brophy defines critical thinking in music as "the ability to *consciously apply* cognitive processing to musical experiences." Brophy acknowledges that this involves self-awareness and personal growth, but there is no explicit acknowledgment of the political nature and purpose of musical critical thinking. Musical critical thinking remains socially abstract and value-neutral (234).

31. Liora Bresler, "Research: A Foundation for Arts Education Advocacy," in *The New Handbook of Research on Music Teaching and Learning*, 1072.

32. Constance Bumgarner Gee, "The 'Use and Abuse' of Arts Advocacy and Its Consequences for Music Education," in *The New Handbook of Research on Music Teaching and Learning*, 955.

33. For a discussion on this point, see Claire Detels, "Hard Boundaries and the Marginalization of the Arts in American Education," *Philosophy of Music Education Review* 7, no. 1 (Spring 1990): 19–30.

34. Milan Kundera, *The Unbearable Lightness of Being,* trans. Michael Henry Heim (New York: Harper Colophon Books, 1985), 93. As reported by the Associated Press, labor unions in Austria similarly charge that the practice of incessantly piping Christmas carols into stores is a form of "psychological terrorism" that renders store workers resentful and aggressive. See "A Blue Christmas for Austria," *London Free Press,* 6 December 2003.

35. Schafer, *Voices of Tyranny,* 152.

36. This was the Second International Research in Music Education Conference, 3–7 April 2001, at the School of Education, University of Exeter.

37. Shinichi Suzuki, *Nurtured by Love: A New Approach to Education,* trans. Waltraud Suzuki (New York: Exposition Press, 1969), 8.

38. As Schafer pointedly observes, "This argument collapsed when Beethoven was adopted by the Nazis—who were not gentlemen." R. Murray Schafer, *The Rhinoceros in the Classroom* (London: Universal, 1975), 19.

39. Frederic Spotts, *Hitler and the Power of Aesthetics* (Woodstock, N.Y.: Overlook Press, 2003). See also Christopher Norris, *Contest of Faculties: Philosophy and Theory after Deconstruction* (London: Methuen, 1985), 138.

40. Jay, *American Literature and the Culture Wars,* 50.

41. Ibid., 48–49.

42. Menand, "Re-imagining Liberal Education," 17–18.

43. Judith A. Jellison, "How Can All People Continue to Be Involved in Meaningful Music Participation?" in *Vision 2020,* 118.

44. Leo Buscaglia, *Love* (New York: Fawcett Crest, 1972). I once overheard a prominent member of the cultural Left in music education disparage a colleague for including some of Buscaglia's publications in her course materials. The issue, as I seem to recall, was not about the validity of Buscaglia's ideas but, rather, the fact that he was not sufficiently scholarly. This, to me, just reinforces ironic criticisms about the elite status of members of the cultural Left.

6. Music Education as an Occasion for Intelligence

1. Ernst Cassirer expresses this idea thusly: "Man cannot find himself, he cannot become aware of his individuality, save through the medium of social life. But to him this medium signifies more than an external determining force. Man, like the animals, submits to the rules of society but, in addition, he has an active share in bringing about, and an active power to change, the forms of social life." Ernst Cassirer, *An Essay on Man* (New Haven, Conn.: Yale University Press, 1944), 223.

2. Beane, "Reclaiming a Democratic Purpose for Education," 10–11. Beane asserts that the moral challenge for "citizen educators" is to develop curricula fostering democratic values and ends.

3. Kundera's character Franz, in *The Unbearable Lightness of Being,* asks, "Who can help getting drunk on Beethoven's Ninth, Bartok's 'Sonata for Two Pianos and Percussion,' or the Beatles' *White Album?*" Franz yearned for "unbounded music, absolute sound, a pleasant and happy, all encompassing, overpowering, window

rattling din to engulf, once and for all, the pain, the futility, the vanity of words" (93–94).

4. Martha C. Nussbaum, *Upheavals of Thought: The Intelligence of Emotions* (Cambridge: Cambridge University Press, 2001), 269. Nussbaum attributes to Schopenhauer this idea that music can reveal or express aspects of personality normally operating "beneath its conscious self-understanding."

5. Warrick L. Carter, former director of Disney Entertainment Arts for Walt Disney Entertainment in Lake Buena Vista, Florida, acknowledges that people are bombarded in our society with music (142). He doesn't think that merely "hearing" music is necessarily bad, as probably everyone uses music as background for doing other things. Warrick L. Carter, "Response to Judith A. Jellison's 'How Can All People Continue to Be Involved in Meaningful Music Participation?'" in *Vision 2020,* 139–52.

6. Richard Bonnycastle, in *In Search of Authority: An Introductory Guide to Literary Theory* (Peterborough, Ont.: Broadview Press, 1991), explains how children whose parents "listen with love" can gain a sense of personal authority, whereas those whose "parents cannot or will not listen" may lack personal confidence and authority (183).

7. John Dewey, *Liberalism and Social Action* (New York: Minton, Balch, 1935), in Dewey, *Intelligence in the Modern World,* 452–53. See also Mursell, *Music Education: Principles and Programs,* 121.

8. Gutmann, paraphrased by Jay in *American Literature and the Culture Wars,* 48.

9. Rorty, "Solidarity or Objectivity?" 575. One of the ways in which I personally attempted to bridge disciplinary boundaries was by hosting an interdisciplinary conference on Music and Lifelong Learning at the University of Western Ontario, 8–10 May 2003. Among the fields or disciplines represented were musicology, music performance, music education, music therapy, occupational therapy, dance, medicine, education, continuing education, sociology, cultural studies, and business.

10. Mursell, *Music Education: Principles and Programs,* 121.

11. Maxine Greene, in "Imagination, Community, and the School," singles out John Cage as an example of an individual who enabled "us to hear sounds somehow silenced by the habitual, excluded by what we ordinarily name as music, offering us a metaphor for what it can mean to open up a world" (225). Cage, however, with his self-declared "open war on the idea of music," was not necessarily as open-minded as Greene thinks. For a brief discussion of Cage's ideas, see Glenn Watkins, *Soundings: Music in the Twentieth Century* (New York: Schirmer Books, 1988), 656–57. The Canadian composer and educator R. Murray Schafer also challenged music teachers and others to rethink their own limited understandings. He was known, however, for his acerbity.

12. There is a wealth of published material about the politics of popular music. I particularly recommend Robin Denselow's book *When the Music's Over: The Story of Political Pop* (London: Faber, 1989). Note especially the Rock Against Racism movement of the 1970s (140–55). More recently, some hip-hop artists in the United States have formed a coalition with social activists and business leaders to promote social change. The nonprofit organization is known as the Hip-Hop Summit Action Network. With respect to classical music, music teachers tend to forget that classical musicians and composers including Mozart, Beethoven, and

Wagner were political beings in their own time. This is unfortunate because it contributes to the misconception that classical music is divorced from politics.

13. Lee Willingham and Lee Bartel, "Proposals for Change to the Face of Music Education," *Canadian Music Educator* 43, no. 4 (Summer 2002): 2

14. Dewey, *How We Think*, in *John Dewey: The Later Works, 1925–1953*, 8:343.

15. Mary Field Belenky, Blythe McViker Clinchy, Nancy Rule Goldberger, and Jill Mattuck Tarule, *Women's Ways of Knowing: The Development of Self, Voice, and Mind* (New York: Basic Books, 1986), 4.

16. Ibid., 34.

17. William Perry, *Forms of Intellectual and Ethical Development in the College Years* (New York: Holt, Rinehart and Winston, 1968); see also Manny Brand, "Toward a Better Understanding of Undergraduate Music Education Majors: Perry's Perspective," *Bulletin of the Council for Research in Music Education* 98 (Fall 1988): 22–31.

18. Belenky et al., *Women's Ways of Knowing*, 134.

19. Brand, "Toward a Better Understanding," 25.

20. Belenky et al., *Women's Ways of Knowing*, 87.

21. Howard Gardner says something very similar in *Leading Minds: An Anatomy of Leadership* (New York: Basic Books, 1995). Whereas less mature people tend to think along the lines of Perry's first three stages of ethical development, the "seasoned adult" is able to distance himself somewhat from the group and its beliefs. This individual is also able to appreciate that he "might well have belonged to a different set of groups, and thence entertained a quite different philosophy of life. But rather than defending each set of groups as equally viable (as the relativistically oriented counterpart is wont to do), such an adult at least attempts to justify the particular ensemble of group memberships to which he is fated to belong" (54).

22. Tanner, "Dewey's Model of Inquiry," 471–75. For a critique of how the western concept of reason, which is implicated in critical thinking, has been bastardized by self-serving and elite technocrats, see Saul's book *Voltaire's Bastards*.

23. Stein, *The Cult of Efficiency*, 221–22.

24. Saul, *The Unconscious Civilization*, 195. See also Dewey's classic book, *The Quest for Certainty*.

25. Westbrook, *John Dewey and American Democracy*, 369.

26. Schafer, *The Rhinoceros in the Classroom*, 2.

27. Saul, *The Unconscious Civilization*, 39. Buscaglia, in *Love*, states that the opposite of love is not hate but apathy (43). Education philosopher Israel Scheffler contends that "positive thinking is highly overrated" because it renders us "forever captives of the past." See his book *In Praise of the Cognitive Emotions* (New York: Routledge, 1991). Criticism of the sort employed throughout this book is essential not just to understanding but to envisioning new possibilities while leaving "pious pedantries behind" (130). I wish to thank Estelle R. Jorgensen for bringing this book to my attention.

28. Since the 1980s, Christian fundamentalists aligned with the neoconservative movement have lobbied hard to keep secular humanist ideas out of public schools. Tanner cites this as contributing to the lack of emphasis on Deweyan-based critical thinking in American school curricula. Tanner, "Dewey's Model of Inquiry," 477.

29. Dewey, "Democracy and Educational Administration," 402.

30. Westbrook, *John Dewey and American Democracy*, 111.
31. Ibid., 109.
32. Ibid., 109–10.
33. The Progressive Education Movement, too, ultimately "failed the larger public" and for many of the same reasons. O'Toole, "Examining the Political Projects of Four Pedagogies," 128. This movement, however, was not as indebted to Dewey's ideas as many people believe. Dewey distanced himself from many "self-styled progressive innovations" while complaining that his ideas were "only partially understood and implemented." Ellen Condliffe Lagemann, "From Discipline-Based to Problem-Centered Learning," in *Education and Democracy*, 24, 28.
34. I am indebted for both of these points to my colleague Carol Beynon at the University of Western Ontario. Reporting on a study of community choirs in Canada, Beynon pointedly observes, "Those who promote lifelong musical involvement are actually providing an advantage for the advantaged and doing little for mainstream Canadian society." Beynon, "Singing and Lifelong Learning: Privileging the Privileged," paper presented at the Music and Lifelong Learning Conference, 8–10 May 2003, University of Western Ontario, London.
35. Lucy Green, *How Popular Musicians Learn: A Way Ahead for Music Education* (Aldershot: Ashgate, 2001), 186.
36. Katherine Smithrim and Rena Upitis, in "Contaminated by Peaceful Feelings: The Power of Music," *Canadian Music Educator* 44, no. 3 (Spring 2003): 12–17, refer to a folk guitarist they know who regularly leads community singing in a small school. This kind of activity in which the entire school participates and in which everyone learns to love singing is described as "music education of the highest order" (16). Conservative, standardized curricula can have the opposite effect. They can intimidate classrooms teachers, constrain specialists, and thus limit children's learning.
37. For more about this folk song and how it has been altered over time, see Paul Woodford, "Is Kodály Obsolete?" *Alla Breve* 24, nos. 1/2 (June 2000): 10–18.
38. Rice, "Ethical Issues for Music Educators in Multicultural Societies," 8.
39. Jackson, introduction to 1990 edition of *School and Society*, xxv.
40. I know of only one attempt thus far to investigate whether teaching for democratic citizenship in music classes can actually work, contributing to the improvement of music education and thus also to the life of the school and community. Prompted by a decision by government to make the teaching of democratic citizenship a compulsory part of the English National Curriculum for students ages 11–16, researchers at the University of Cambridge undertook an eight-week case study of about sixty children ages 11 and 12 in which course content about the life and music of composer John Cage was coupled with lessons in democratic citizenship. The researchers' stated aim was to promote the children's musical learning while also inculcating in them a disposition to democracy. The scheme of work for the children was organized along democratic lines and involved them participating regardless of ability in the roles of composer, conductor, performer, audience member, and critic. Throughout the study, children were encouraged to discuss, reflect upon, justify, and amend their respective values and classroom behaviors while attempting to reach consensus on matters such as what counts as music and criteria for success in tasks. The teacher's views were also "equally open to question," and students were repeatedly reminded to reflect on issues of power

and control with respect to decision making. Further, specific citizenship values identified in curricular documents were explicitly acknowledged and taught. Based on their own observation, the researchers concluded that their efforts were successful. However, the results were presented only anecdotally and in the form of teacher testimony, making it difficult to tell in what ways and to what extent the researchers were successful in accomplishing their goals. For that reason, and while an interesting and potentially valuable piece of research, it is best considered only a pilot study. More in-depth studies are obviously needed, utilizing more rigorous qualitative assessment strategies and techniques. See John Finney and Jo Plumb, "Practising Democracy in a Cambridgeshire Village College," paper presented at the Research in Music Education Conference, School of Education and Lifelong Learning, University of Exeter, April 2001.

BIBLIOGRAPHY

Alexander, Lamar. "A Horse Trade for K–12 Education." *Phi Delta Kappan* 83, no. 9 (May 2002): 698–99.

Apple, Michael. *Education and Power*. Boston: Routledge, 1982.

Argyros, Alexander J. *A Blessed Rage for Order: Deconstruction, Evolution, and Chaos*. Ann Arbor: University of Michigan Press, 1991.

Ash, Stacey. "Globally, Reforms Have Been Drastic." *Toronto Star*, 26 January 2002, A4.

Attali, Jacques. *Noise: The Political Economy of Music*. Translated by Brian Massumi. Minneapolis: University of Minnesota Press, 1985.

Barber, Benjamin R. *Jihad vs. McWorld: How Globalism and Tribalism Are Reshaping the World*. New York: Ballantine Books, 1996.

Barnes, Stephen H. *Muzak: The Hidden Messages in Music*. Lewiston, N.Y.: Edwin Mellen Press, 1988.

Barry, Andrew, Thomas Osborne, and Nikolas Rose, eds. *Foucault and Political Reason: Liberalism, Neo-Liberalism, and Rationalities of Government*. Chicago: University of Chicago Press, 1996.

Bartel, Lee. "Cultural Equity in Music Education." *Recorder* 37, no. 2 (March/April 1995): 51–54.

Barwell, Ismay. "Towards a Defense of Objectivity." In *Knowing the Difference: Feminist Perspectives in Epistemology*, ed. Kathleen Lennon and Margaret Whitford. London: Routledge, 1994.

Beane, James A. "Reclaiming a Democratic Purpose for Education." *Educational Leadership* 56, no. 2 (October 1998): 8–11.

Beane, James A., and Michael W. Apple, eds. "The Case for Democratic Schools." In *Democratic Schools*. Alexandria, Va.: Association for Supervision and Curriculum Development, 1995.

Belenky, Mary Field, Blythe McViker Clinchy, Nancy Rule Goldberger, and Jill Mattuck Tarule. *Women's Ways of Knowing: The Development of Self, Voice, and Mind*. New York: Basic Books, 1986.

Bennett, Paul. Letter to British Columbia premier Gordon Campbell. *Canadian Association of University Teachers Bulletin* 49, no. 3 (March 2002): A2.

Bennett, William. *Reclaiming a Legacy*. Washington, D.C.: National Endowment for the Humanities, 1984.

Bernstein, Richard J. *Beyond Objectivism and Relativism: Science, Hermeneutics, and Praxis*. Philadelphia: University of Pennsylvania Press, 1988.

Bérubé, Michael, and Cary Nelson, eds. *Higher Education under Fire: Politics, Economics, and the Crisis of the Humanities*. New York: Routledge, 1995.

Beynon, Carol A. "From Music Student to Music Teacher: Negotiating an Identity." In *Critical Thinking in Music: Theory and Practice*, ed. Paul Woodford. *Studies in Music from the University of Western Ontario* 17 (1998): 83–105.

———. "Singing and Lifelong Learning: Privileging the Privileged." Paper presented at the Music and Lifelong Learning Conference, 8–10 May 2003, University of Western Ontario, London.

Birge, Edward Bailey. *History of Public School Music in the United States.* 1928; reprint, Washington, D.C.: Music Educators National Conference, 1966.

Bloom, Allan. *The Closing of the American Mind: How Higher Education Has Failed Democracy and Impoverished the Souls of Today's Students.* New York: Simon and Schuster, 1987.

Bonnycastle, Richard. *In Search of Authority: An Introductory Guide to Literary Theory.* Peterborough, Ont.: Broadview Press, 1991.

Botstein, Leon. "The Training of Musicians." *Musical Quarterly* 84, no. 3 (Fall 2000): 327–32.

Bowman, Wayne D. "Sound, Sociality, and Music." *Quarterly Journal of Music Teaching and Learning* 5, no. 3 (Fall 1994): 50–67.

———. *Philosophical Perspectives on Music.* New York: Oxford University Press, 1998.

———. "Universals, Relativism, and Music Education." *Bulletin of the Council for Research in Music Education* 135 (Winter 1998): 1–20.

———. "Music as Ethical Encounter." *Bulletin of the Council for Research in Music Education* 151 (Winter 2001): 11–20.

———. "Educating Musically." In *The New Handbook of Research on Music Teaching and Learning,* ed. Richard Colwell and Carol P. Richardson. New York: Oxford University Press, 2002.

Brand, Manny. "Toward a Better Understanding of Undergraduate Music Education Majors: Perry's Perspective." *Bulletin of the Council for Research in Music Education* 98 (Fall 1988): 22–31.

Bresler, Liora. "Research: A Foundation for Arts Education Advocacy." In *The New Handbook of Research on Music Teaching and Learning,* ed. Richard Colwell and Carol P. Richardson. New York: Oxford University Press, 2002.

"Britain: Caning the Teachers." *Economist,* 23 October 1999.

Britton, Allen P. "Music Education: An American Specialty." In *Perspectives in Music: Source Book III,* ed. Bonnie C. Kowall. Washington, D.C.: Music Educators National Conference, 1966.

Britzman, Deborah P. *Practice Makes Practice.* Albany: State University of New York Press, 1991.

Brophy, Timothy S. *Assessing the Developing Child Musician: A Guide for General Music Teachers.* Chicago: GIA Publications, 2000.

Bruner, Jerome. *On Knowing: Essays for the Left Hand.* New York: Atheneum, 1970.

Buscaglia, Leo. *Love.* New York: Fawcett Crest, 1972.

Cahoone, Lawrence E. *The Dilemma of Modernity: Philosophy, Culture, and Anti-Culture.* Albany: State University of New York Press, 1988.

Campbell, Patricia Shehan. *Lessons from the World: A Cross-Cultural Guide to Music Teaching and Learning.* New York: Schirmer Books, 1991.

Canadian Band Association. *National Voluntary Curriculum and Standards for Instrumental Music (Band).* 2nd ed. Saskatoon: Saskatchewan Band Association, 2003.

Carr, Wilfred, and Anthony Hartnett. *Education and the Struggle for Democracy: The Politics of Educational Ideas.* Buckingham: Open University Press, 1996.

Carter, Warrick L. "Response to Judith A. Jellison's 'How Can All People Continue to Be Involved in Meaningful Music Participation?'" In *Vision 2020: The Housewright Symposium on the Future of Music Education,* ed. Clifford K. Madsen. Reston, Va.: Music Educators National Conference, 2000.

Casement, William. "Unity, Diversity, and Leftist Support for the Canon." *Journal of Aesthetic Education* 27, no. 3 (Fall 1993): 35–49.

Cassirer, Ernst. *An Essay on Man.* New Haven, Conn.: Yale University Press, 1944.

Choksy, Lois. *The Kodály Method II: Folksong to Masterwork.* Upper Saddle River, N.J.: Prentice Hall, 1999.

Chomsky, Noam. *American Power and the New Mandarins.* New York: Pantheon Books, 1967.

———. *Equality and Social Policy.* Urbana: University of Illinois Press, 1978.

———. "Equality: Language, Development, Human Intelligence, and Social Organization." In *The Chomsky Reader,* ed. James Peck. New York: Pantheon Books, 1987.

———. "The Responsibility of Intellectuals." In *The Chomsky Reader,* ed. James Peck. New York: Pantheon Books, 1987.

Cloonan, Martin, and Bruce Johnson. "Killing Me Softly with His Song: An Initial Investigation into the Use of Popular Music as a Tool of Oppression." *Popular Music* 21, no. 1 (January 2002): 27–39.

Cole, Hugo. *The Changing Face of Music.* London: Victor Gollancz, 1978.

Connor, Steven. *Postmodern Culture: An Introduction to Theories of the Contemporary.* Oxford: Basil Blackwell, 1989.

Critchley, Simon. "Derrida: Private Ironist or Public Liberal." In *Deconstruction and Pragmatism,* ed. Chantal Mouffe. London: Routledge, 1996.

Cusic, Don. *Music in the Market.* Bowling Green, Ohio: Bowling Green State University Popular Press, 1996.

Davis, Hilary E. "The Temptations and Limitations of a Feminist Deaesthetic." *Journal of Aesthetic Education* 27, no. 1 (Spring 1993): 99–105.

DeNora, Tia. *Music in Everyday Life.* Cambridge: Cambridge University Press, 2000.

Denselow, Robin. *When the Music's Over: The Story of Political Pop.* London: Faber, 1989.

Detels, Claire. "Hard Boundaries and the Marginalization of the Arts in American Education." *Philosophy of Music Education Review* 7, no. 1 (Spring 1999): 19–30.

———. "Towards a Redefinition of the Role of the Arts in Education: Extrapolations from Ernest Gellner's *Plough, Sword, and Book.*" Paper presented at the Philosophy of Music Education Symposium, Birmingham, UK, 7–10 June 2000.

Dewey, John. *Psychology.* 1887. In *John Dewey: The Early Works, 1882–1898,* vol. 2. Carbondale: Southern Illinois University Press, 1975.

———. "Ethics of Democracy." 1888. In *John Dewey: The Early Works, 1882–1898,* vol. 1. Carbondale: Southern Illinois University Press, 1967–72.

———. "My Pedagogic Creed." *School Journal* 54, no. 3 (January 1897): 77–80.

———. *The School and Society.* 1900. Reprint and expanded edition with a new introduction by Philip W. Jackson. Chicago: University of Chicago Press, 1990.

———. *How We Think.* 1910. In *John Dewey: The Middle Works, 1899–1924,* vol. 6. Carbondale: Southern Illinois University Press, 1976–83.

———. "Learning and Doing." In *Interest and Effort in Education,* 65–84. Boston: Houghton Mifflin, 1913. Reprinted in *Intelligence in the Modern World: John Dewey's Philosophy,* ed. Joseph Ratner, 607–14. New York: Modern Library, 1939.

———. *Essays in Experimental Logic.* Chicago: University of Chicago Press, 1917.

———. "Need for a Recovery of Philosophy." 1917. In *John Dewey: The Middle Works, 1899–1924,* vol. 10. Carbondale: Southern Illinois University Press, 1976–83.

———. *Democracy and Education: An Introduction to the Philosophy of Education.* New York: Macmillan, 1921, 1933.

————. *The Public and Its Problems*. New York: Henry Holt, 1927. Reprinted in *Intelligence in the Modern World: John Dewey's Philosophy*, ed. Joseph Ratner. New York: Modern Library, 1939.

————. *The Quest for Certainty: A Study of the Relation of Knowledge and Action*. New York: Minton, Balch, 1929.

————. "America's Responsibility." In Vol. 2 of *Characters and Events*, ed. Joseph Ratner. New York: Henry Holt, 1929. Reprinted in *Intelligence in the Modern World: John Dewey's Philosophy*, ed. Joseph Ratner, 503–508. New York: Modern Library, 1939.

————. *Philosophy and Civilization*. New York: Minton, Balch, 1931.

————. *Ethics*. 1932. In *John Dewey: The Later Works, 1925–1953*, ed. Jo Ann Boydston. Carbondale: Southern Illinois University Press, 1981–91.

————. *How We Think*. 1933. In *John Dewey: The Later Works, 1925–1953*, vol. 8, ed. Jo Ann Boydston. Carbondale: Southern Illinois University Press, 1989.

————. *A Common Faith*. New Haven, Conn.: Yale University Press, 1934.

————. *Art as Experience*. 1934; reprint, New York: Perigee Books, 1980.

————. *Liberalism and Social Action*. New York: Minton, Balch, 1935. Reprinted in *Intelligence in the Modern World: John Dewey's Philosophy*, ed. Joseph Ratner, 449–55. New York: Modern Library, 1939.

————. "Educators and the Class Struggle." *Social Frontier*, May 1936. Reprinted in *Intelligence in the Modern World: John Dewey's Philosophy*, ed. Joseph Ratner, 696–702. New York: Modern Library, 1939.

————. "Democracy and Educational Administration" (an address made to the National Education Association, 22 February 1937). In *Intelligence in the Modern World: John Dewey's Philosophy*, ed. Joseph Ratner, 400–404. New York: Modern Library, 1939.

————. *Logic: The Theory of Inquiry*. London: George Allen and Unwin, 1938.

————. *Intelligence in the Modern World: John Dewey's Philosophy*, ed. Joseph Ratner. New York: Modern Library, 1939.

————. "The Economic Basis of the New Society." In *Intelligence in the Modern World: John Dewey's Philosophy*, ed. Joseph Ratner, 416–33. New York: Modern Library, 1939.

————. *Reconstruction in Philosophy*. 3rd ed. New York: Mentor Books, 1950.

————. "What Is Freedom?" In *John Dewey on Education: Selected Writings*, ed. Reginald D. Archambault. New York: Random House, 1964.

————. *Experience and Education*. London: Collier Books, 1969.

Dewey, John, and James H. Tufts. *Ethics*. Rev. ed. New York: Henry Holt, 1932. Reprinted in *Intelligence in the Modern World: John Dewey's Philosophy*, ed. Joseph Ratner, 761–78. New York: Modern Library, 1939.

"Dissenters Fight Spain's Reform Law: Mass Protests, Demonstrations, and Strikes in Wake of New Plans to Reform the Country's University System." *Canadian Association of University Teachers Bulletin* 49, no. 3 (March 2002): A3.

Dorter, Kenneth. "Multiculturalism and Cultural Diversity in Music." *Proceedings for Music and Cross-Cultural Understanding Colloquium*. Twenty-fifth Annual Richard R. Baker Philosophy Colloquium, cosponsored by the Departments of Philosophy and Music, University of Dayton, Ohio, 25–27 September 1997.

Drafall, L. "The Use of Developmental Clinical Supervision with Student Teachers in Secondary Choral Music: Two Case Studies." Ph.D. diss., University of Illinois at Urbana-Champaign, 1991.

Edwards, Malcim V. "Music Education as a Conserving Activity." *Canadian Music Educator* 43, no. 4 (Summer 2002): 14–17.

Eisner, Elliott. "The Celebration of Thinking." *Educational Horizons* 66, no. 1 (Fall 1987): 24–29.

———. "Why Standards May Not Improve Our Schools. "*Recorder* 38, no. 2 (Winter 1996): 62–64.

Elliott, David J. "Music as Culture: Toward a Multicultural Concept of Arts Education." *Journal of Aesthetic Education* 24, no. 1 (Spring 1990): 147–66.

———. "Music as Knowledge." *Journal of Aesthetic Education* 25, no. 3 (Fall 1991): 21–40.

———. "Rethinking Music Teacher Education." *Journal of Music Teacher Education* 2, no. 1 (Fall 1992): 6–15.

———. "On the Values of Music and Music Education." *Philosophy of Music Education Review* 1 (Fall 1993): 81–93.

———. *Music Matters: A New Philosophy of Music Education.* New York: Oxford University Press, 1995.

Ellsworth, Elizabeth. "Why Doesn't This Feel Empowering? Working through the Repressive Myths of Critical Pedagogy." *Harvard Educational Review* 59, no. 3 (August 1989): 297–324.

Elshtain, Jean Bethke. *Democracy on Trial.* Concord, Ont.: House of Anansi Press, 1993.

Emberley, Peter C. *Zero Tolerance: Hot Button Politics in Canada's Universities.* Toronto: Penguin Books, 1996.

Finney, John, and Jo Plumb. "Practising Democracy in a Cambridgeshire Village College." Paper presented at the Research in Music Education Conference, School of Education and Lifelong Learning, University of Exeter, April 2001.

Fiske, Harold. Review of *Music Matters: A New Philosophy of Music Education,* by David J. Elliott. *Notes: Quarterly Journal of the Music Library Association* 53, no. 3 (March 1997): 770–73.

Freeman, Samuel, ed. *The Cambridge Companion to Rawls.* Cambridge: Cambridge University Press, 2003.

Freire, Paulo. *Cultural Action for Freedom.* Cambridge, Mass.: Harvard Educational Review and Center for the Study of Development and Social Change, 1974.

Frith, Simon. *Performing Rites: On the Value of Popular Music.* Cambridge, Mass.: Harvard University Press, 1996.

Frum, David. *Dead Right.* New York: Basic Books, 1994.

Gadamer, Hans Georg. *Philosophical Hermeneutics.* Translated and edited by David E. Linge. Berkeley: University of California Press, 1976.

Gardner, Howard. *The Unschooled Mind: How Children Think and How Schools Should Teach.* New York: Basic Books, 1991.

———. *Leading Minds: An Anatomy of Leadership.* New York: Basic Books, 1995.

Gee, Constance Bumgarner. "The 'Use and Abuse' of Arts Advocacy and Its Consequences for Music Education." In *The New Handbook of Research on Music Teaching and Learning,* ed. Richard Colwell and Carol P. Richardson. New York: Oxford University Press, 2002.

Gilligan, Carol. *In a Different Voice: Psychological Theory and Women's Development.* Cambridge, Mass.: Harvard University Press, 1982.

Giroux, Henry A. *Disturbing Pleasures: Learning Popular Culture.* New York: Routledge, 1994.

Goodrich, R. A. "Kivy on Justifying Music in Liberal Education." *Journal of Aesthetic Education* 36, no. 1 (Spring 2002): 50–59.

Grant, Judith. *Fundamental Feminism: Contesting the Core Concepts of Feminist Theory.* New York: Routledge, 1993.

Green, Lucy. "Music, Gender, and Education: A Report on Some Exploratory Research." *British Journal of Music Education* 10, no. 3 (November 1993): 219–53.

———. *Music, Gender, Education.* Cambridge: Cambridge University Press, 1997.

———. *How Popular Musicians Learn: A Way Ahead for Music Education.* Aldershot: Ashgate, 2001.

———. "From the Western Classics to the World: Secondary Music Teachers' Changing Attitudes in England, 1982 and 1998." *British Journal of Music Education* 19, no. 1 (March 2002): 5–30.

Greene, Maxine. "Imagination, Community, and the School." *Review of Education* 15 (1993): 223–31.

Gutmann, Amy. Introduction to *Multiculturalism and "The Politics of Recognition,"* by Charles Taylor. Princeton, N.J.: Princeton University Press, 1992.

Hanley, Betty. "Creating a National Vision for Arts Education in Canada: Pipe-Dream or Possibility?" *Canadian Music Educator* 40, no. 1 (Fall 1998): 9–13.

Hanley, Betty, and Janet Montgomery. "Contemporary Curriculum Practices and Their Theoretical Bases." In *The New Handbook of Research on Music Teaching and Learning,* ed. Richard Colwell and Carol P. Richardson. New York: Oxford University Press, 2002.

Harris, Wendell V., ed. *Beyond Poststructuralism: The Speculations of Theory and the Experience of Reading.* University Park: Pennsylvania State University Press, 1996.

Hennessey, Sarah. "Overcoming the Red-Feeling: The Development of Confidence to Teach Music in Primary School amongst Student Teachers." *British Journal of Music Education* 17, no. 2 (2002): 183–96.

Hirsch, E. D., Jr. *Cultural Literacy: What Every American Needs to Know,* with an appendix "What Literate Americans Know," by E. D. Hirsch, Jr., Joseph Kett, and James Trefill. Boston: Houghton Mifflin, 1987.

Hlebowitsh, Peter S. "Critical Theory versus Curriculum Theory: Reconsidering the Dialogue on Dewey." *Educational Theory* 42, no. 1 (Winter 1992): 69–82.

Hoffmann, Banesh. *The Tyranny of Testing.* New York: Collier Books, 1962.

Holt, David K. "Postmodernism: Anomaly in Art-Critical Theory." *Journal of Aesthetic Education* 29, no. 1 (Spring 1995): 85–93.

Holub, Robert C. *Crossing Borders: Reception Theory, Poststructuralism, Deconstruction.* Madison: University of Wisconsin Press, 1992.

hooks, bell. "Feminism: A Transformational Politic." In *Talking Back.* Boston: South End Press, 1989.

Jay, Gregory S., ed. *American Literature and the Culture Wars.* Ithaca, N.Y.: Cornell University Press, 1997.

Jellison, Judith A. "How Can All People Continue to Be Involved in Meaningful Music Participation?" In *Vision 2020: The Housewright Symposium on the Future of Music Education,* ed. Clifford K. Madsen. Reston, Va.: Music Educators National Conference, 2000.

Jones, Kathleen. *The Making of Social Policy in Britain: From the Poor Law to New Labour.* 3rd ed. London: Athlone Press, 2000.

Jordan, Joyce. "Multicultural Music Education in a Pluralistic Society." In *Handbook of Research on Music Teaching and Learning*, ed. Richard Colwell. New York: Schirmer Books, 1992.

Jorgensen, Estelle R. "Justifying Music Instruction in American Schools: An Historical Perspective." *Bulletin of the Council for Research in Music Education* 120 (Spring 1994): 16–31.

———. "Music Education as Community." *Journal of Aesthetic Education* 29, no. 3 (1995): 71–84.

———. *In Search of Music Education*. Urbana: University of Illinois Press, 1997.

———. "Musical Multiculturalism Revisited." *Journal of Aesthetic Education* 32, no. 2 (Summer 1998): 77–88.

Kailin, Julie. "How White Teachers Perceive the Problem of Racism in Their Schools: A Case Study in 'Liberal' Lakeview." *Teachers College Record* 100, no. 4 (Summer 1999): 724–50.

Kaplan, Max. *Foundations and Frontiers of Music Education*. New York: Holt, Rinehart and Winston, 1966.

Kemp, Anthony E. *The Musical Temperament: Psychology and Personality of Musicians*. Oxford: Oxford University Press, 1996.

Kimball, Bruce A. "Naming Pragmatic Liberal Education." In *Education and Democracy: Re-imagining Liberal Learning in America*, ed. Robert Orrill. New York: College Entrance Examination Board, 1997.

Kingsbury, Henry O. "Music as Cultural System: Structure and Process in an American Conservatory." Ph.D. diss., Indiana University, 1984.

———. *Music, Talent, and Performance: A Conservatory Cultural System*. Philadelphia: Temple University Press, 1988.

Kivy, Peter. "Music and the Liberal Education." *Journal of Aesthetic Education* 25, no. 3 (Fall 1991): 79–93.

———. *Authenticities: Philosophical Reflections on Musical Performance*. Ithaca, N.Y.: Cornell University Press, 1995.

Klein, Naomi. *No Logo: Taking Aim at the Brand Bullies*. Toronto: Vintage Books, 2000.

Kloppenberg, James T. "Cosmopolitan Pragmatism: Deliberative Democracy and Higher Education." In *Education and Democracy: Re-imagining Liberal Learning in America*, ed. Robert Orrill. New York: College Entrance Examination Board, 1997.

Knight, John. "Fading Poststructuralisms: Post-Ford, Posthuman, Posteducation?" In *After Postmodernism: Education, Politics, and Identity*, ed. Richard Smith and Philip Wexler. London: Falmer Press, 1995.

Koskoff, Ellen. "What Do We Want to Teach When We Teach Music? One Apology, Two Short Trips, Three Ethical Dilemmas, and Eighty-two Questions." In *Rethinking Music*, ed. Nicholas Cook and Mark Everist. New York: Oxford University Press, 1999.

Koza, Julia Eklund. "Corporate Profit at Equity's Expense: Codified Standards and High-Stakes Assessment in Music Teacher Preparation." *Bulletin of the Council for Research in Music Education* 152 (Spring 2002): 1–16.

———. "A Realm without Angels: MENC's Partnerships with Disney and Other Major Corporations." *Philosophy of Music Education Review* 10, no. 2 (Fall 2002): 72–79.

Kundera, Milan. *The Unbearable Lightness of Being*. Translated by Michael Henry Heim. New York: Harper Colophon Books, 1985.

Kymlicka, Will. *Contemporary Political Philosophy: An Introduction.* Oxford: Oxford University Press, 1990.

Labuta, Joseph A., and Deborah A. Smith. *Music Education: Historical Contexts and Perspectives.* Upper Saddle River, N.J.: Prentice Hall, 1997.

Lagemann, Ellen Condliffe. "From Discipline-Based to Problem-Centered Learning." In *Education and Democracy: Re-imagining Liberal Learning in America,* ed. Robert Orrill. New York: College Entrance Examination Board, 1997.

Lankford, E. Louis. "Aesthetic Experience in a Postmodern Age: Recovering the Aesthetics of E. F. Kaelin." *Journal of Aesthetic Education* 32, no. 1 (Spring 1998): 23–30.

Laxer, James. *In Search of a New Left: Canadian Politics after the Neoconservative Assault.* Toronto: Penguin, 1996.

Lehman, Paul. "How Can the Skills and Knowledge Called For in the National Standards Best Be Taught?" In *Vision 2020: The Housewright Symposium on the Future of Music Education,* ed. Clifford K. Madsen. Reston, Va.: Music Educators National Conference, 2000.

Leonhard, Charles, and Robert House. *Foundations and Principles of Music Education.* 2nd ed. New York: McGraw-Hill, 1972.

Lipman, Samuel. *Arguing for Music, Arguing for Culture.* Boston: Godine, 1990.

Lundquist, Barbara Reeder. "Music, Culture, Curriculum, and Instruction." In *The New Handbook of Research on Music Teaching and Learning,* ed. Richard Colwell and Carol P. Richardson. New York: Oxford University Press, 2002.

Mark, Michael L. *Contemporary Music Education.* 2nd ed. New York: Schirmer Books, 1986.

———. "A History of Music Education Research." In *Handbook of Research on Music Teaching and Learning,* ed. Richard Colwell. New York: Schirmer Books, 1992.

Marshall, Peter H. *Demanding the Impossible: A History of Anarchism.* London: HarperCollins, 1992.

McCarthy, Marie. "The Foundations of Sociology in American Music Education (1900–1935)." In *On the Sociology of Music Education,* ed. Roger Rideout. Norman: University of Oklahoma School of Music, 1997.

McClary, Susan. *Feminine Endings: Music, Gender, and Sexuality.* Minneapolis: University of Minnesota Press, 1991.

Menand, Louis. "Re-Imagining Liberal Education." In *Education and Democracy: Re-imagining Liberal Learning in America,* ed. Robert Orrill. New York: College Entrance Examination Board, 1997.

Miles, Stephen. "Critical Musicology and the Problem of Mediation." *Notes: Quarterly Journal of the Music Library Association* 53, no. 3 (March 1997): 722–50.

Mill, John Stuart. *On Liberty.* Edited by David Spitz. New York: W. W. Norton, 1975.

Morton, Charlene. "Critical Thinking and Music Education: Nondiscursive Experience and Discursive Rationality as Musical Friends." In *Critical Thinking in Music: Theory and Practice,* ed. Paul Woodford. *Studies in Music from the University of Western Ontario* 17 (1998): 63–78.

———. "Boom Diddy Boom Boom: Critical Multiculturalism in Music Education." *Philosophy of Music Education Review* 9, no. 1 (Spring 2001): 32–41.

Mursell, James L. *Human Values in Education.* New York: Silver Burdett, 1934.

———. *Principles of Democratic Education.* New York: W. W. Norton, 1955.

———. *Music Education: Principles and Programs.* Morristown, N.J.: Silver Burdett, 1956.

Nagel, Thomas. "Rawls and Liberalism." In *The Cambridge Companion to Rawls,* ed. Samuel Freeman. Cambridge: Cambridge University Press, 2003.

National Commission on Excellence in Education. *A Nation at Risk: The Imperative for Educational Reform.* A Report to the Nation and the Secretary of Education, Department of Education. Washington, D.C.: National Commission on Excellence in Education, 1983.

National Standards for Arts Education: What Every Young American Should Know and Be Able to Do in the Arts. Reston, Va.: Music Educators National Conference, 1994.

Norris, Christopher. *Contest of Faculties: Philosophy and Theory after Deconstruction.* London: Methuen, 1985.

North, Adrian C., David J. Hargreaves, and Mark Tarrant. "Social Psychology and Music Education." In *The New Handbook of Research on Music Teaching and Learning,* ed. Richard Colwell and Carol Richardson. New York: Oxford University Press, 2002.

Nussbaum, Martha C. *Poetic Justice: The Literary Imagination and Public Life.* Boston: Beacon Press, 1995.

———. *Upheavals of Thought: The Intelligence of Emotions.* Cambridge: Cambridge University Press, 2001.

O'Toole, Patricia. "I Sing in a Choir but I Have 'No Voice'!" *Quarterly Journal of Music Teaching and Learning* 4, no. 4 (Winter/Spring 1993/1994): 65–76.

———. "Examining the Political Projects of Four Pedagogies: Progressive, Humanistic, Critical, and Feminist." *Dialogue in Instrumental Music Education* 21, no. 2 (Fall 1997): 126–41.

Perry, William. *Forms of Intellectual and Ethical Development in the College Years.* New York: Holt, Rinehart and Winston, 1968.

Postman, Neil. *Amusing Ourselves to Death: Public Discourse in the Age of Show Business.* New York: Penguin Books, 1985.

Regelski, Thomas A. "Scientism in Experimental Music Research." *Philosophy of Music Education Review* 4, no. 1 (1996): 3–19.

———. "Critical Theory as a Foundation for Critical Thinking in Music Education." In *Critical Thinking in Music: Theory and Practice,* ed. Paul Woodford. *Studies in Music from the University of Western Ontario* 17 (1998): 1–21.

———. "Critical Education, Culturalism, and Multiculturalism." *Finnish Journal of Music Education* 5, nos. 1/2 (2000): 120–46.

Reimer, Bennett. *A Philosophy of Music Education.* Englewood Cliffs, N.J.: Prentice Hall, 1970.

———. "Music Education as Aesthetic Education: Past and Present." *Music Educators Journal* 75, no. 6 (February 1989): 22–28.

———. *A Philosophy of Music Education.* 2nd ed. Englewood Cliffs, N.J.: Prentice Hall, 1989.

———. "Music Education Philosophy and Psychology after Mursell." In *Basic Concepts in Music Education, II,* ed. Richard J. Colwell. Niwot: University Press of Colorado, 1991.

———. "Can We Understand Music of Foreign Cultures?" In *Musical Connections: Traditions and Change,* ed. Heath Lees. Auckland: International Society for Music Education, 1994.

———. "Viewing Music Education in the United States through Irish Eyes." *College Music Symposium* 38 (1998): 74–79.

Rice, Timothy. "Ethical Issues for Music Educators in Multicultural Societies." *Canadian Music Educator* 39, no. 2 (Winter 1998): 5–8.

Richardson, Carol P., and Nancy Whitaker. "Critical Thinking and Music Education." In *Handbook of Research on Music Teaching and Learning*, ed. Richard Colwell. New York: Schirmer, 1992.

Richmond, Stuart. "Liberalism, Multiculturalism, and Art Education." *Journal of Aesthetic Education* 29 no. 3 (Fall 1995): 15–25.

Rideout, Roger, and Allan Feldman. "Research in Music Student Teaching." In *The New Handbook of Research on Music Teaching and Learning*, ed. Richard Colwell and Carol P. Richardson. New York: Oxford University Press, 2002.

Riebling, Barbara. "Remodelling Truth, Power, and Society: Implications of Chaos Theory, Nonequilibrium Dynamics, and Systems Science for the Study of Politics and Literature." In *After Poststructuralism: Interdisciplinarity and Literary Theory*, ed. Nancy Easterlin and Barbara Riebling. Evanston, Ill.: Northwestern University Press, 1993.

Rinaldo, Vince. "A Fragmentary View of Education." *Canadian Music Educator* 44, no. 3 (Spring 2003): 23–25.

Roberts, Brian A. *A Place to Play: The Social World of University Schools of Music*. St. John's: Memorial University of Newfoundland, 1991.

———. "Music Teacher Education as Identity Construction." *International Journal of Music Education* 18 (1991): 30–39.

———. "Editorial." *International Journal of Music Education* 32 (1998): 1–2.

———. "Gatekeepers and the Reproduction of Institutional Realities: The Case of Music Education in Canadian Universities." *Musical Performance* 2, no. 3 (2000): 63–80.

Rorty, Richard. "Response to Ernesto Laclau." In *Deconstruction and Pragmatism*, ed. Chantal Mouffe. London: Routledge, 1996.

———. "Solidarity or Objectivity." In *From Modernism to Postmodernism: An Anthology*, ed. Lawrence Cahoone. Cambridge, Mass.: Blackwell, 1996.

Rose, Andrea M. "A Place for Indigenous Music in Formal Music Education." *International Journal of Music Education* 26 (1995): 39–54.

Rosenfeld, Anne H. "The Sound of Selling." *Psychology Today* (December 1985): 56.

Ross, Malcolm. "What's Wrong with School Music?" *British Journal of Music Education* 12, no. 3 (November 1995): 185–201.

Rushkoff, Douglas. *Coercion: Why We Listen to What "They" Say*. New York: Riverhead Books, 1999.

Said, Edward W. *Culture and Imperialism*. New York: Vintage Books, 1994.

Saul, John Ralston. *Voltaire's Bastards: The Dictatorship of Reason in the West*. Toronto: Penguin Books, 1992.

———. *The Unconscious Civilization*. Concord, Ont.: House of Anansi Press, 1995.

Sayers, Elizabeth. "Deconstructing McClary: Narrative, Feminine Sexuality, and Feminism in Susan McClary's *Feminine Endings*." *College Music Symposium* 33/34 (1993/1994): 41–55.

Schafer, R. Murray. *The Rhinoceros in the Classroom*. London: Universal, 1975.

———. *Voices of Tyranny: Temples of Silence*. Indian River, Ont.: Arcana, 1993.

Scheffler, Israel. *In Praise of the Cognitive Emotions*. New York: Routledge, 1991.

Schmidt, Catherine M. "Who Benefits? Music Education and the National Standards." *Philosophy of Music Education Review* 4, no. 2 (Fall 1996): 71–82.

Schön, Donald A. *Educating the Reflective Practitioner.* San Francisco: Jossey-Bass, 1987.
———. "The Theory of Inquiry: Dewey's Legacy to Education." *Curriculum Inquiry* 22 (1992): 119–39.
Schwadron, Abraham A. *Aesthetics: Dimensions for Music Education.* Washington, D.C.: Music Educators National Conference, 1967.
Shepherd, John. "Music and the Last Intellectual." *Journal of Aesthetic Education* 25, no. 3 (Fall 1991): 95–114.
Shepherd, John, and Graham Vulliamy. "The Struggle for Culture: A Sociological Case Study of the Development of a National Music Curriculum." *British Journal of Sociology of Education* 15, no. 1 (1994): 27–40.
Shusterman, Richard. *Pragmatist Aesthetics: Living Beauty, Rethinking Art.* 2nd ed. Lanham, Md.: Rowman and Littlefield, 2000.
Siegel, Harvey. "Is Inclusion an Epistemic Virtue?" In *Philosophy of Education Yearbook, 1997,* ed. Susan Laird. Urbana, Ill.: Philosophy of Education Society, 1997.
Singley, Mark K., and John R. Anderson. *The Transfer of Cognitive Skill.* Cambridge, Mass.: Harvard University Press, 1989.
Small, Christopher. *Music, Society, Education.* London: John Calder, 1980.
———. *Music of the Common Tongue: Survival and Celebration in Afro-American Music.* London: John Calder, 1987.
———. *Music, Society, Education.* 3rd ed. Hanover, N.H.: Wesleyan University Press, 1996.
———. *Musicking: The Meanings of Performing and Listening.* Hanover, N.H.: Wesleyan University Press, 1998.
Smith, Ralph. "Recent Trends and Issues in Policy Making." In *The New Handbook of Research on Music Teaching and Learning,* ed. Richard Colwell and Carol P. Richardson. New York: Oxford University Press, 2002.
Smithrim, Katharine, and Rena Upitis. "Contaminated by Peaceful Feelings: The Power of Music." *Canadian Music Educator* 44, no. 3 (Spring 2003): 12–17.
Spiro, Rand J., Walter P. Vispoel, John G. Schmitz, Ala Samarapungaven, and A. E. Boerger. "Knowledge Acquisition for Application: Cognitive Flexibility and Transfer in Complex Content Domains." In *Executive Control Processes in Reading,* ed. Bruce K. Britton and Shawn M. Glynn. Hillsdale, N.J.: Lawrence Erlbaum Associates, 1987.
Spotts, Frederic. *Hitler and the Power of Aesthetics.* Woodstock, N.Y.: Overlook Press, 2003.
Spychiger, Maria B. "Aesthetic and Praxial Philosophies of Music Education Compared: A Semiotic Consideration." *Philosophy of Music Education Review* 5, no. 1 (Spring 1997): 33–41.
Stallings, D. T. "A Brief History of the U.S. Department of Education, 1979–2002." *Phi Delta Kappan* 83, no. 9 (May 2002): 677–83.
Stein, Janice Gross. *The Cult of Efficiency.* Toronto: House of Anansi Press, 2001.
Stubley, Eleanor V. "Musical Performance, Play and Constructive Knowledge: Experiences of Self and Culture." *Philosophy of Music Education Review* 1, no. 2 (Fall 1993): 94–102.
———. "The Performer, the Score, the Work: Musical Performance and Transactional Reading." *Journal of Aesthetic Education* 29, no. 3 (Fall 1995): 55–69.
Subotnik, Rose Rosengard. *Deconstructive Variations: Music and Reason in Western Society.* Minneapolis: University of Minnesota Press, 1996.

Suzuki, Shinichi. *Nurtured by Love: A New Approach to Education*. Translated by Waltraud Suzuki. New York: Exposition Press, 1969.

Swanwick, Keith. *Music, Mind, and Education*. London: Routledge, 1988.

———. *Teaching Music Musically*. London: Routledge, 1999.

Tanner, Laurel N. "The Path Not Taken: Dewey's Model of Inquiry." *Curriculum Inquiry* 18, no. 4 (1988): 471–79.

Taruskin, Richard. *Text and Act: Essays on Music and Performance*. New York: Oxford University Press, 1995.

Taylor, Charles. *Multiculturalism and "The Politics of Recognition."* Edited by Amy Gutmann with commentary by Gutmann, Steven C. Rockefeller, Michael Walzer, and Susan Wolf. Princeton, N.J.: Princeton University Press, 1992.

Thomas, Gary. "What's the Use of Theory?" *Harvard Educational Review* 67, no. 1 (Spring 1997): 75–104.

Tilley, Terrence W., ed. *Postmodern Theologies: The Challenge of Religious Diversity*. Maryknoll, N.Y.: Orbis Books, 1995.

Tupman, Dennis F. "A Rant about Elementary Music Education—Whither Goest Thou?" *Canadian Music Educator* 43, no. 4 (Summer 2002): 43–44.

Tyler, Ralph. *Basic Principles of Curriculum and Instruction*. Chicago: University of Chicago Press, 1949.

Usher, Robin, and Richard Edwards. *Postmodernism and Education*. London: Routledge, 1994.

Väkevä, Lauri. "Interviewing Richard Shusterman." *Finnish Journal of Music Education* 5, nos. 1/2 (2000): 187–95.

Walters, Jane. "Response to Paul Lehman's 'How Can the Skills and Knowledge Called For in the National Standards Best Be Taught?'" In *Vision 2020: The Housewright Symposium on the Future of Music Education*, ed. Clifford K. Madsen. Reston, Va.: Music Educators National Conference, 2000.

Watkins, Glenn. *Soundings: Music in the Twentieth Century*. New York: Schirmer Books, 1988.

Watson, Ian. *Song and Democratic Culture in Britain: An Approach to Popular Culture in Social Movements*. London: Croom Helm, 1983.

Westbrook, Robert B. *John Dewey and American Democracy*. Ithaca, N.Y.: Cornell University Press, 1991.

Whitehead, Alfred North. *The Aims of Education and Other Essays*. New York: Macmillan, 1929; reprint, New York: Free Press, 1967.

Willingham, Lee, and Lee Bartel. "'Music Makes You Smarter'—Is There Any Evidence?" *Canadian Music Educator* 43, no. 2 (Winter 2001): 11–12.

———. "Proposals for Change to the Face of Music Education." *Canadian Music Educator* 43, no. 4 (Summer 2002): 2

Wilsmore, S. J. "Against Deconstructing Rationality in Education." *Journal of Aesthetic Education* 25, no. 4 (Winter 1991): 99–113.

Woodford, Paul G. "Development of a Theory of Transfer in Musical Thinking and Learning Based on John Dewey's Conception of Reflective Thinking." Ph.D. diss., Northwestern University, 1994.

———. "A Critique of Fundamentalism in Singing: Musical Authenticity, Authority, and Practice." In *Sharing the Voices: The Phenomenon of Singing, Proceedings of the International Symposium*, ed. Brian A. Roberts. St. John's: Memorial University of Newfoundland, 1998.

————. "Is Kodály Obsolete?" *Alla Breve*. Special research edition of the newsletter of the Kodály Society of Canada 24, nos. 1/2 (June 2000): 10–18.

————. "Music, Reason, Democracy, and the Construction of Gender." *Journal of Aesthetic Education* 35, no. 3 (Fall 2001): 73–86.

————. "The Social Construction of Music Teacher Identity in Undergraduate Music Education Majors." In *The New Handbook of Research on Music Teaching and Learning*, ed. Richard Colwell and Carol P. Richardson. New York: Oxford University Press, 2002.

Woodford, Paul, and Robert E. Dunn. "Beyond Objectivism and Relativism in Music." In *Critical Thinking in Music: Theory and Practice*, ed. Paul Woodford. *Studies in Music from the University of Western Ontario* 17 (1998): 45–62.

Wright, Robert. "'I'd Sell You Suicide': Pop Music and Moral Panic in the Age of Marilyn Manson." *Popular Music* 19, no. 3 (October 2000): 365–85.

York, Norton. "Valuing School Music: A Report on School Music." London: University of Westminster and Rockschool, 2001.

Index

PAUL G. Woodford is Chair of the Department of Music Education, the Don Wright Faculty of Music, at the University of Western Ontario, London, Ontario. He has published a history of music in Newfoundland, two music collections, and a book of essays.